# STEPHEN F. AUSTIN'S

## REGISTER

OF

## FAMILIES

Edited by
Villamae Williams

From the originals in the
General Land Office
Austin, Texas

CLEARFIELD

Reprinted for
Clearfield Company, Inc. by
Genealogical Publishing Co., Inc.
Baltimore, Maryland
1996, 2000

# INTRODUCTION

Stephen F. Austin's Register of the Families is one of those basic documents, once published, the question is asked: "Why was this never published before?" Accessible until now only in the original at the General Land Office in Austin, it provides data available nowhere else on a cross section of early Anglo settlers of Mexican Texas.

The Register is a legacy of the formal, thorough Mexican colonization system. Article J of the massive colonization law of the State of Coahuila and Texas dated March 24,1825, required that "any foreigner, already in the limits of the state of Coahuila and Texas, who wishes to settle himself in it, shall make a declaration of that effect before the Ayuntamiento of the place which he selects as his residence." To complete the process of settlement, a local official had to administer to the foreigner an oath of allegiance to both the religion and laws of Mexico. Afterward, he recorded that the oath had been taken. More importantly for research, he was required to gather pertinent information on the immigrant. This included name, marital and/or family status, place of birth and/or place from where moved, and occupation. Only after completing this process, "and not before," the law specified emphatically, would a person be considered "domiciliated," the word Austin used in his translations for the Laws, Orders, and Contracts of Colonization, the book published for his colonists in late 1829, the first book printed in Texas.

Until February, 1828, Austin himself provided the local government for his colonies.  Thus he began this register of settlers as the law required.  Apparently he and his secretary, Samuel May Williams, maintained the book even after the growth of Austin's colonies brought a full Mexican local government system into effect.  Entries, which had been antedated to include arrivals as early as 1823, continue through February, 1836, less than a week before the signing of the Texas Declaration of Independence.

The Register provides the historian and the sociologist with an extensive body of data by which to study the demography of a major portion of Mexican Texas  For the genealogist, this list is a superb source of information, giving, as it often does, data on family members as well as the immigrant. Actually, this resource is so useful, I suspect few will have time to ask why it was never published before.  They will be too busy using it!

David B. Gracy II
Texas State Archives

## ACKNOWLEDGEMENTS

Appreciation goes to the employees of the General Land Office who so generously made their records available; to Mr. Alan Probert whose assistance with the translation of this document was invaluable, and most of all to Mr. Gifford White, without whose help this book would not have been published.

Villamae Williams

1984

# CONTENTS

STEPHEN FULLER AUSTIN
Courtesy Texas State Archives

Empresario Grants.

1 Felisola's Grant.
2 Burnet's  "
3 Vehlin's  "
4 Zavalla's  "
5 Austin's Colony.
6 Robertson's Grant.
7 S. F. Austin's  "
8 Milam's  "
9 DeWitt  "
10 DeLeon's  "
11 Bexar District
12 McMullin & McGloire's  Grant.
13 Power's  "
14 John Cameron's  "

TEXAS

In 1834

Scale

Miles 10  20  30  40  50           100

San Antonio
&
Environs
Old Mill

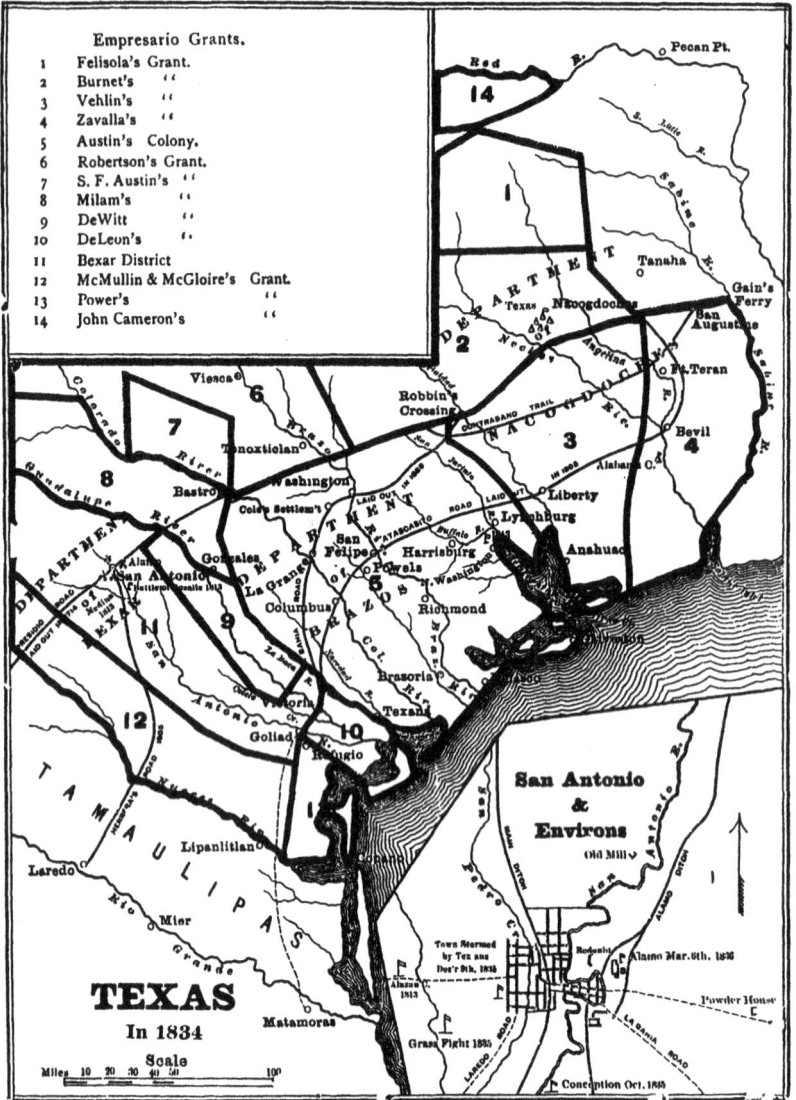

A PICTORIAL HISTORY OF TEXAS
Rev. Homer S. Thrall, St. Louis, 1879

# PREFACE

Texas was thinly settled under Spanish rule, with
only two settlements of consequence in 1820: San
Antonio and Nacogdoches.  In 1821, revolt freed
Mexico from Spanish rule and it became the Repub-
lic of Mexico.  Under a new colonization policy,
Mexico made contracts with Empresarios to bring
specific numbers of families into Texas.  Stephen
F. Austin was the first and most successful and he
began granting lands to settlers in 1824. His
first colony for 300 families came to be known as
"Austin's Old Three Hundred."

Under a new Colonization Law passed in 1825, each
Empresario was required to record personal information on every immigrant.  In the Austin Colony
(the only colony in full function at the time),
this information was written into a ledger called
the "Regis de las Familias."  Most of the first
entries were in Spanish, and then later in English, by Samuel May Williams.  Williams was lit-
erate in Spanish and English and was Secretary and
business manager to Austin for 11 years until the
movement for independence exploded in 1835.

The "Register" is now in the Spanish Archives of
the General Land Office, Austin, Texas.  The original manuscript was bound into two volumes called
Volume A and Volume 2.  Vol. 2 is the earlier of
the two.  In this publication they are referred
to as Volume 1 and 2 in the order of writing.

Original page numbers have been copied into the
body of the transcription in ( ).  These numbers
have been used in making the Personal Names Index.
If photostats of a particular record are wanted,
these page numbers will facilitate ordering the
correct page.

In translating from Spanish, the modern English place names have been used if there is no uncertainty about the place. It may be noted that Texas still uses most of the old Spanish place names. See the Appendix for a short list of place name equivalents, and for names not now in use.

Personal names have been copied as written within the limits of legibility of the original. They were carefully written and there are few outright errors. None has been "corrected."

Entries were made on two facing pages for much of the "Register." The right hand page was used for notes and land descriptions, in a fine hand that cannot now be read with certainty. Both pages of entries have been folded into one page here in the transcription.

Frequent use was made of id, idem, do and ". They all mean "repeat the entry above."

Inquiries about copies may be made to the General Land Office, Archives & Records Div., 1700 North Congress, Austin TX 78701.

# IMPORTANT EVENTS

## That Affected the Making of the "Register"

1821  Mexico became independent of Spain.

1823 April.  Stephen F. Austin finally obtained approval in Mexico City to settle families in Texas.

1824 May.  Samuel May Williams arrived in Texas to assume duties as secretary and business manager to Austin for the next 11 years.

1824 July.  Titles began to be issued to the settlers waiting for Austin to return. They were the "Old Three Hundred."

1825 March 24.  The Colonization Law was passed that caused the keeping of the "Register" in the hands of Samuel May Williams.

1833 April 22.  Austin left San Felipe de Austin on political business, leaving Williams in charge. Austin was "detained" in Mexico.

1835 September 1835.  Austin returned to Texas.

1835 October 17.  The Permanent Council ordered all the land offices closed. Titles with a later date were declared invalid.

1836 Feb 26.  Last entry in the "Register."

1836 March 2.  Texas declared its independence.

# PLACE NAMES

Place names no longer in common use may have the following modern equivalents. It will be noted that Texas retained a majority of its Spanish place names.

Francisco. Probably San Francisco de Bexar, to be equated with modern San Antonio.

Aises. Probably the same as Ayish, a bayou between the Sabine and Neches Rivers, and a settlement of the same name.

Palogacho. Possibly Palo Gaucho Bayou in now San Augustine County, and a settlement of the same name.

Atacapas. In early Louisiana, a district, and then a county. Not now in use, it covered Lafayette, St. Martin and later parishes.

Opelousas. An early Louisiana fort and settlement around the present town of the same name.

# LAND TERMS AND MEASURES

Vara. A Spanish linear measure of varying value. Defined to be 33-1/3 inches in Texas.

League. A linear measure of 5000 varas; a land measure of a square league, or 4428.3 acres.

Labor. 1,000,000 square varas or 177.1 acres.

Augmentation. An increased amount due a settler because of a change in status (e.g. marriage) or because he brought an industry etc.

# Registro

De las

# Familias

## NOTICE

Each Emigrant who has removed to this Colony, as a
part of the Colonists, which I am authorized to
settle, under my contract with the Government, as
Empresario, and who has not received a title, is
notified to present himself to me, after the 1st
day of December next, in person, and hand in a
list in writing, in conformity with the 3rd article of the Colonization Law, containing the name
and ages of the head of the family and his wife,
the names and ages and sex of each child, the number of dependents, or servants, his occupation or
trade, where removed from, and the date of arrival
in this colony with his family, which list must be
signed by the applicant. Single men will also
present themselves and hand in the above list, so
far as it is applicable to them...in order that if
the applicant should be received as a settler by
me, his name may be registered, the oath prescribed by the 3d article of the said law administered, and a certificate to that effect issued to him or her.

S.F. Austin

Town of Austin, 29th November, 1829

[Excerpt from a handbill]

| (1)(2) Date | Name of Family | Age | Status | Ages of Sons | Daus | Slaves | Place of Origin |
|---|---|---|---|---|---|---|---|
| 1825 July 11 | Robert Patton | 38 | Single | | | 4 | |
| | East Bank of the Colorado River south of the Bexar Road beginning at the low country road | | | | | | |
| | Jesse H. Cartwright | 38 | Married | 7,3,1 | 16,14 | 8 | Woodville, Mississippi |
| | Nancy his wife | 26 | | | | | |
| | One labor near the east bank of the Navidad | | | | | | |
| | Robert Cartwright | | Single | | | | |
| | East bank of the Navidad at the place where the Atascosito crosses | | | | | | |
| Septr 1 | David Hamilton | 27 | Married | | | 4 | Pike Cty, Mississippi |
| | Dianah his wife | 16 | | | | | |
| | Above the road to the Labahia on the Colorado River | | | | | | |
| 10 | Robert Nalls | 25 | Single | | | | Arkansas |
| | On the plain called McGinty's Prairie | | | | | | |
| | Juan Tobar | 39 | Married | 11,8 | 13 | | Mexico |
| | Teresa his wife | 30 | | | | | |
| | On the Arroyo of the Jaranames | | | | | | |
| 10 | Jose Sandoval | 33 | Married | | 3 | 1 | |
| | Gertrudes Rodrigues | 20 | | | | | |
| | At Arroyo Palmito | | | | | | |
| | Daniel Lyon | 33 | Single | | | | Claiborne Cty, Mississippi |

| Date | Name of Family | Age | Status | Ages of Sons | Daus | Slaves | Place of Origin |
|---|---|---|---|---|---|---|---|
| Novemr 12 | Samuel Craft | 51 | Married | 22,14 8,4 | 16,12 5,7 | | Virginia |
| | On the Colorado at the place where old Fulcher wants his land | | | | | | |
| " | Jenkins Shelby | 21 | Single | | | | Tennessee |
| | Warren Buford | 45 | Married | 21,19,17 | 7 | 9 | Attacapas, Louisiana |
| " | Armstead Moore | 51 | Married | 29,16 14,11 4 | 21,19 15,6 | 30 | Smith County,Tennessee Round Li-- Post Office |
| (3)(4) Novemr 20 | William Moore | 25 | Single | | | Smith Cty | Tennessee Farmer |
| | Samuel A. Bowen | 35 | Married | 3 | 6 mos | 5 | id idem |
| | Harrison | 48 | " | 5 sons 4 daus | | 10 | id idem |
| | Daniel M. Frazier | 26 | Single | | | | id idem |
| | Moses B. Frazier | 35 | Married | 9,4,2 | 12,10,3 | 11 | id idem |
| Decr 20 | Francis F. Wells | 26 | Married | | | | Louisiana Farmer & Stockraiser |
| | Elizabeth McNut | 40 | Widow | 18,14 | 12,10 8,6,2 | 15 | idem idem |
| 1826 Jan 7 | William Barrat | 26 | Single | | | | Pennsylvania Farmer |
| | Abraham H. Philips | 40 | Widower | 11,6 | 8,4 | | Alabama Artisan & Farmer |

John W. Williamson 37 Widower 16    1    Mississippi
    On the same day took the oath in proper form

John S. Wallace    60 Married    17    Ohio

John P. Wallace    30 Single    do

Lemuel Dickinson    36 Married    2,1    Louisiana

John McCoy    58 Married 21,17,15    9    Missouri

Joseph McCoy    38 Married 15,13,8    11    do

Ira Ingram    37 Widower    Pennsylvania
    To the east of the limits of the Village of Matagorda

March 15    Zeddock Woods    52 Married 20,18,11    1    Missouri
    Above the Labahia Road on the west bank of the Colorado

John Crier    24 Widower 7    5    Arkansas
    Next to the half sitio of S. Castleman

Norman Woods    22 Single    Missouri

Philo Fairchild    28 idem    New York
    A quarter sitio joining the labor of Morton's on the western strip
    of Brown

Hosea H. League    36 Married    5    Tennessee
    Took the required oath

William D. Horton    24 Married    6    Tennessee

| Date | Name of Family | Age | Status | Ages of Sons | Daus | Slaves | Place of Origin | Place Moved From |
|---|---|---|---|---|---|---|---|---|
|  | Thomas K. Porter | 25 | idem |  |  | 4 | Tennessee |  |
|  | Edwd H. Tarrant | 28 | idem |  |  | 4 | Tennessee |  |
| Apr 1 | Robt Guthrie | 30 | idem | 9,11 | 7 |  | Missouri |  |
|  | On the Arroyo Bernard near the land of John Andrews |  |  |  |  |  |  |  |
|  | Arche Hodge | 30 | idem | 2,4,6 | 11,13 |  | Arkansas |  |
|  | Geo W. Himer |  | Married |  |  |  | Missouri |  |
|  | John Boyce | 32 | idem |  |  |  | Louisiana |  |
|  | Josiah Horton | 55 | idem | 14,18 |  |  | Tennessee |  |
|  | Henderson W. Horton | 20 | Single |  |  |  | idem |  |
| May 3 | Israel L. Ludlow | 27 | idem |  |  |  | Ohio |  |
|  | Took the proper oath |  |  |  |  |  |  |  |
|  | Nicholas Clopper | 59 | Widower | 15,14 |  |  | Ohio |  |
|  | With 10 servants |  |  |  |  |  |  |  |
|  | Benjamin Osborn | 54 | Married | 19,17, 15,13,1 | 11,9, 5,2 |  | Mississippi |  |
|  | Came in the month of March |  |  |  |  |  |  |  |
| (5)(6) July 1 | William H. Skerrett | 34 | Married |  |  |  | Philadelphia | Ohio |
|  | Land back of Sitio No. 4 east of the Barnard |  |  |  |  |  |  |  |

| Name | Age | Status | | | | | |
|---|---|---|---|---|---|---|---|
| Andrew Churchill<br>Will come in 4 months | 32 | idem | 4,6 | | 6 | Kentucky | Kentucky |
| William C. Carson<br>Has had his family in the Colony for 4 months | 36 | Married 2,10 | 1,5,14 | | | Delaware | Indiana |
| Nancy Smaley | 19 | Single | | | | Kentucky | Kentucky |
| Susana Smaley | 17 | idem | Heirs of Andrew Smaley who died here | | | | |
| Elizabeth Smaley | 14 | " | at the mouth of the Brazos in the | | | | |
| John Smaley | 12 | " | month of July 1826 | | | | |
| Abner Smaley | 10 | " | | | | | |
| John Pate | 25 | " | | | | | Mississippi |
| John Parker | 25 | " | | | | | Kentucky |
| Wyatt Hanks<br>Arrived March 20 | 32 | Married 13<br>3,1 | 11<br>5,1 | | 2 | Kentucky | Arkansas |
| John Brown | 37 | Single | | | | idem | idem |
| George Hudson | 47 | idem | | | | Philadelphia | idem |
| Isaac Vandorn | 25 | idem | | | | Pennsylvania | Kentucky |
| James Tate | 52 | Widower 14 | | | 2 | idem | Louisiana |
| George Alexander | 47 | Single | | | | N.Carolina | Mississippi |
| John McLaren | 30 | idem | | | | Virginia | Kentucky |

7

| Date | Name of Family | Age | Status | Ages of Sons | Daus | Slaves | Place of Origin [?] | Place Moved From |
|---|---|---|---|---|---|---|---|---|
|  | Presley Gill | 26 | idem |  |  |  |  | Kentucky |
|  | Arrived here in June of the year 1824 |  |  |  |  |  |  |  |
|  | Daniel Herrington | 23 | idem |  |  |  | England | Louisiana |
|  | Samuel Shup | 25 | idem |  |  |  | Pennsylvania | Indiana |
|  | Arrived here in the spring of the past year |  |  |  |  |  |  |  |
|  | Charles Breen | 39 | Married | 8,4 | 11,9 |  | Georgia | Alabama |
|  | Richard Greaves | 60 | Married | 12,10,3 | 7 |  | Georgia | Louisiana |
|  | James Stephenson | 36 | idem | 7,6,5 | 3 |  | North Carolina | Georgia |
|  | Mary Kiggins | 38 | Widow | 12,10,8 | 14,4 |  | Pennsylvania | Missouri |
|  | Jacob Stephens | 22 | Married |  | 1 |  | Tennessee | Missouri |
|  | John A. Warren | 25 | Single |  |  |  | Massachusetts | Louisiana |
|  | Arrived in the year 1825 |  |  |  |  |  |  |  |
|  | John York | 25 | Married | 2 | 5 |  | Georgia | Mississippi |
|  | John Jones | 41 | Single |  |  |  | New Jersey | Virginia |
|  | John Dziekanski | 29 | idem |  |  |  | Germany |  |
|  | Aaron Parker | 51 | Married | 13,16 |  |  | North Carolina | Mississippi |
|  | Montreville Woods | 20 | Married |  |  |  | Missouri | Missouri |
|  | Land on the west bank of the Colorado crossing of the LaBahia Road |  |  |  |  |  |  |  |

| Name | Age | Status | | | Birthplace | From |
|---|---|---|---|---|---|---|
| Thos York | 56 | idem | 20 | 8,10,12 14,17 | South Carolina | Mississippi |
| John T. Edwards | 20 | Single | | | Tennessee | Alabama |
| William H. Sewall | 24 | Married | 1 | 3 | Georgia | Louisiana |
| Land on the west branch of the San Jacinto | | | | 4 | | |
| Robert Browne Shoemaker | 30 | Single | | | Ireland | Pennsylvania |
| (7)(8) 1827 Sep 1 | | | | | | |
| Elizabeth McKensey | 43 | Widow | 14 | 12,17,19 | North Carolina | Kentucky |
| J.H. Bell to select land & are allowed until April next to move to the Country | | | | | | |
| Francis Giraud | 27 | Married | | | Massachusetts | do |
| Wm W. McKensey | 23 | Single | | | North Carolina | Tennessee |
| George Miliken | 23 | idem | | | | do |
| James Kegans | 25 | Married | 3 | | Missouri | Missouri |
| Labor on the Llegua League on New Year's Creek below Simon Millers | | | | | | |
| Mary Kegans | 45 | Widow | 11,9,5 | 4,13 | Pennsylvania | do |
| Jacob Stevans | 24 | Married | 1 | | Missouri | do |
| John Fields | 44 | Single | | | New Hampshire | South Carolina |
| Labor No. 6 east of Brazos near mouth | | | | | | |

9

| Date | Name of Family | Age | Status | Ages of Sons | Slaves Daus | Place of Origin | Place Moved From |
|------|----------------|-----|--------|--------------|-------------|-----------------|------------------|
| | Joseph Lindley | | | Solomon Bowlin | Heseka Waldrop ) | | |
| | James Thompson | | | Wiley Waldrop | Abraham Smelser ) | | |
| | Jeremiah Bowlin | | | Fredk Grimes | George Reynolds ) | | H.H. League |
| | Wm Bowlin | | | James Harper | Peter Nicholson ) | | |
| | George Grimes | | | Claiborne Waldrop | Earnest ) | | |
| ( | Elisha Moore | 35 | Married | 5,2 | 8 | Maryland | Missouri |
| ( | Catherine Gillet | | Canadan | | | | |
| | Geo Heny Grovesnor | 38 | Married | 9 | 12,1 | Connecticut | Louisiana |
| | Josiah Squires | 27 | Married | 5 | 2 | Pennsylvania | Ohio |
| | John Dickson | | | 5 Labor west of the Colorado | | | |
| | Wm Munson | | Married | 3 Labor west of the Colorado | | | |
| Jun 2 | John Cocke | | Married | Wife & child | | Kentucky | Arkansas |

3 labors west of Colorado - next above Andrew Castleman. Wants
to [be] investigated as another claims priority & settlement

| | | | | | | | |
|---|---|---|---|---|---|---|---|
| | Samuel Highsmith | | Married | wife | | do | Missouri |

1 League on the east side of Colorado opposite the head of
McGintys Prairie

| | | | | | | | |
|---|---|---|---|---|---|---|---|
| | Edward Beaty | | Married | wife | | | Arkansas |

On the east side of the Colorado River next above Saml Highsmith one league

| | | | | | | | |
|---|---|---|---|---|---|---|---|
| | Abijah Highsmith | | Married | wife & 5 children | | | Missouri |

One league on the east side of the Colorado in a prairie about 15 miles
below the San Antonio Road

| | | | | | | | |
|---|---|---|---|---|---|---|---|
| | Winslow Turner | | Married | 10 children | | | Missouri |

One league east side of Colorado about 4 miles above McGintys Prairie
next below the location of Abijah Highsmith to begin below the ---

(9)  1828

Stephen Cottle - at the lower end of McGinty's
    Prairie one league.
John Litton 1/4 at the forks of Buckners Creek.
Jonathan D. Morris - has improved the place that
    Cocke has applied for
Norman Woods - west of Colorado above the place
    applied for by Cocke.
Montreville Woods west side of Colorado next above
    Norman Woods.
John Denton  single - 1/4 League between Miller &
    Laky to lay between the wood and the river.
John Thompson (lives near Burnham) 2 children,
    applies for land at the LaBahia crossing on
    the east side of Colorado.
Robert Nalls - single, 1/4 League on the west of a
    Lake above the middle of McGintys Prairie
    west side Colorado.
June 16
John Clark (father-in-law of Wm Andrews) family
    removed from Opelousas, has permission to
    choose land 1/4 league.
Mary Beckham, widow one child, daughter of Jno
    Clark, has permission to choose 1 League.
Smetser family, 1 League in a small prairie on the
    west side of Colorado about 4 miles above
    McGintys Prairie.
[Mr] Earnest, single, 1/4 League to be chosen by
    Wilbarger.
July 27
John R. Ray family, carpenter, 1 League on San
    Jacinto.
Christian Smith Junr single 1/4 League  ditto
Andrew Lewis Castleman, single, 1/4 League at the
    lower end of McGinty Prairie provided it had
    not been previously selected by Cottle.
Abrella Herrington, widow, 3 children under age
    wants land on Tumlinson Creek at the head of
    the creek.
William Munson - League on New Years Creek to join
    Miller.
July 31
George Grymes family, wife, 9 children 4 male & 5
    female, born in North Carolina, removed from
    Tennessee, age 43, occupation a farmer, has
    permission verbally to select land.
1829 Jany 1
T.J. Gasley, wife 1 child.   Elisha Moore League
    above G. Hutt.
Jany 25
Peyton R. Splane, widower, one daughter, 30 years
    of age, the said Splane and the little girl 3
    years wants land on the La Bahia between the
    Brazos and Colorado.
Feby 15
Wm McFarlan  8th League west of Colorado opposite
    to Clark.

12
(10) April 7
Thos McCoy, single, upper 1/4 of next league below
    16 Mile Point.
Wm B. Demesse - enters a plan at the crossing of
    the Gonzales Road on the east side of Navidad
    to make up his quantity. Laid over for Comr.
Wm McLaughlin - at the crossing of Town Road on
    Buffalo Bayou above Pine Point.
Mathew Hubbard family wife and two children on San
    Jacinto next below John Edwards.
Robert A. Burney, single, arrived 25 Decr 1828,
    will bring one servant and others. Took the
    oath 18 Novbr 1829.
    Issued the certification the same day.
Certification issued to Mr. William Collins of Op-
    elousas. Must emigrate within five months,
    family him and his wife, son, daughter, 8
    servants, 1 orphan dependent, 13 souls. The
    sitio below and adjoining with that of Isaac
    Lee on Cummins Creek. 5 December 1829.
Mathew Duty for the minor heirs of Solomon Duty,
    wants to take the land for them adjoining and
    above his situated on the east bank of the
    Colorado River above the Bexar Road.
Joseph Duty wants to take some land in augmenta-
    tion of what he has and registered on the
    Colorado River bank on the left side about
    three miles below the Bexar Road between the
    land of Winslow Turner and the said road on
    a plain that is there.
Mr. George Ewing for Mr. Davis wants to take a
    sitio on the east bank below the junction of
    said Navidad and Sandy Creek between the
    sitio of Crozier and Scott, if there is room
    and if there is not, west bank of the Navidad
    opposite Crozier.
M. Cummins wants land near the Bexar Road west of
    the Brazos adjoining the land measured for
    Spears and land of John Williams.
21 Dec 1829.
Mr. Thomas J. Chambers wants to settle in this
(11)
    Colony on the Navasota River toward the east
    of the Brazos, beginning at the place called
    Rocky Shoals, and from there westward to the
    point and to the south and to the east and
    north to the point to complete one quarter.
1829 Decr 19.
Today Certifications have been issued to the fol-
    lowing men who have returned to bring their
    families, and have been granted a Term of
    sixteen months beginning after the 1st of
    next January to bring them here.
They are    Anthony Winston
            William O. Winston
            Isaac Winston

                    John T. Dillard
                    Benjamin A. Jones
                    Gibson Wooldrige
                    William J. Adair
                    Milton Winston
                    William Winston
                    George Carrol
                    Joel W. Winston
                    Richard S. Jones
Which gentlemen have chosen their land on the
Navidad River and Lavaca

Decr 20. Today certifications have been given to
the following men of the State of Missouri who
have returned to bring their families and goods,
and have been given [blank] months from [blank]
to bring them here. [No list of names.]

(12) [1830]
24 January. Today issued certificates to the following gentlemen of the State of Alabama who have
the term of 16 months after the first of this
month to effect moving their families into this
Colony, and they are
                    George Sutherland
                    John Sutherland
                    William Manifee
                    Thomas Manifee
                    William H. Heard
                    Joseph Rector
                    William Pride
                    Jessey White
                    Benjamin White
                    Samuel Rogers
                    Robert G. Crosier
                    William Haskins
                    Pulaskey Dudley
                    James N. Smith
                    Mary Smith
                    Richard R. Royall
                    Thacker Winter
                    John Caldwell
                    Washington J. Cockrill
These gentlemen have designated their land on the
Arroyo Karankahuas and Arroyo Navidad.

24 January. Today was issued a certification to
Mr. Joseph Davis and given the term to the 1st of
May of the year 1831 to bring his family and he
has chosen on the left bank of the Navidad River.

Certifications have been issued to the following
gentlemen of the State of Missouri and given the
term to the 15 of June of the following year to
bring their families.
                    Stephen F. Danklin
                    George Hammond

William W. Hunter
Henry Bates
[Marginal note]: Not in Texas
(13)
Today a certification was issued to T. McQueen,
was granted a term for moving here until 20 Feby
of the coming year.

Today certifications were issued for the following gentlemen who were granted the term to 24 Feb
1831.

| | |
|---|---|
| James Wright | Married |
| Rensalleer W. Lee | idem |
| Simon Calkins | idem |
| Henry Thorp | idem |

Today issued certifications to Messers. Alexr H.
Morton and James G. Boughan and gave a term until
15 April of coming year of 1831 to bring their
families.

Today certifications were issued to the following
gentlemen, were granted until 1st February of 1831
to bring their families from Missouri.
> John Jones
> Myers F. Jones
> John Hawkins

Today certifications were issued to the following
gentlemen giving them a term until the 1st of
March 1831 for bringing their families from Mississippi.
> Hugh McDonald Senior
> Hugh McDonald
> Daniel McDonald
> Roderick Nicholson

1st March 1830
Today certifications were issued to Messrs. Santi-
ago Bowie and Isaac Donoho who were received and
took the proper oath 20 day Feby just past.

(14)
21 June    Jn H. Moore left bank of the Colorado
above Thompson and above the Labahia Road adjacent
to Thompson.

21 August    I issued 15 passports with the term of
18 months.

6 August    Knight and White a site on the right
bank of the Colorado above and adjoining with that
of Jenkins.

14 Sept    J.H. Bell by virtue of the commission
made by the Supreme Government of the State dated

22 of May of the immediate past year should have
one of the sites of land as follows, that is the
sitio promised to R.C. Crozier on Lavaca, or the
site at the junction of the creek "Mustang Creek"
with the Navidad. The first in case that George
Sutherland does not take that promised Crozier,
and in case that he takes it, Bell is to take the
site at the said junction.

1 Novbr   David Grammer wants a quarter which was
chosen by Panky and abandoned, joining Sam Gates
and Widow Panky. It is subject to choice of land
made by H. Chriesman, also said Grammer must present recommendations to prove his good behavior.

8 Novr   Have issued certifications to Messrs.
J.W. and Benjamin F. Hughes with the term of 6
months from this date.

18 Novr   To Charles Donoho, Elijah Conklin, Alexander Odom certifications were issued, gave them a
term of three months.

18 Novr   Mr. George Ewing should have the site in
front of that chosen by Crozier on the right bank
of the Navidad River and which he chose for Davis,
in case that Mr. Davis does not come.

18 Novr   Mr. Saml P. Browne should have one of
the sites on Navidad and Lavaca chosen by the Alabamans if some of them do not come. The site
chosen for Richard Ellis is reserved for said
Browne in case that Ellis does not come.

(15)
December 7   A passport was issued to John Flanders - six months.

December 10, 1830   James B. Phillips took to the
north, 16 passports for as many other families
who must immigrate from Alabama in one year.

Decr 12   The tract between John Austin and John
D. Taylor on Buffalo Bayou is entered for Wm T.
Austin, brother of John Austin.

P.W. Grason has applied for a tract on the east
fork of Karankawy and is to have a preference
there, if the Alabamans who selected land there
should fail.   S.F. Austin

Tomas Barnet has requested the sitio on the west
bank of the Brazos River above and adjoining the
sitio of Joel Lakey, which was conceded to John
Elam in the First Colony of the Empresario Estevan
F. Austin and abandoned by the said John Elam and

16

the title lapsed. The said Barnet is to have the
preference of said sitio over anyone else, being
the first to ask for it, and for being a man of
the highest character and much merit, and an old
colonist.          Estaven F. Austin
     17 December 1830     San Felipe de Austin

Mr. R.R. Royall wants the sitio at the junction of
Carancahuay and Colorado which was chosen by Mrs.
Smith, in case she does not come.

Samuel Chance wants the piece of land due him adjoining Joseph San Pierre on the east bank of the
Navidad in front of Hardy and Alley.

10 March [1831]   Lewis Lamas of New York, 30 years
of age, Mary his wife 27 years of age. One son,
two daughters. Has until Febr 18<u>31</u> [sic]to bring
his family.

(16)
David Harris is to have one or the other of the
tracts of Wm Hunter or Mr. Sarton, provided they
do not get them.

John H. Jones single man wants a place below the
tract where John Williams lives adjoining Spears
tract and the tract granted to William Raleigh,
and as he is an entire stranger, I have required
him to produce me satisfactory evidence of his
moral conduct.

David Randon wants half a league of land on the
east side of the Bernard adjoining George & John
G. McNeel below.

Capt Wyly Martin wants back of Joseph & Abner
Kuykendall.

19 Feb   A.B. Sterrett & Stephen Bowie took the
oath before the Commissioners.

20 April 1831   Albert G. Reynolds  26
                Wife Elizabeth      33
                2 Male, 2 female children
From Missouri, has 6 months from date to bring his
family. Land between John Austin and Pine Point.

(17)
          John Goodman    48    From Tennessee
          Rebecca         42
          8 Male, 2 female [children]

J.J. Hughes 26 years of age from Mississippi.

James P. Caldwell 36 years of age, widower from

the State of Kentucky. 14 months from the 1' Decr 1830. Wants land below Dillard on Cedar Lake.

May 12   Samuel Coates takes his league of Augmentation at the crossing of the St Antonio Road on the Yegua.

John McClaren wants a place on the peninsula on the east side of the Pass Caballo.

James Hughson   32 years of age Family in Illinois
Temperance   22 years of age
One male child
Has until first of February 1832 to move his family and has selected League No 1 mouth of the Carancahua Bay east side, which entry he is to have reserved until that time.

May 13   Patrick Allison, single man, from Baltimore.

(18)
Isaa[c] Dunbar & wife   ) Arrived 1 May and wish to
Edwd Winston & wife   ) be recd as part of the
500 families
Williamson Daniels   33 years of age of age
Cynthia his wife   26
3 Male 1 female [children]
From Missouri. Arrived 3d Jany 1831.
Took the oath 17 May 1831. Issued certificate.
Ratcliffs entry on Lavaca.

Isaac R. Hawkins 24 years of age, moved from Missouri and arrived 1 Jany 1831.

Thomas H. Austin from Florida, arrived in May 1831. A quarter in the Coast Colony.

Thomas Hill, Mary his wife, 2 male children. Removed from Missouri, arrived in Jany 1831, recd provisionally and is to be subject to future confirmation or not as the Empresario may deem proper. Applied 17 June 1831. Issued certificate.

Henry Martin, Mary his wife, 1 male child, 3 female children. Family on the Sabine. Has presented no recommendations. His reception as a colonist is to be subject to future consideration. No certificate is issued to him and it is entirely optional with the empresario to receive him or not. June 17, 1831.

Jesse Bartlet, Francis his wife, 39 years, 6 male children, 4 female. Illinois. To remove in November next. June 18, 1831.

18
Nathan A. McFadden, Eliza his wife, 27 years,
1 female child.  Illinois.  To remove Novr next.
June 18, 1831.

James Cooper    22 years of age ) Married in the
Miranda         19 years of age )      Colony

(19)
John A. Thompson  22 years of age, from the State
of New York and arrived in this Colony 14 June
1831.  Took the oath 5" July & recd certificate.

Edmund St John Hawkins 20 years of age, moved from
Kentucky and arrived in the Colony 22d April 1831.
Took the oath 18 Feb 1832.

Henry Husted 33 years of age, moved from the State
of New York.  Passport 28 May.  Hatter.  Issued
certificate 24" June.

Winston S. McDaniel 28 years of age, married, from
Tennessee where his family now reside.
Arrived 24" May 1831.
Lydia his wife    24   One female [child]
Passport dated 16 May.  Has permission to locate
land which is to be held up for him until 1 Decr
1831.  Took oath.
Certificate issued 27 June and note given.

Bernard Rogan.  54 years of age, single man from
Ireland and arrived 24 May 1831.  Took the oath.
Has permission to select land.
Passport dated 16 May.

John Berry    33 years of age
Nancy my wife 33  years of age
2 Male 2 female children
Farmer from Virginia, to be here by 30 Novr 1831.
[Marginal note]: Declined coming

David Berry        33 years of age    Farmer from
Elizabeth my wife 28 years of age    Tennessee
3 Male 1 female children
To be here by 30 Novr 1831.

Lacy Kerr    50 years of age.  From Tennessee
5 Children 3 male 2 female

(20)
William Brookfield 44 years of age
Emma my wife        36 years of age
4 Male 3 female children.
Occupation farmer.  Moved from Indiana and arrived
in this Colony in June 1831.
Took the oath 22d June.  30 May passport.

James O. Farrel 29 years of age, a native of Ireland. Emma my wife 18 years of age, one male child. Moved from Phila and arrived in this Colony in June 1831. 30 May Passport. Took the oath 22d June.

Solomon Lapham 34 years of age    From New York Lovicy my wife 28 years of age    3 female children Passport 30 May. Issued certificate 24 June. Family resides in N. York. To be here 30 Novr 1831

Edward Coibble 25 years of age & wife. From State of N. York. Passport 28 May. Arrived 14" June 1831.

(21) Abednigo Biddy 33 years of age, born in S. Carolina. Patsy 26   3 Male 1 female children Moved from Alabama and arrived in this Colony in Decr 1830.           Cold

John Talbott 45 years of age. Susanna my wife 32 years of age One male 2 female children Moved from Arkansas and arrived 23d Decr 1830. 23d June took the oath.

Thomas Toulson, single, 40 years of age, of the State of Virginia. Arrived in June 1830, wants his land in the contract of 100 families. Took the oath today 25 June 1831 (lives with Rosseau).

John Kerley, 36 years of age, arrived in Feb 1830, single, took the oath June 25, 1831.

Isaac Marshall, single, 35 years of age, moved from Georgia and arrived in the Colony 24 May 1831. Passport 16 May. Took the oath 28 June.

Joseph M. McCormick 25 years of age, single, moved from Kentucky and arrived in this Colony 24 May 1831. Passport dated 16 May. Took the oath 28 June. Issued Certificate.

(22) On Walnut Creek the upper league entered for James Burleson 26 June.

Adam Heldebrand 35 years of age, married, 2 sons and one daughter. In Ohio. I League above Dottery. Entered by W.R. Dickenson. To move by Decr 1831.

Isaac Harris 25 years of age Martha my wife 18 years of age. One male child. Mr. Harris has been living on the Trinity for almost 7 years and being desirous to move into the

Colony wishes to obtain a place on Cypress Bayou.
He has a large stock of cattle.  He also has a
brother married and a single brother anxious to
move here.  The place he wants is about 4 to 6
miles from the mouth of Cypress Bayou on the west
side, and is promised the place on the first
vacancy.

John Hubbell 24 years of age, born in Upper Louisiana and came to this province about 4 years, came
to the Colony in Augt 1830.

John Mahuna 30 years of age, native of Ireland and
arrived in this country in 1824 unmarried, took
the oath and obtained a certificate July 18.

Andrew Northington, aged 39 years, widower, one
male and one female child, both in Kentucky.  Born
in North Carolina, arrived in this Colony in Jany
7, 1831.  Took the oath.  Certificate issued July
18, 1831.  (Lives with J.H. Bell).

Pierre Blanchet, single, 42 years of age, native
of France, arrived in this Colony in June 1831,
took the oath, certificate issued.  July 18, 1831.

(23)
July 18, 1831.
George P. Dykes aged 56 years.
Judy S. Dykes his wife
Two male, two female children.
From Alabama, arrived in March 1831, living on
Labaca.  Took oath.  Certificate issued.

Lovick P. Dykes, aged 25 yeats
Roady V. Dykes his wife
From Alabama, arrived in March 1831.  Living on
Navidad.  Took oath, certificate issued.
Land opposite but on east side of Navidad.

William M. Alley, single, 29 years of age, of Missouri, arrived in 1828.  West bank of the Navidad
adjoining, above Hardy.

Robert Mills, single, of Kentucky, arrived in
1830.  Took the oath and received certificate.
Living in Brazoria.

Andrew G. Mills single of Kentucky.  Arrived in
March 1831.  Took the oath, received certificate.

Jacob Phillipson, single, Hanover in Germany, arrived in 1831.  Took the oath, certificate.

Wm H. Cox, single, of England, arrived in 1830.

Elijah Howell 26 years of age, single, moved from
Ohio and arrived in this Colony 30" May 1831.

Thomas Hushan wishes his quarter of a league of
land back of the lands on the Colorado east of
Eagle Lake.

Lemuel Dickinson 37 years of age, widower,
2 female children. Moved from Louisiana and
arrived in this Colony in 1825.

(24)
Jesse M. Evans 29 years of age, unmarried, moved
from Tennessee and arrived in this Colony October
1830. Surveyor & farmer.

James Hall 28 years of age, married.
Nancy his wife 27
3 Male 1 female children
Moved from Arkansas and arrived in this Colony
4" Augt 1831. Issued certificate. League No 9 on
San Antonio Road.

John Thomas 30 years of age from Louisiana.
Entered 22d October 1831.

James Higgins 28 years of age    One male child
Maria my wife 17 years of age
Moved from Louisiana where his family resides, and
will be here in March 1832. Took the oath before
Col Austin in Septr.

Henry Louis wants his league on the head of west
fork of Mustang Creek. 16 Novr 1831.

Peter L. Berry 25 years of age, moved from Phila
and arrived in this Colony in October 1831.
Issued a certificate Coast Colony 22 Novr 1831.

1' Decr issued two passports, one year.
    Walter Shinault          Absalom Kennedy

(25)
John Yorke 32 years of age
Iutitia his wife 27 years of age
3 Male 2 female children
Arrived in this Colony in 1822.
Issued certificate 22 Novr 1831.

Patrick Reels wants his half league back of
leagues on Eagle Lake.

Henry Applewhite 33 years of age. Moved from
Tennessee and arrived in this Colony 1' Feby 1831.

Gowin Harris married, wife not in the Country. Two

sons with him. Issued a certificate this day
Coast Colony 19 Decr 1831.

T.F.L. Parrott 28 years of age from South Carolina
and arrived in this Country in Novr 1831.
Physician. Certificate Coast Colony 2d Feby 1832.

William Miller 18 years of age, single (brother of
Dr. Miller) from Kentucky and arrived in February
1831, entered as a colonist in the Coast Colony.

William Eaton 23 years of age from Ohio and arrived in this Colony in February 1827, entered as
a colonist in the Coast Colony 27 February 1831.
Issued a certificate and recd his note, took the
oath under the State Constitution.

(26)
Anne Catherine Douglass 19 years of age, single,
orphan both parents being dead. To have a quarter
of a league of land in the Coast Colony, arrived
in this Colony Jany 1832.

Samuel C. Douglass 39 years of age widower, moved
from Georgia and arrived in this Colony in May
1831. 2 Males and 3 females. Entered the Coast
Colony. Took the oath and issued the certificate
3d March 1832.

William Eckle single man arrived in this Colony in
1830 took the oath & has a certificate of admission in the Coast Colony.

Arhibald Austin widower with two children belongs
to the Contract of July 1828.

Andrew Y. Austin 28 years old wife & one child
belongs to the same contract.

John G. Rowland 32 years of age. One female child
Frances W        23
Took the oath 27 March 1832 Coast Colony

Thomas Andrews  35 years of age  One aged female
Nancy           30                One female child
Alabama. To move in the Spring of 1832.

(27)
Berry Haney 26 years of age  2 Female children
Philadelphia my wife 22 years of age
Moved from Illinois where his family resides.  Has
until 1" Jany 1833 to bring his family to the
Colony, the Little Colony on the Colorado.

18 August 1832
D.W. Anthony colonist for the Coast Colony.

Jacob Anthony if there is a location joining his
brother on the Bernard.

C.A. Bettner enters the upper quarter of League No
2 east of Bernard sold by Simon Miller to Steritt
forfeited on acct of non residence.

Mrs Bostic enters No 4 north of Navasota joining
Richd Carter. Novr 10, 1832.

Mr. Woodruff wants the fraction on Spring Creek
after Dr. Hunters Labor is run off, opposite from
the Town. Novemr 20, 1832.

Daniel F. Donaldson native of the State of Maryland 26 years of age, unmarried, arrived on the
Sabine in Novemr.

Nancy Blakey widow & eight children wants a place
above the San Antonio Road, on the N.E. corner of
a ten league tract made by Brown, if possible.

Richard Wilhelm 46 years of age married
Sarah my wife    42      do
5 Female 2 male children.  Just arrived in the
country.  Moved from Illinois.  Passport from the
Consul of St. Louis.  15" Sepr 1832.

(28)
Abraham Gallatin        Minor children
Moved from Missouri and arrived in this Colony
1" Decr 1832 is to be admitted if there is room.
Should the tract of land granted to John R. Wil-
liams be declared vacant Mr. Gallatin wants it.

Albert Gallatin  23 years of age. Single.
Moved from Missouri, to be admitted if room.

James Winn
Elizabeth his wife        To be admitted

Euclid M. Cox 22 years old.
Quarter below Parkers half lea.

Austin M. Coats 39 yrs of age
Lucinda my wife.  One child. Family in Missouri.

Adam Smith 41 years of age.  Widower.
Seven children in Illinois.

John G. Robinson 44 years    One male child
Francis

Samuel O. Pettus            One child
Patsey
McLaughlin league back of Dottery.

24
(29)
P.K. Bartelson 32 years of age
Caroline

Miles G. Stevens 30 years of age
Mary my wife        One male child

Reuben P.F. Stone 34 years of age.
Quarter of a league on the Colorado joining Bowman
& Williams.  Took the oath. Title issued.

John P. Borden single man.

Anthony D. Kennard 45 years of age
Sarah my wife        42        7 Children
Arkansas Territory.  Took the oath and title
issued for his land.

Herschel H. Hunt 30 years of age, single. Arrived
2 years ago.  Takes the quarter on the Navidad
relinquished by Mr. Dwyer.  Title issued.

Phinneas M. Smith, son of Phinneas Smith. Moved
from New York. Single. Teaching at Brazoria.

Alvin Weatherby 28 years of age (Boston)

T.G. Western      40        "        N. York

(30)
Isaac C. Hoskins 34 yrs of age
Nancy his wife    28      do
5 Children, 3 males, 2 females
24 Decr 1832 took the oath.  Moved from Kentucky.

William A. Hall 31 yrs of age      Took the oath
Elizabeth his wife 27    do        One female child

Thomas Lewis 18 years of age. Has parents in this
Country.  Came in with Mr. Baird.  Took the oath.

Joseph Flanigan 27 years of age.
Came in with Mr. Baird.

Fayett Bankson 32 years of age.
Came in with Mr. Baird

Joseph Thompson 63 years of age.    From Alabama
Nancy            55 years of age.    Took the oath
3 Female, 3 Male children

Stephen Manner, his wife, from Alabama.

John H. Dabney, his wife, from Alabama. 5 Children
Took the oath & recd his title.
Land on Scull Creek

Charles H. Smith 23 years of age    From New York
Susan Anne      20      do          Took the oath

Henry Austin wishes to locate a league of land
lying on the Bastrop Creek in such parcels as the
local situation will admit.

(31)
Edmund H. Martin 23 years of age from Kentucky.
Quarter of a league above Jno H. Moore on the
Colorado.

George Robbins 28 yrs of age.
Cynthia his wife 23
Moved from Louisiana. Took the oath 24 Decemr.

James McLaughlin 49 years of age.      Moved from
Lucy Kerr my wife 33 years of age.     Trinity
4 Male, 1 Female [children]

James J. Dewitt 50 years of age, widower.
2 Male, 1 female children.
Been in the Country 7 years. Made a petition for
his title.

Thomas J. Wootten 40 years of age.
Paulina my wife    32 years of age.
6 Children. 3 Male, 3 Female.
Mr. W. came out as one of the families introduced
by Thompson & Robertson. Arrived in the beginning
of 1831. Took the oath 26 Decr. League between
Jones & McKinney east side of the Brazos.

John W. Buckner 43 years of age
Elizabeth my wife 28 years of age
2 Male 2 Female [children]
Family residing in in the State of Missouri. 26
Decemr 1832 took the oath, issued a certificate.

Jacob Ebberle 34 years of age    From Kentucky
Catherine my wife 32 years of age
2 Male, 5 Female children

(32)
Richard Breeden 50 years of age, unmarried.
Moved from Kentucky.

Albert Elgin 21 years of age, unmarried.
Moved from Kentucky.

Mary Young, widow of Adam Lawrence with 1 male and
7 female children, been in the Country 13 months.
Paid the Commissioner 9$ on acct of his fees & no
more.

Saml Houston 38 years of age from Tennessee.

James Bradley 22 years of age from Tennessee.

Wm Hawkins 20 years of age from Missouri.

John Thomas 50 years of age        Moved from Alabama
Phoebe his wife 50 years of age
6 Male 2 Female children

Peter Cartwright 55 years of age    From Alabama
Elizabeth 50 years of age
7 Male, 4 female children

John Springer 27 years of age       From Alabama
Elizabeth        22 years of age
1 Male, 2 female children

Wm Morris, widower, 29 years of age & one female
child.  From Alabama.  Wants the place on Sn
Jacinto called Cedar Point.

Ezekiel Springer 21 years of age
Erises Springer  21 years of age

[In the original Register, a marginal note applies
to all the names from John Thomas through Ezekiel
Springer]:   Want land in the San Jacinto District
& have gone to examine it.

(33)
Wilifred Cartwright 30 years of age, single man
from Alabama.

William Cartwright

James Peterson 28 years of age unmarried, moved
from Alabama.

Robert Stevenson 28 years of age
Narcissa his wife 22 years
One male, one female [children]
Moved from Tennessee.  Took the oath.  Land north
of Navasota.  Title delivered.

Andrew Graham 36 years of age
Sibby his wife 27 years of age
2 Male, 2 female children
Moved from East Tennessee and arrived in Feby 1832

John Edward Lewis 26 years of age      From New York
Anne his wife        21 years of age
Mr. Lewis family is in New York & will have them
here in 3 or 4 months.

William Lewis 24 years of age unmarried.
From New York.

William Gorham 30 years of age unmarried.
Connecticut. Arrived in Feby 1831, enters the
quarter on Navidad No 5.

Radford Berry 32 years of age single from the
State of Mississippi. Has eight years of residence in Texas. Wants his land on the east side
of the Brasos near Navasota.

William McGuffin 24 years of age.     Native of
Margaret his wife 17 years of age      Ireland
Moved here from Tennessee, wants land in the
neighborhood of Black.

(34)
Samuel Millet  32 years of age
Clementine his wife 17 years of age
Moved from District State of Main and arrived in
this Colony April 1831.

John F. Whiteside 20 years of age
Elizabeth his wife 18      do

Reuben D. Wood 23 years of age
Martha his wife 22    do        One female child
From Tennessee, moved into Texas in 1827.
Took the oath.

Samuel F. Allen  23 years of age
Unmarried.  Quarter above Wootens on Brazos.

Isaac Casner 47 years of age
Mary his wife 30 years of age
2 Male 2 female children.
Land in Contract of Novr 1827.

William Hillhouse 66 years of age
Lucretia my wife  65 years of age
Wants land in Neighborhood of Bowman

William Medford 46 years of age
Elizabeth his wife 35 years of age
One male 3 female children
Lives on Mill Creek with Cooper and wants his land
cleared out.

Jesse Halderman 31 years of age, moved from
Kentucky.

David Halderman 25 years of age, moved from
Kentucky.

(35)
Henry Cooke 32 years of age
Mary his wife, 30 years of age
2 Male 1 female children
Moved from the upper part of Mississippi and just
arrived.  Land not selected.

Samuel Wood 26 years of age
Mary his wife 26 years of age
2 Male 1 female children
Moved from Little Missouri. Just arrived. Land not
selected.

David A. Hoffman 28 years of age
Mary his wife 20 years of age
Moved from Missouri and arrived in this Colony in
1831.  Took the oath and title issued.
No 7 East Labaca.

Henry Anthony single man from Kentucky.

James Ryan 57 years of age    Land on the Navasota.
Henry Durbain 44 years of age       Title issued.
6 Children                          Took the oath

Alfred R. Guild 25 years of age, unmarried.
From Boston. Land on Davidson Creek.
14 Feby took the oath.

Jacob G. Lentz 38 years of age.
Sarah his wife 37 years of age.
3 Male 3 female children.
15 Feby took the oath.

James Wilkinson 30 years of age   Tennessee
Amanda his wife 27 years of age   Been in 2 years.

Howard Decrow 26 years of age unmarried, been 2
years in the Country.  Land on the Juanita.

(36)
Hugh M. Childers 23 years of age
Susannah his wife 23 years of age
One male child                    Contract of 1827
Moved here from Alabama and arrived in April 1831.

Samuel Denton 30 years of age
Sarah Ann     22 years of age
From Michigan where his family resides.

David Ayers 39 years of age    From New York where
Anne M.     33    do           his family resides
2 Male 4 female children
15 February 1833 took the oath before Mr.
Arcineaga

John H. Pickens 25 years of age     From Kentucky
Elizabeth his wife 28    do         Took the oath
1 Male 3 female children

William L. Litle 25 years of age    From Kentucky
Matilda his wife 24      do         Took the oath
One male child

William Ponton 60 years of age
Isabella his wife 50 years
One female child

James Foster 61 years of age        Moved from
Pamelia his wife                    Mississippi
3 Male 3 female children

Macklin, Bracy  28 years
Julia his wife
3 Male 1 female [children]
[Margin]: Connections of J.E. Groce.

(37)
William C. Sparks 33 years of age
Sarah his wife 22 years of age
1 Male 4 Female children
Moved from Tennessee and arrived on the
1st of Jany 1833.

Jacob Casner 42 years of age    Widower
3 Males 1 female
Moved from Mississippi, arrived 1st Feby 1833.

Jesse Barker 28 years of age    From Missouri
Milinda his wife 23    do
3 Male 1 female children
Arrived in the Colony Decemr 1833. Took the oath.

James Crawford  23                  took the oath
Sarah his wife  22
1 Male 1 female [children]
Arrived in this Country from Tennessee in 1830.

William Avery  24 years of age
Elsina his wife 17 years of age    2 boys
Arrived in Decr from Missouri. Took the oath.

John Hallett  50 years of age
Margaret his wife 42 years of age
3 Male 1 female children
Mr. Hallets wife & 2 children are in New York, has
2 sons with him at Labahia.  Wants a place east of
Brookfield.

Thomas Lester 33 years of age    Moved from Ohio
Sarah his wife 21 years of age
2 Male 1 female children

B.L. Hanks 28 years of age      Moved from Tennessee
Sarah Anne his wife 18 do

(38)
Daniel Parker 52 years of age
Patsey his wife 41 years of age
6 Male 5 female children
Moved from Illinois where his family now resides
to be here by the 1st of Jany next.  Took the oath
March 18, 1833.  Chriesman to make the selection.

Grey B. King 29 years of age      Took the oath
Susan S. his wife 21 years of age
One male one female children
Moved here from Tennessee and arrived in
March 1833.

Littleberry Franks 36 years of age. Widower with
five children.  2 Male 3 female [children]
Moved from Louisiana and arrived in this Country
in August 1832.  Took the oath 19 March 1833.

James W. Foster  25  Single. Wants land near Bracy

Wm W. Carson 26 years of age.    Single.
From Pennsylvania.

Buckman Canfield 37 years of age
Harriet his wife 23 years of age
One male child
Moved from the State of New York and arrived
6 Feby 1833.  Took the oath 26 March.

James Campbell 26 years of age
Anne his wife 18 years of age
One male child
League below Pontons on the Lavaca.

Elisha Wheeler joining Henry at the mouth of the
Brazos.  Entered by Borden.

(39)
Jesse B. Atkinson 25 years of age
Margaret his wife 18 years of age
Moving from Tennessee and arrived in the Colony in
September 1833.

John Foster
William Sanders      [Nothing entered]
Elisha Mackey

William Arnold 38 years of age
Martha Eliza his wife 26 years of age
2 Female children
From the State of Tennessee and just arrived.
Took the oath and entered in Coast Colony.

J.E. Robertson 37 years of age
Euphemia Lemely 27 years of age
3 Female children. Moved from the State of
Alabama where his family now resides.
Selected League No 2 on Highland Creek.

John Curlew 27 years of age, single. Native of
England. Took the oath and issued a certificate
for the Coast Colony.

(40)
William Hunt 35 years of age, married.
Mary his wife 21 years of age
One male child. From the State of Ohio where his
family now resides.

Robert J. Calder 23 years of age, unmarried.
Apr 16. Contract of 1827.

Jane E. Caldwell widow of James H. Calder.
Widow with one child.

Henry B. Prentiss enters the league of land on
Sims Bayou joining the Harrisburg tract.

Allen Norton 33 years of age, widower with one
child from Connecticut where his child lives.

April 18, 1833
Alexander Ewing 25 years of age, unmarried. Moved
from Pennsylvania, an European by birth.
Took the oath.

William F. Garner 26 years of age, unmarried.
Moved from Alabama and arrived in the present
month. Took the oath.

John Hoffman 35 years of age, unmarried. Moved
from Tennessee and arrived in this Colony in March
1832. Took the oath.

James J. Foster 33 years of age
Mary his wife 21 years of age
Wants land on San Jacinto.

(41)
Fielding Ruble 31 years of age.
Francis his wife 21 years of age.
Wants the place on Mill Creek between Bostics
place and S.F. Austin's Reserve. Augt 14, 1833.

Dunlevy, D. Wants land in the Little Colony.
Children. 6 Male 4 female.

Henry Parker 43 years of age
Henrietta his wife 30 years of age
2 Male 1 female children
Moved from South Carolina and arrived in the
Colony 1st July 1833.

James Ross 40 years of age from Kentucky. Arrived
in this Country 1st March 1833. Unmarried.

Bird L. Hanks wants the place formerly entered by
Mr. Medley. Cleared out by Mr. Ayres.

L.C. Manson widower arrived Decr 1832, made an application for admission Jany 1833, took the oath
before H. Smith alcalde Brazoria 9th Novr 1833.
Issued a certificate same day.

(42)
John Merry 48 years of age
Marrill 47        do
3 Male 1 female children
Tennessee, arrived last fall, is to have the
league of land surveyed by Hirams for John Moore.

Hall Roddy single man 30 years of age moved from
the State of Tennessee, moved into the Country 1st
April 1831. Wants the place joining McCains League
entered by Mr. Raney & is to have it if Raney
moves away. Feby 6, 1834.

Isaac Batterson 42 years of age
Amelia            39        do
4 Female children
From the State of New York where his family resides. Wants the league of land surveyed by Hirams
for John L. Moore.

Mr. Shubael Marsh wants the proportion of land
which he is entitled to joining Maclin Bracy.
April 15, 1834

Thomas Bridges 37 years of age
Hannah H. his wife
One female child
Coast Colony

Municipality of Austin

Register of the families introduced by the Citizen Empresario Estevan F. Austin by virtue of the contract made to the effect with the Government which have taken the due oath prescribed by Article No. 3 of the Colonization Law of the State of Coahuila and Texas dated 25 [24] March 1825

| No. | Name | Age | State | Children M | Children F | Other dep. | Profes- sion | Origin | Arrived | Took Oath | Total Souls |
|---|---|---|---|---|---|---|---|---|---|---|---|
| 1 | George B. McKinstry | 27 | Single | | | | Trader | Georgia | 20 Apr 1829 | 19 May[1829] | 1 |
| 2 | Luis DeMoss | 26 | Married | | 1 | | Farmer | Missouri | yr 1823 | | 3 |
| | Catherine his wife | 20 | | | | | | | | | |
| 3 | Abraham Roberts | 56 | Widower | 1 | | 9 | idem | Louisiana | 2 Jan 1827 | Nov | 11 |
| 4 | Robert Burney | | Single | | | 1 | Farmer | Louisiana | Novr 1828 | 18 Nov | 2 |
| 5 | Robert Pebles | 30 | Married | 1 | | 5 | Doctor | Louisiana | 10 Sep 1829 | 27 Oct | 8 |
| | Pamelia his wife | 25 | | | | | | | | | |
| 6 | John Peterson | 23 | Single | | | | Farmer | idem | Nov 1824 | 1 Dec | 1 |
| | Adjoining land of Holland | | | | | | | | | | |
| 7 | James B. Miller | 29 | idem | | | | Doctor | Kentucky | 10 May 1829 | 1 Dec | 1 |
| | Claimed site of P.H. Kerr | | | | | | | | | | |
| 8 | Henry Chever | 30 | idem | | | | Trader | Louisiana | Jul 1826 | 1 Dec | 1 |
| | Adjoins that of Millers the No. 3 west bank of Palmito Creek | | | | | | | | | | |
| 9 | Thomas J. Gasley | 31 | Married | 2 | | 1 | Doctor | Ohio | 16 Nov 1828 | 12 Jan | 5 |
| | Wants his land at upper end of McGinty's Prairie and at upper end of a little prairie on the | | | | | | | | | | |
| | Colorado between this and that of a tiny plain above | | | | | | | | | | |
| 10 | G.B. Cotten | 38 | Single | | | | Printer | Louisiana | 10 Aug 1829 | 2 Dec | 1 |
| 11 | Joseph McGeorge | 25 | idem | | | | Trader | idem | 26 Jul | 2 idem | 1 |
| 12 | Thos F. Converse | 32 | idem | | | | Printer | idem | 10 Aug | 2 idem | 1 |
| 13 | Horatio H. Hickoke | 22 | idem | | | | idem | Alabama | Oct | 2 idem | 1 |
| 14 | William Robinson | 39 | Widower | 2 | 2 | 10 | Farmer | Arkansas | Aug 1827 | 2 idem | 13 |
| 15 | James Stephenson | 39 | Married | 3 | | | idem | Georgia | Mar 1826 | 3 idem | 7 |
| | Amelia his wife | 30 | | | | | | | | | |
| 16 | E. Alexander J. Blair | 21 | Single | | | | Trader | Louisiana | 13 Jul 1829 | 5 | 1 |
| 17 | Edward Lang | 22 | do | | | | idem | idem | idem | 5 | 1 |

33

| No. | Name | Age | State | Child-ren | Other dep. | Profes-sion | Origin | Arrived | Took Oath | Total 34 Souls |
|---|---|---|---|---|---|---|---|---|---|---|
| 18 | Charles Bury | 36 | Single | | | idem | idem | idem | | 1 |
| 19 | William Munsen | 39 | Widower | 1 | | Farmer | Arkansas | 29 Jul 1824 | | 2 |
| 20 | Thomas Bell | 35 | Married | | | Farmer | Georgia | year 1824 | | 2 |
| | Abigail his wife | 21 | | | | | | | | |
| 21 | Florence Stack | 30 | Single | | | Carpenter | Ireland | year 1825 | | 1 |
| | Wants the quarter of sitio chosen by Henderson on Carancuhua Bayou | | | | | | | | | |
| 22 | Joshua Fletcher | 47 | idem | | | Trader | Louisiana | 18 Jul 1829 | 5 Dec | 1 |
| | Site No. 6 above the headwaters of west bank of Palmito Creek | | | | | | | | | |
| 23 | Thomas Cox | 37 | Married | 1 | | Farmer | Alabama | Mar 1822 | | 3 |
| | Cynthia his wife | 28 | | | | | | | | |
| 24 | Patrick Scott | 54 | Widower | 5 | 2 | Farmer | Alabama | Feb 1829 | | 11 |
| 25 | Henry W. Munson | 36 | Married | 3 | 19 | idem | Louisiana | yr 1828 | | 24 |
| | Anne B. his wife | | | | | | | | | |
| 26 | Jefferson George | 22 | Single | | | idem | idem | | | 1 |
| (45)(46) | | | | | | | | | | |
| 27 | Robert Hodges | 26 | Married | 1 | 1 | Farmer | Louisiana | Mar 1829 | 10 Dec 1829 | 4 |
| | Susan his wife | 20 | | | | | | | | |
| 28 | Henry Scott | 38 | Married | 5 | 3 | Farmer | Alabama | Feb 1829 | 10 Dec | 10 |
| | Patsey his wife | 33 | | | | | | | | |
| | Next to --- of the plot of Saml Isaacs west bank of the Brazos | | | | | | | | | |
| 29 | Thomas J. Pilgrim | 24 | Single | | | Schoolmaster | New York | Jan 1829 | 10 Dec | 1 |
| 30 | Nestor Clay | 31 | Married | 2 | 5 | Farmer | Kentucky | Dec 1827 | 7 Dec | 10 |
| | Nancy his wife | | | | | | | | | |
| 31 | John Litle | 31 | Married | 1 | | Farmer | Ohio | 22 Jun 1825 | 10 Dec | 3 |
| | Winniford his wife | 21 | | | | | | | | |
| 32 | James Moore | 32 | Married | 4 | 10 | idem | Tennessee | Feb 1824 | 10 Dec | 18 |
| | Olive his wife | | | | | | | | | |
| 33 | Job Williams | 45 | Married | 2 | 4 | idem | Missouri | Dec 1825 | 10 Dec | 8 |
| | Nancy his wife | | | | | | | | | |
| | Wants his land above the Navidad west bank adjoining above that of Brown | | | | | | | | | |

| No. | Name | Age | Status | | | | Occupation | Origin | Date | Date | No. |
|---|---|---|---|---|---|---|---|---|---|---|---|
| 34 | Isaac McGary | 27 | Single | | | | idem | Mississippi | Mar 1825 | 11 Dec | 1 |
| | A sitio adjoining the Widow Powell on the upper Barnard | | | | | | | | | | |
| 35 | Fredk J. Calvit | 42 | idem | | | | idem | Louisiana | Jun 1828 | 11 Dec | 1 |
| | West of the Oyster Creek below Austin's land | | | | | | | | | | |
| 36 | John Partin | 27 | Married | 1 | 2 | | idem | Tennessee | Jun 1828 | 12 Oct | |
| | Nancy Partin his wife | 26 | | | | | | | | | |
| | Wants his land on the east side of --- Bayou | | | | | | | | | | |
| 37 | James Small | 34 | Single | | 2 | | idem | Louisiana | May 1825 | 8 Oct | 3 |
| | The 2nd quarter east of the Carankaway between the lower part of the sitio adjoining Cook | | | | | | | | | | |
| | and Davis and Osborn and Winston and --- | | | | | | | | | | |
| 38 | Moses Cummins | 44 | Widower | 1 | 3 | 2 | Schoolmaster | Kentucky | Feb 1829 | 14 Oct | 7 |
| | His children are in Kentucky | | | | | | | | | | |
| 39 | John Williams | 41 | Married | 2 | 4 | 12 | Farmer | Arkansas | in 1823 | 14 Oct | 20 |
| | Rebecca his wife | | | | | | | | | | |
| 40 | Johnson Hensley | 22 | Married | | 2 | | Farmer | Arkansas | 8 Nov 1828 | 17 Oct | 11 |
| | Sarah his wife | | | | | | | | | | |
| 41 | Daniel Etherton | 26 | Single | | | | Farmer | Louisiana | Apr 1825 | | 1 |
| 42 | William D. Finley | 29 | Married | 2 | 1 | | Doctor | Ohio | 18 Jan 1829 | | 5 |
| | Lydia V. his wife | 27 | | | | | | | | | |
| | Has six months delay to bring his family from --- | | | | | | | | | | |
| 43 | Edwd N. Cullum | 29 | Single | | | | Carpenter | Louisiana | Oct 1826 | 15 Oct | 1 |
| | Adjoins land of Holland | | | | | | | | | | |
| 44 | Rice F. Murray | 22 | idem | | | | Farmer | Kentucky | Mar 1826 | 18 Oct | 1 |
| 45 | Luke Lesassier | 38 | Married | 1 | 6 | | Farmer & Lawyer | Louisiana | Dec 1829 | 19 Oct | 9 |
| | Eliza his wife | 30 | | | | | | | | | |
| 46 | John S. Evans | 31 | Married | 2 | 4 | | Farmer | idem | Dec 1829 | 19 Oct | 8 |
| | Sarah his wife | 29 | | | | | | | | | |
| 47 | John W. Moore | 31 | Single | | | | Trader | Tennessee | Jul 1828 | 20 Oct | 1 |
| | A quarter below the place that encircles the labor of Isaacs on the Brasos | | | | | | | | | | |
| 48 | William Hensley | 29 | idem | | | | Farmer | Arkansas | Nov 1828 | 20 Oct | 1 |
| 49 | Robt M. Williamson | 23 | idem | | | | Lawyer | Alabama | 13 Jun 1827 | 20 Oct | 1 |

Total 36

| No. | Name | Age | State | Children | Other dep. | | Profession | Origin | Arrived | Took Oath | Total Souls |
|---|---|---|---|---|---|---|---|---|---|---|---|
| 50 | Wm Dunlap | 52 | Married | 5 | 2 | | Trader | Georgia | 25 Apr 1828 | 20 Oct | 9 |
| | Dolly his wife | 40 | | | | | | | | | |
| | Wants land as a bachelor, more when his family comes the amount will be increased | | | | | | | | | | |
| 51 | Anthony Winston | 45 | Married | 4 | 3 | 85 | Farmer | Alabama | Nov 1829 | 19 Dec | 86 |
| | Sally Anne his wife | 39 | | | | | | | | | |
| (47)(48) | | | | | | | | | | | |
| 52 | George Sutherland | 42 | Married | 3 | 2 | 6 | Farmer | Alabama | Nov 1829 | 19 Dec 1829 | 13 |
| | Frances his wife | 40 | | | | | | | | | |
| 53 | Jessie White | 46 | Married | 4 | 2 | 3 | idem | idem | Nov 1829 | 19 Dec | 11 |
| | Mary his wife | 45 | | | | | | | | | |
| 54 | James N. Smith | 27 | Married | 1 | 1 | 25 | idem | idem | Nov 1829 | 19 Dec | |
| | Sarah Anne his wife | 22 | | | | | | | | | |
| 55 | R.C. Crozier | 24 | Married | | 5 | | idem | idem | Nov 1829 | 16 Dec | 7 |
| | Sarah H. his wife | 20 | | | | | | | | | |
| 56 | George Ewing | 38 | Single | | 1 | | idem | idem | Nov 1829 | 19 Dec | 1 |
| | He wants a place on the east side of the Colony above the mouth of Ten Mile Creek | | | | | | | | | | |
| 57 | Haney | 38 | Single | | | | idem | idem | Nov 1829 | 19 Dec | 1 |
| 58 | William Hardy | 36 | Married | 2 | 3 | 2 | idem | Tennessee | Dec 1822 | 19 Dec | 9 |
| | Margaret his wife | 27 | | | | | | | | | |
| 59 | Samuel C. Hirons | 43 | Single [sic] | 2 | | | Carpenter | Atacapas | Jan 1826 | | 4 |
| | Nancy W. his wife | 29 | | | | | | | | | |
| 60 | Sylvanus Hatch | 48 | Married | 4 | 1 | 3 | Farmer | Louisiana | 15 Aug 1829 | 21 Oct | 10 |
| | Pamelia his wife | 39 | | | | | | | | | |
| 61 | James D. Allcorn | 30 | Single | | | | Farmer | Arkansas | in 1824 | | 1 |
| 62 | Warren D.C. Hall | 34 | idem | 1 | | 13 | idem | Louisiana | 12 Nov 1828 | 21 Dec | 16 |
| | Julietta his wife | 29 | | | | | | | | | |
| 63 | Matthew Duty | 36 | Single | | | | Farmer | Louisiana | 15 Jul 1829 | | 1 |
| | On the east bank of the Colorado above the road from Bexar to the point above the third plain | | | | | | | | | | |
| 64 | Elizabeth Powell | 30 | Widow | 2 | 2 | | idem | idem | Nov 1828 | 21 Dec | 5 |

| 65 | Nelson Smith | 25 | Married | 1 | | | Farmer | Arkansas | Mar 1829 | 21 Dec | 5 |
|---|---|---|---|---|---|---|---|---|---|---|---|
| | Darkay his wife | 23 | | | | | | | | | |
| | Wants his land adjoining the land of --- on Palmito Creek | | | | | | | | | | |
| 66 | John W. Litle | 55 | Married | 2 | 2 | | Farmer | Louisiana | Nov 1829 | 21 Dec | 6 |
| | Edith his wife | 48 | | | | | | | | | |
| 67 | William Barret | 30 | Married | | | | idem | | | | |
| | Elizabeth his wife | 25 | | | | | | | | | |
| 68 | Bryant Dottery | 32 | Married | 3 | 1 | 4 | Farmer | Louisiana | Dec 1829 | 22 Dec | 8 |
| | Anne his wife | 29 | | | | | | | | | |
| | Wants his land on the west branch west bank of Palmito Creek | | | | | | | | | | |
| 69 | Andrew Miller | 44 | idem | 3 | 1 | 5 | idem | do | Dec 1829 | 22 Dec | 11 |
| | Celia his wife | 32 | | | | | | | | | |
| | Behind A.Robinson's land beginning at Doe Run where Panky road crosses on the North | | | | | | | | | | |
| 70 | Elisha Roberts | 54 | idem | 3 | 3 | 30 | idem | do | Dec 1829 | 22 Dec | 38 |
| | Patsey his wife | 50 | | | | | | | | | |
| | Took three months delay beginning January 1 | | | | | | | | | | |
| 71 | Aaron Colvin | 33 | idem | 1 | 2 | | idem | do | Dec 1829 | 22 Dec | 5 |
| | Margaret his wife | 30 | | | | | | | | | |
| | His family is in Nacogdoches District and will come very soon. Took 3 months from January 1. | | | | | | | | | | |
| 72 | John W. Noble | 29 | idem | 2 | 1 | 4 | idem | Mississippi | Dec 1829 | 22 Dec | 9 |
| | Fanny his wife | 35 | His family should arrive in two months | | | | | | | | |

(49)(50)

| 73 | David Selkriggs | 18 | Single | Orphan | | | Farmer | | | | |
|---|---|---|---|---|---|---|---|---|---|---|---|
| Mississippi | 1825 | 22 Dec 1829 | | 1 | 1 | | | | | | |
| 74 | Edmund R. Miller | 25 | Married | 1 | 1 | | idem | Arkansas | 1824 | 23 Dec | 4 |
| | Lucinda his wife | | | | | | | | | | |
| 75 | Simon Miller | 22 | Single | | | | idem | Arkansas | 1824 | 23 Dec | 1 |
| 76 | James Thompson | 36 | Married | 6 | | | idem | Tennessee | 1827 | 23 Dec | 8 |
| | Agnes Dinning his wife | 34 | | | | | | | | | |
| | Wants his land on the Bay Rad, east bank | | | | | | | | | | |
| 77 | Anthony R. Clarke | 55 | Single | | | | idem | New York | 1824 | 23 Dec | 1 |
| 78 | Wm Chase | 37 | Married | 2 | | | idem | Massachusetts | 1826 | 23 Dec | 4 |
| | Eliza his wife | 40 | | | | | | | | | |

Total 38 Souls

| No. | Name | Age | State | Children | Other dep. | Profession | Origin | Arrived | Took Oath | Total Souls |
|---|---|---|---|---|---|---|---|---|---|---|
| 79 | Isaac House | 49 | Married | 2 | 1 | idem | Luisiana | 1823 | 23 Dec | 6 |
|  | Kizia his wife | 23 |  |  |  |  |  |  |  |  |
| 80 | Widow of G.B. Hall and the heirs | | | | | | | | | |
| 81 | Alexander Hodge for the heirs of his son. Lot No. 3 above --- of San Jacinto. | | | | | | | | | |
| 82 | Henry Harrison | 32 | Single | | | Blacksmith & Farmer | idem | 1825 | 23 Dec | 1 |
| 83 | Henry L. Baire | 22 | Married | | | Farmer | idem | 1824 | | |
|  | Louisa Hamey wife | 17 |  |  |  |  |  |  |  |  |
|  | Did not want to take a Certificate. | | | | | | | | | |
| 84 | Thomas Jefferson Pryor | 23 | Single | | | idem | Alabama | 1824 | 25 Dec | |
|  | Above and adjoining Gasley. | | | | | | | | | |
| 85 | William Hunter | 51 | Married | 4 | 18 | idem | Mississippi | | 25 Dec | 28 |
|  | Nancy his wife | 49 |  |  |  |  |  |  |  |  |
|  | Has extension until December 1 of 1830 to take his land on Buffalo Bayou adjoining the lot granted to Taylor. | | | | | | | | | |
| 86 | Peyton R. Splane | 32 | Widower | 1 | 6 | idem | Louisiana | | 25 Dec | 8 |
| 87 | Levi Bostic | 51 | Married | 2 3 | 9 | Farmer & Artisan | Tennessee | 1829 | 23 Dec | 16 |
|  | Patsey his wife | 47 |  |  |  |  |  |  |  |  |
| 88 | Joseph Davis | 48 | Married | | | Farmer | Arkansas | 1829 | 26 Dec | 2 |
|  | Rachel his wife | 44 |  |  |  |  |  |  |  |  |
|  | One plot adjoining Saml Gates below on Jackson's Creek. | | | | | | | | | |
| 89 | John Whiteside | 30 | Married | 1 | 1 | idem | Missouri | 1826 | 26 Dec | 3 |
|  | Elizabeth his wife | 18 |  |  |  |  |  |  |  |  |
| 90 | James Wallace | 56 | Married | | | idem | Georgia | 1826 | 26 Dec | 2 |
|  | Patsey his wife | 50 |  |  |  |  |  |  |  |  |
|  | Wants his land next that of Groce's Retreat above. | | | | | | | | | |
| 91 | Jonathan Newman | 30 | Married | 1 | 1 | idem | Missouri | 1826 | 26 Dec | 4 |
|  | Polley his wife | 20 |  |  |  |  |  |  |  |  |
| 92 | Elish Jackson | 23 | Single | | | idem | Illinois | 1827 | 26 Dec | 1 |
| 93 | Mary Ann Pankey | 44 | Widow | 2 | 5 | idem | Louisiana | 1824 | 26 Dec | 8 |
|  | Widow of M. Early | | | | | | | | | |

| No. | Name | Age | Status | | | Occupation | Origin | Year | Date | |
|---|---|---|---|---|---|---|---|---|---|---|
| 94 | James Pankey | 46 | Single | | | Farmer | idem Luisiana | 1827 | 26 Dec | 1 |

North of Franco Holland and east of William Holland adjoining with two plots

| 95 | John F. Edwards | 22 | idem | | | | " Alabama | 1822 | | |

Wants the land adjoining Morton's and Randall Jones' labors and also to include
a small fraction existing between Morton's and the Widow Long.

(51)(52)

| 96 | Isaac Jackson | 32 | Married | 3 | | Farmer | Ohio | 1827 | 26 Dec | 5 |
| | Samantha his wife | 30 | | | | | | | | |

Wants his land on the arroyo known as Jackson's Creek.

| 97 | James Bell | 38 | Single | | | idem | Georgia | 1824 | 26 Dec | 1 |
| 98 | Jacob Stevens | 24 | Married | 1 | | idem | Missouri | 1826 | 26 Dec | 4 |
| | Nancy his wife | 20 | | | | | | | | |
| 99 | Archie Hodge | 39 | Married | 3 | | idem | Arkansas | 1826 | 26 Dec | 7 |
| | Charlotte his wife | 37 | | | | | | | | |

Sitio No. 1 on Lake Creek below parallel base.

| 100 | James Peveyhouse | 25 | Married | 3 | 2 | idem | idem | 1826 | 26 Dec | 7 |
| | Mary his wife | 25 | | | | | | | | |

Sitio No. 2 below parallel base on San Jacinto.

| 101 | Alexr E. Hodge | 29 | Single | | | idem | idem | 1826 | 26 Dec | 1 |
| 102 | Richd R. Royall | 31 | Married | 3 | 2 20 | idem | Alabama | 1829 | 26 Dec | 27 |
| | Anne R. his wife | 29 | | | | | | | | |
| 103 | E.P. Myrick | 24 | idem | 1 | | idem | idem | 1826 | 26 Dec | 3 |
| | Niema his wife | 22 | | | | | | | | |
| 104 | David Harris | 33 | Single | | | Trader | Louisiana | 1828 | 26 Dec | 1 |

The land granted to William Hunter in case Hunter does not arrive before 25th of the month.

| 105 | Benjn Osborn | 60 | Widower | 4 | 3 | Farmer | Mississippi | 1826 | 26 Dec | 8 |

On the same creek where Wilbarger lives.

| 106 | John Brown | 33 | Married | 2 | | idem | Missouri | 1829 | 26 Dec | 4 |
| | Nancy his wife | 23 | | | | | | | | |
| 107 | John Keller | | Widower | 2 | 3 | | | | | |
| 108 | Patrick Greene | 35 | Married | 3 | | Farmer & Carpenter | Kentucky | 1829 | 27 Dec | 5 |
| | Elizabeth his wife | 25 | | | | | | | | |

| No. | Name | Age | State | Children | Other dep. | Profession | Origin | Arrived | Took Oath | Total Souls |
|-----|------|-----|-------|----------|-----------|-----------|--------|---------|-----------|-------------|
| | | | | | | | | | | 40 |
| 109 | Allen Larrison | 32 | Single | | | Artisan | Ohio | 1825 | 27 Dec | 1 |
| | Adjoins above with --- on the Palmito Creek west bank. | | | | | | | | | |
| 110 | Samuel Love | 38 | Married | 2 | 1 5 | Farmer | Louisiana | 1825 | | 10 |
| | Nancy his wife. | 35 | | | | | | | | |
| 111 | Abraham Darst | 43 | Married | 7 | 3 | idem | Missouri | 1829 | 28 Dec | 12 |
| | Jemimah his wife | 32 | | | | | | | | |
| 112 | Jn W. Mitchell | 52 | Single | | | idem | Georgia | 1822 | | 1 |
| | Adjoins Kincaid | | | | | | | | | |
| 113 | Edwd Baty | 24 | Widower | 1 | | idem | Arkansas | 1829 | 28 Dec | 2 |
| | Does not want to take his certificate. | | | | | | | | | |
| 114 | Thos S. Saul | 34 | Married | 1 | | idem | Louisiana | 1829 | 28 Dec | 3 |
| | Malissa his wife | 23 | | | | | | | | |
| | Wants his land adjoining ---, Kuykendall and Cole. | | | | | | | | | |
| 115 | James Stephens | 35 | Married | 4 | 2 | idem | Missouri | 1829 | 28 Dec | 8 |
| | Mary his wife | 34 | | | | | | | | |
| | Adjoins Stephens on Caney Creek | | | | | | | | | |
| 116 | Sarah Parker | 40 | Widow | 1 | 5 | | idem | 1827 | | 7 |
| | Wants the land adjoining that of John Elam. | | | | | | | | | |
| 117 | George Dennett | 38 | Married | | | Artisan | Kentucky | 1828 | 29 Dec | 2 |
| | Sarah his wife | 31 | | | | | | | | |
| 118 | John Denton | 29 | Single | | | Farmer | Tennessee | 1827 | 7 Dec | 1 |
| | One quarter adjoining John Brown on Carancahua Creek. | | | | | | | | | |
| (53)(54) | | | | | | | | | | |
| 119 | Francis Keller | 50 | Married | 2 | 2 4 | Farmer | Mississippi | 1829 | | 10 |
| | Anne his wife | 34 | | | | | | | | |
| 120 | Heirs of Cassy Steward | 16 ) | | | | idem | Alabama | 1823 | | 2 |
| | two children | 14 ) | | | | | | | | |
| | They have chosen the land on the Colorado River on the west side to the end of | | | | | | | | | | |
| | the plain known as Tanner's  4 Feb 1830 | | | | | | | | | | |

| No. | Name | Age | Status | | | | Occupation | Origin | Year | Date | Total |
|---|---|---|---|---|---|---|---|---|---|---|---|
| 121 | Elijah Curtis | 22 | Single | | | | idem | idem | 1823 | | 1 |
| | Together with the same. The same date. | | | | | | | | | | |
| 122 | Adolphus Hope | 22 | Single | | | | idem | Louisiana | 1827 | | 1 |
| 123 | Washington Curtis | 25 | idem | | | | idem | Alabama | 1823 | | |
| | Adjoining the same. The same date. | | | | | | | | | | |
| 124 | Prosper Hope | 26 | idem | | | | idem | Louisiana | 1825 | | 1 |
| 125 | Daniel Arnold | 48 | Married | 2 | 2 | 5 | idem | Mississippi | 1826 | 29 Dec | 11 |
| | Rachael his wife | 43 | | | | | | | | | |
| | Wants his land adjacent to two labors granted to Keller which he chose on Navasota Creek. | | | | | | | | | | |
| 126 | James Gilliland | 30 | Married | 1 | 2 | | idem | Arkansas | 1828 | 29 Dec | 5 |
| | Dianah his wife | 25 | | | | | | | | | |
| | Wants his land on left bank of the Colorado adjoining and above that of Tobin and Webber above the Bejar Road. | | | | | | | | | | |
| 127 | Thos J. Williams | 22 | Single | | | | idem | idem | 1822 | 29 Dec | 1 |
| | Wants his land adjoining above the land of Wilbarger. | | | | | | | | | | |
| 128 | Nicholas George | 36 | Married | 2 | 3 | 12 | idem | Louisiana | 1829 | 29 Dec | 19 |
| | Nancy his wife | 25 | | | | | | | | | |
| | On the east bank of the Navidad above the Atascosito Road. | | | | | | | | | | |
| 129 | Alexr McCoy | 37 | Single | | | | Carpenter | Pennsylvania | 1823 | | 1 |
| 130 | Samuel Pharr | 28 | idem | | | | Farmer | Louisiana | 1823 | | 1 |
| 131 | John Hodge | 24 | Married | 3 | 3 | | idem | Arkansas | 1824 | | 8 |
| | Polley his wife | 32 | | | | | | | | | |
| 132 | Leander Woods | 21 | Single | | | | idem | Missouri | 1824 | | 1 |
| | East of the Colorado the third creek that runs above McGinty's Prairie. | | | | | | | | | | |
| 133 | John H. Edwards | 31 | Married | 1 | 1 | 2 | idem | Luisiana | 1827 | | 6 |
| | Sarah Anne | 23 | | | | | | | | | |
| 134 | Robert Brown | 34 | Single | | | | Shoemaker | Pennsylvania | 1826 | | 1 |
| 135 | Amos Edwards | 53 | Married | 4 | 10 | | Farmer | Kentucky | 1829 | | 16 |
| | Penelope his wife | 43 | Took the oath in Nacogdoches | | | | | | | | |
| 136 | Darius Gregg | 25 | Single | | | | Farmer | Kentucky | 1829 | 31 Dec | 1 |
| 137 | Jonathan Vess | 50 | Married | 2 | 4 | | idem | Missouri | 1829 | 31 | 8 |
| 138 | Moses Rosseau | 37 | Widower | 1 | 2 | 3 | idem | Alabama | 1828 | 31 | 7 |
| | | | | | | | | | | | 41 |

| No. | Name | Age | State | Children | Other dep. | Profession | Origin | Arrived | Took Oath | Total 42 Souls |
|---|---|---|---|---|---|---|---|---|---|---|
| 139 | John H. Allcorn | 25 | Single | | | idem | Arkansas | 1823 | | 1 |
| | Wants his land adjoining land of his father on New Years Creek. | | | | | | | | | |
| 140 | Wm E. Allcorn | 24 | Married | | | idem | idem | 1823 | | 2 |
| | Sarah his wife | 16 | | | | | | | | |
| | Wants a plot of land that was granted to Andrew Roberts. | | | | | | | | | |
| 141 | Sylvester Bowen | 38 | Married | 1 | | idem | Rhode Island | 1827 | | 3 |
| | Almira | 20 | | | | | | | | |
| 142 | Thomas Jefferson Allcorn | 21 | Single | | | idem | Arkansas | 1823 | | 1 |
| 143 | Thomas Peyton Kuykendall | 21 | Single | | | idem | idem | 11825 | | 1 |
| | read Thornton P.K. [sic] | | | | | | | | | |
| (55)(56) | | | | | | | | | | |
| 144 | James Kegans | 27 | Married | 2 | | Farmer | Missouri | 1826 | 31 Dec 1829 | 4 |
| | Nancy his wife | 24 | | | | | | | | |
| 145 | Hugh Kilgore ) | | | | | | | | | |
| | Delia Armstrong ) | 32 | Widow | 4 | 1 | idem | Louisiana | Jul 1829 | 1 Jan 1830 | 6 |
| 146 | George Grimes | 46 | Married | 4 | 5 | idem | Tennessee | 1827 | 1 Jan | 11 |
| | Disey his wife | 43 | | | | | | | | |
| 147 | Robert Ray | 29 | Married | | | idem | New York | 1824 | 1 Jan | 2 |
| | Margaret his wife | 14 | | | | | | | | |
| | To the north and adjoining James Holland. | | | | | | | | | |
| 148 | Fredk Grimes | 22 | Single | | | idem | Tennessee | 1827 | 1 Jan | 1 |
| 149 | Leonard W. Groce | | Single | | | idem | Alabama | 1822 | | 1 |
| | [all the above entry was crossed out. Ed] | | | | | | | | | |
| 149 | James Bennett | | Single | | | | Ohio | | | |
| | The land surveyed by Pankey. | | | | | | | | | |
| 150 | Leonard W. Broce | | Single | | | idem | Alabama | | | |
| | Sitio No. 6 on Palmito Creek. | | | | | | | | | |
| 151 | Harman Hensley | 50 | Married | 2 | 2 | idem | Arkansas | | | |
| | Betsey his wife | 54 | | | | | | | | |

| No. | Name | Age | Status | | | | | Origin | Date | |
|---|---|---|---|---|---|---|---|---|---|---|
| 152 | James Clark | 40 | Married | 6 | 1 | | idem | Missouri | 1828 | 2 Jan | 9 |
| | Rhoda his wife | 33 | | | | | | | | | |
| | Wants his land on New Year's Creek. | | | | | | | | | | |
| 153 | William Burney | 31 | Married | 2 | 1 | | idem | Opelousas | 1828 | | 5 |
| | Susan his wife | 24 | | | | | | | | | |
| 154 | James Holland | 21 | Single | | | | idem | Ohio | 1824 | | 1 |
| 155 | Joseph Miller | 37 | Married | 3 | 2 | 1 | idem | Missouri | 1829 | | 8 |
| | Hannah his wife | 34 | | | | | | | | | |
| 156 | Nathaniel Hutcheson | 40 | Married | 1 | 3 | | idem | Missouri | 1829 | 3 Jan | 6 |
| | Mary his wife | 28 | | | | | | | | | |
| 157 | Josiah Wilbarger | 29 | Married | 1 | | | idem | Missouri | 1827 | 3 Jan | 3 |
| | Margarette his wife | 19 | | | | | | | | | |
| 158 | Abijah Highsmith | 34 | Married | 3 | 3 | | idem | idem | Jan 1828 | 4 Jan | 8 |
| | Debora his wife | 35 | | | | | | | | | |
| | A year ago he chose his land on the east bank of the Colorado on a small plain some 15 miles below where the Bejar Road passes. | | | | | | | | | | |
| 159 | Thomas Garretson | 17 | Single | | | | idem | Alabama | 1828 | 4 Jan | 1 |
| 160 | William Barton | 47 | Married | 2 | 3 | 5 | idem | idem | 1828 | 4 Jan | 12 |
| | Stacy his wife | 31 | | | | | | | | | |
| | West bank of the Colorado above the Bahia Road above Barton. | | | | | | | | | | |
| 161 | Edward Jinkins | 34 | Married | 2 | 1 | | idem | idem | 1829 | 4 Jan | 5 |
| | Sarah his wife | 30 | Same (i.e. same land location as above. Ed] | | | | | | | | |
| 162 | Montraville Woods | 23 | Married | 1 | | | idem | Missouri | 1824 | | 3 |
| | Isabelle his wife | 17 | | | | | | | | | |
| | West of the Colorado above the Bahia Road 8 to 10 miles ----. | | | | | | | | | | |
| 163 | J.D. Morris | 42 | Single | | | | idem | idem | 1828 | | 1 |
| | East of the Colorado opposite a creek at the upper end of McGinty's Prairie. | | | | | | | | | | |
| 164 | Stephen Cottle | 43 | Married | 4 | 6 | | idem | idem | 1828 | | 12 |
| | Sally his wife | 42 | | | | | | | | | |
| | West of the Colorado where the Bahia Road passes along side of Buckner's Creek. | | | | | | | | | | |

Total Souls 44

| No. | Name | Age | State | Children | Other dep. | Profession | Origin | Arrived | Took Oath | Total Souls |
|---|---|---|---|---|---|---|---|---|---|---|
| (57)(58) | | | | | | | | | | |
| 165 | John Cocke | 29 | Married | 1 | 1 | Farmer | Arkansas | 1825 | 4 Jan | 3 |
| | Anna his wife | 29 | | | | | | | | |
| | Adjoins land of Norm Woods on the Colorado. | | | | | | | | | |
| 166 | Thos Powell | 37 | Single | | | idem | Illinois | 1829 | 4 Jan | 1 |
| 167 | Nicholas Lynch | 41 | Married | 4 | | idem | Alabama | 22 Mar 1828 | 4 Jan | 6 |
| | Nancy his wife | 45 | | | | | | | | |
| 168 | Louis Geffray | 41 | Married | 3 | 1 | idem | Louisiana | Aug 1829 | 5 Jan | 6 |
| | Irene his wife | 28 | | | | | | | | |
| | East bank of the Navidad at the place where it crosses the Gonzales Road --- . | | | | | | | | | |
| 169 | Francis W. Johnson | 30 | Single | | | idem | Missouri | Sep 1829 | 5 Jan | 1 |
| 170 | Elisha Hall | 30 | Married | 1 | | idem | Arkansas | Nov 1829 | 5 Jan | 3 |
| | Jemima his wife | 21 | | | | | | | | |
| 171 | Elizabeth Campbell | 45 | Widow | 3 | 2 | idem | idem | 1829 | 5 Jan | 6 |
| 172 | Isaac Lee | 60 | Married | | 1 | idem | Arkansas | 1829 | 3 Jan | 3 |
| | Patsey his wife | 54 | | | | | | | | |
| 173 | Sandford Woodward | 30 | idem | 1 | 3 | idem | idem | 1829 | 5 Jan | 6 |
| | Nancy his wife | 26 | | | | | | | | |
| 174 | Hiram Lee | 23 | Single | | | idem | idem | 1829 | 5 Jan | 1 |
| | A quarter together with Lakey and on the east side with Elam. | | | | | | | | | |
| 175 | Davis Chandler | 30 | Married | 1 | 1 | idem | idem | 1829 | 5 Jan | 4 |
| | Prissa his wife | 23 | | | | | | | | |
| 176 | Frances Bland | 60 | Widower | 4 | 4 | " | Illinois | | | 5 |
| 177 | Alvin B. Clark | 31 | Married | 1 | 1 | " | Mississippi | 1829 | | 1 |
| | Elizabeth his wife | | | | | | | | | |
| 178 | Lewis Hearst | 40 | Widower | 4 | | " | Arkansas | 1826 | | 5 |
| 179 | Adam Stafford | 25 | Single | | | " | Tennessee | 1824 | | 1 |
| 180 | Elisha W. Barten | 39 | Married | 3 | 2 | | Alabama | 1 Jan 1830 | 6 Jan | 8 |
| | Susana his wife | 39 | | | | | | | | |
| 181 | Francis J. Haskins | 35 | Single | Void, returned note | | | New York | 12 Dec 1829 | | 1 |
| 182 | Thos Alley | 25 | idem | | | " | Missouri | 1825 | 6 Jan | 1 |
| | Wants his land behind the sitio adjoining the deceased Williams. | | | | | | | | | |

| No. | Name | Age | Status | | | | Occupation | Origin | Date | | |
|---|---|---|---|---|---|---|---|---|---|---|---|
| 183 | W.B. White | 27 | Single | | | | Farmer | Missouri | Sep 1826 | | 1 |
| 184 | Jesse B. McNeily | 27 | Married | 1 | | | " | Louisiana | Dec 1829 | 7 Jan | 3 |
| | Elizabeth his wife | 18 | | | | | | | | | |
| | Land adjoining Wm Holland | | | | | | | | | | |
| 185 | Sarah Kennedy | 36 | Widow | 3 | 3 | 8 | " | idem | Jan 1829 | | 15 |
| | --- above the land of Nancy Spencer | | | | | | | | | | |
| 186 | Franklin Lewis | 28 | Single | | | | " | Alabama | 1827 | | 1 |
| 187 | William McFarlane | 54 | Married | | | | " | Kentucky | 1827 | | 4 |
| | Martha his wife | 50 | | | | | | | | | |
| | Sitio Ho. 8 west of the Colorado below the Atascosito Road. | | | | | | | | | | |
| 188 | Paschal P. Borden | 23 | Single | | | | Blacksmith | Indiana | 18 Dec 1829 | | 1 |
| | Quarter No. 2 above Prior on Palmito Creek. | | | | | | | | | | |
| 189 | Henry F. Armstrong | 20 | idem | | | | Farmer | idem | idem | | 1 |
| | Quarter No. 1 on said creek | | | | | | | | | | |
| 190 | Gail Borden | 52 | Widower | 1 | | | Tanner & Farmer | idem | idem | | |
| | Sitio No. 4 on the west side of said creek. | | | | | | | | | | |

(59)(60)

| No. | Name | Age | Status | | | | Occupation | Origin | Date | | |
|---|---|---|---|---|---|---|---|---|---|---|---|
| 191 | William Deaver | 25 | Single | | | | Farmer | Missouri | '27 | | 1 |
| | Wants his land adjoining on the west with that of Byrd and south with the land of Dillard | | | | | | | | | | |
| 192 | Lemon Barker | 43 | Widower | 1 | | | idem | idem | '29 | 9 Jan | 1 |
| 193 | John B. Walters | 29 | Single | | | | idem | idem | '25 | | 1 |
| | Wants his land on the first plain below Ross to be above said plain. | | | | | | | | | | |
| 194 | John T. Webber | 35 | idem | | | | idem | idem | '25 | | 1 |
| | Wants his land above the road of plain called Ross beginning next to where it reaches the branch of Sandy Creek. | | | | | | | | | | |
| 195 | Wm Murphee | 53 | idem | | | | idem | Tennessee | '26 | | 1 |
| 196 | Jos K. Looney | 28 | idem | | | | idem | Kentucky | '28 | | 1 |
| 197 | William New | 32 | idem | | | | idem | idem | Dec '29 | | 1 |
| 198 | Charles McLaughlin | 32 | idem | | | | idem | Luisiana | " '29 | | 7 |
| 199 | Peter Bertrand | 38 | Married | 3 | 1 | 6 | idem | Tennessee | Jan '30 | 12 Jan | 7 |
| | Anna W. his wife | 30 | | | | | | | | | |

45

| No. | Name | Age | State | Children | Other dep. | Profession | Origin | Arrived | Took Oath | Total Souls |
|---|---|---|---|---|---|---|---|---|---|---|
| 200 | Gail Borden Jr | 28 | Married | | 1 | idem | Mississippi | Dec '29 | id | 4 |
| | Pennelope his wife | 18 | | | | | | | | |
| 201 | Eli Mercer | 40 | Married | 3 | 2 | idem | idem | Nov '29 | id | 17 |
| | Nancy his wife | 33 | | | | | | | | |
| 202 | James McCoy | 39 | idem | 2 | | idem | Pennsylvania | Nov '29 | | 4 |
| | Matilda his wife | 17 | | | | | | | | |
| 203 | Amasa Ives | 49 | Single | | | idem | Louisiana | Dec 1829 | | 1 |
| | Married after receiving his certificate. Adjoins T. Bell near above that of the Cushatti | | | | | | | | | |
| 204 | Ezekiel Clampit | 24 | Married | 1 | | idem | idem | Dec 1825 | | 3 |
| | Catharine his wife | 17 | | | | | | | | |
| | Between Singleton and Kerr west bank of the Brazos | | | | | | | | | |
| 205 | Caliste de Jesus Solis | 17 | Orphan | | | idem | Bexar | | | 1 |
| | Wants his land adjoining and behind the Widow Long | | | | | | | | | |
| 206 | John T. Terry | 29 | Married | | | idem | Arkansas | 1828 | | 2 |
| | Nep--cy his wife | 19 | | | | | | | | |
| | Wants his land east side of --- adjoining above that of John Ingram | | | | | | | | | |
| 207 | John B. Taylor | 30 | Married | 1 | | Carpenter | New York | 1830 | 14 Jan | 3 |
| | Mary his wife | 26 | | | | | | | | |
| 208 | Charles W. Ewing | 31 | Married | | 1 | Lawyer | Michigan | 1830 | 14 Jan | 3 |
| | Abbie B. his wife | 20 | | | | | | | | |
| | His family is still in USA | | | | | | | | | |
| 209 | Louisiana Kenney | 39 | | | | Farmer | Louisiana | 1822 | | 1 |
| | On the northeast bank of Ahuizote Creek to another creek below the Camino Real about one or two miles | | | | | | | | | |
| 210 | Susannah Clampit | 44 | Widow | 2 | | idem | idem | 1825 | | 3 |
| 211 | Andrew L. Castleman | 21 | Single | | | idem | Missouri | 1825 | | |
| | Devolved to his brother because of his death | | | | | | | | | |
| 212 | Francis Moore | 41 | Married | 2 | 3 | idem | Tennessee | 1830 | 20 Jan | 7 |
| | Sarah his wife | 33 | | | | | | | | |
| | He wants a labor behind the sitio of --- , adjoining Wm McCall | | | | | | | | | |
| 213 | Barnabas Wickson | 55 | Married | 6 | 5 | idem | Ohio | 1827 | 20 Jan | 1 |
| | Hutrah his wife | 43 | | | | | | | | |

| # | Name | Age/Status | | | | Occupation | Origin | Date | Date | No. |
|---|------|------------|--|--|--|------------|--------|------|------|-----|
| 214 | Asa Holdridge | 27 Single | | | | Doctor | Louisiana | 1830 | 21 Jan | 1 |
| 215 | Martin Wells | 55 Married | 5 | | 3 | Farmer | Alabama | Jan " | 22 " | 10 |
| | Sarah his wife | 40 | | | | | | | | |
| 216 | Robert Bullock | 24 Single | | | | idem | idem | idem | idem | 1 |
| (61)(62) | | | | | | | | | | |
| 217 | John Landrum | 29 Married | 1 | 1 | 2 | Farmer | Alabama | 20 Jan | 22 Jan | 6 |
| | Mary his wife | 22 | | | | | | | | |
| 218 | William Landrum | 26 idem | 1 | | 2 | idem | idem | idem | idem | 5 |
| | Nancy his wife | 22 | | | | | | | | |
| | Plot on San Jacinto Creek marked on the map | | | | | | | | | |
| 219 | William Atkins | 29 idem | 2 | | 2 | idem | Louisiana | Dec 1829 | id | 6 |
| | Phoebe his wife | 36 | | | | | | | | |
| 220 | Evan Corner | 23 Single | | | | idem | idem | Dec 1829 | idem | 1 |
| 221 | Abijah W. Draughan | 23 Single | | | | idem | idem | " 1829 | idem | 1 |
| 222 | Asa Wickson | 26 idem | | | | idem | Ohio | " 1827 | 24 Jan | 1 |
| | Above and adjoining B. Wickson on Big Creek | | | | | | | | | |
| 223 | Reuben R. Russel | 23 Married | | | 1 | idem | Arkansas | 2 Jan 1830 | 26 Jan | 3 |
| | Luisiana his wife | 20 | | | | | | | | |
| 224 | Elisha Moore | 40 idem | 3 | | 2 | idem | Missouri | Mar 1827 | | 7 |
| | Jane his wife | 28 | | | | | | | | |
| 225 | M. Sandefur | 28 idem | | | | idem | Arkansas | 1828 | 27 Jan | 2 |
| | Elizabeth his wife | 28 | | | | | | | | |
| | West bank of the Navidad where Gonzales Road crosses | | | | | | | | | |
| 226 | John D. Ziekanski | 30 Single | | | | idem | Virginia | 1824 | | 1 |
| | Ziekanski wants the land he petitioned adjoining --- | | | | | | | | | |
| 227 | James Schrier | 24 Married | 2 | | 1 | idem | Louisiana | Nov 1829 | 29 Jan | 5 |
| | Sarah his wife | 22 | | | | | | | | |
| | Sitio No. 2 east branch of Palmito Creek adjoining above Nelson Smith | | | | | | | | | |
| 228 | Laughlin McLaughlin | 45 Single | | | | idem | Mississippi | Dec 1829 | 29 id | 1 |
| 229 | Peter White | 29 Married | 1 | | 1 | idem | Missouri | 1827 | 30 id | 4 |
| | Nancy his wife | 25 | | | | | | | | |
| | His land east of the Navidad four or five miles above Golden Rod Creek | | | | | | | | | |

| No. | Name | Age | State | Children | Other dep. | Profession | Origin | Arrived | Took Oath | Souls |
|---|---|---|---|---|---|---|---|---|---|---|
| 230 | John Corner | 28 | idem | | | idem | Louisiana | Dec 1829 | 30 id | 2 |
| | Prussia his wife | 19 | | | | | | | | |
| | On the San Jacinto above and outside of the coastal zone | | | | | | | | | |
| 231 | Thos Corner | 22 | Single | | | idem | idem | id | id | 1 |
| | ditto [that is, same as above. Ed] | | | | | | | | | |
| 232 | Silas Clark | 46 | idem | | | Carpenter | idem | idem | 1 Feb | 1 |
| | Above the Grimes northern branch of Caney Creek | | | | | | | | | |
| 233 | Miguel Nicoless | 36 | idem | | | Trader | idem | 1828 | 2 id | 1 |
| 234 | Nichs Whitehead | 35 | idem | | | Farmer | idem | 1825 | 2 id | 1 |
| | Wants his land adjoining to James Bell above | | | | | | | | | |
| 235 | Alexr Thompson | 31 | Married | | | idem | Georgia | 1823 | 2 id | 2 |
| | Asena his wife | 19 | | | | | | | | |
| | Wants his land north or northeast of Gibbons some eight miles on a branch of the Navasota | | | | | | | | | |
| 236 | Wm K. Wilson | 31 | Single | | | Trader | Maryland | 1828 | 2 id | 1 |
| 237 | Phinneas Gleason | 52 | Married | 2 | 3 | Farmer | Ohio | 1822 | 4 id | 7 |
| | Cynthia his wife | 30 | | | | | | | | |
| | His family in Ohio. He wants land while his family is coming as he is | | | | | | | | | |
| | classed as a bachelor on the Colorado with the Curtis boys | | | | | | | | | |
| 238 | Philo Fairchild | 34 | Married | 1 | | Farmer | Illinois | 1826 | | 3 |
| | Mahaley his wife | 23 | | | | | | | | |
| | Below and adjoining the land of Elizabeth Lippincott | | | | | | | | | |
| 239 | Jefferson Singleton | 23 | Single | | | idem | Louisiana | Jan 1830 | 6 Feb | 7 |
| 240 | Wesley Singleton | 20 | idem | | | idem | idem | idem | 6 Feb | 1 |
| | | | | | | | | | | |
| (63)(64) | | | | | | | | | | |
| 241 | Thomas Thompson | 25 | Single | | | Farmer | Arkansas | 1825 | 8 Feb | 1 |
| | William Perkins | 40 | Married | | | Mariner | Louisiana | 1829 | 4 Feb | 2 |
| | Leonora his wife | 30 | | | | | | | | |
| 242 | Arter Crownover | 20 | idem | | | Farmer | Arkansas | 1829 | 8 Feb | 2 |
| | Clarissa his wife | 17 | | | | | | | | |
| | Wants his land on Buffalo Bayou together with Thomas | | | | | | | | | |

| No. | Name | Age | Status | | | | Origin | Date | | No. |
|---|---|---|---|---|---|---|---|---|---|---|
| 243 | Andrew Robinson Jr. | 21 | idem | | | idem | idem | Nov 1821 | 8 Feb | 2 |
| | Mary his wife | 21 | | | | | | | | |
| | Wants his land on Buffalo Bayou below and together with Price | | | | | | | | | |
| 244 | B. Burton | 44 | Single | | | idem | Alabama | Dec 1829 | 9 Feb | 1 |
| 245 | James Trammel | 30 | idem | | | idem | idem | Jul 1829 | 9 Feb | 1 |
| 247 | James Beardslee | 50 | Married | 3 | 3 | idem | New Jersey | Feb 1830 | 16 Feb | 8 |
| | Hester his wife | | | | | | | | | |
| 248 | John M. Hensley | 24 | idem | | | idem | Arkansas | 1828 | 20 Feb | 2 |
| | Mary his wife | 24 | | | | | | | | |
| 249 | Obadiah Hudson | 32 | Widower | 1 | | idem | idem | Feb 1830 | 20 Feb | 2 |
| 250 | John Clark | 68 | Widower | 1 | | idem | Louisiana | 1828 | 20 Feb | 2 |
| 251 | Samuel Fulton | 39 | Married | | 4 | idem | Louisiana | Dec 1829 | 23 Feb | 6 |
| | Elisabeth his wife | 31 | | | | | | | | |
| | Wants his land adjoining Jesse Grimes | | | | | | | | | |
| 252 | Adam Lawrence | 25 | Single | 1 | | idem | Arkansas | 1824 | 23 Feb | 2 |
| | 3/4 between the land of Muslim and Gustavus Edwards | | | | | | | | | |
| 253 | Saml Lawrence | 25 | idem | | | idem | idem | 1829 | 23 Feb | 1 |
| 254 | David Lawrence | 27 | Married | 1 | | idem | idem | Jan 1830 | 23 Feb | 3 |
| | Jenny his wife | 22 | | | | | | | | |
| | On New Years and Cedar Creeks adjoining Walter E. Mullins, ---, and Wm Munson | | | | | | | | | |
| 255 | Young Coleman | 25 | Married | 1 | | idem | Tennessee | Dec 1829 | 8 Feb | 3 |
| | Lucy his wife | 22 | | | | | | | | |
| 256 | Peter Aldrich | 43 | Single | | | idem | New Hampshire | Dec 1829 | 5 Feb | 1 |
| 257 | Chauncey Treat | 31 | Married | | | Trader | New York | Feb 1830 | 24 Feb | 2 |
| | Mary his wife | 31 | His wife is in New York | | | | | | | |
| 258 | Mary Owens | 50 | Widow | | | Farmer | Louisiana | 1826 | 25 Feb | 1 |
| 259 | Joseph B. Chance | 30 | Married | 3 | 1 | idem | Tennessee | 7 Jan | 27 Feb | 6 |
| | Nancy his wife | 29 | | | | | | | | |
| | Beginning at the eastern boundary of J.F. Coles and from there to the end | | | | | | | | | |
| | Singleton on both sides of Mare Creek to the extent of 1 sitio | | | | | | | | | |
| 260 | Thos Jefferson Hall | 21 | Married | | | idem | Louisiana | 1824 | 7 Mar | 2 |
| | Nancy his wife | 20 | | | | | | | | |

| No. | Name | Age | State | Child-ren | Other dep. | Profes-sion | Origin | Arrived | Took Oath | Total 50 Souls |
|---|---|---|---|---|---|---|---|---|---|---|
| 261 | Margaret Wightman | 26 | Single | | | Farmer | New York | Dec 1828 | 6 Mar | 1 |
| 262 | John Hinkson | 32 | Single | | | idem | Missouri | Oct 1826 | 3 Mar | 1 |
| 263 | John E. Bacchus | 42 | Married | 3 | | idem | Louisiana | Apr 1829 | 7 Mar | 5 |
| | Mary his wife | 24 | | | | | | | | |
| 264 | James E. Loving | 21 | Single | | | idem | Ohio | Feb 1830 | 10 Mar | 1 |
| 265 | Isaac Jackson | 40 | Married | 3 | 2 | idem | Alabama | Feb 1830 | 10 Mar | 7 |
| | Tilly his wife | 40 | | | | | | | | |
| | Wants his land on New Years Creek between Walker and Kuykendall | | | | | | | | | |
| (65)(66) | | | | | | | | | | |
| 266 | Thos P. Helm | 24 | Single | | | Farmer | Kentucky | Jul 1828 | 14 Mar 1830 | 1 |
| 267 | Samuel Bruff | 45 | Widower | 1 | 2 | Farmer | Tennessee | Feb 1830 | 13 Mar | 2 |
| 268 | Joseph Rees | 46 | Married | 4 | 9 | idem | idem | idem | 15 Mar | 17 |
| | Margaret his wife | | | | | | | | | |
| | Sitio No. 4 east of the Colorado below Betts land | | | | | | | | | |
| 269 | Christopher G. Cox | 27 | Married | 1 | 1 | Doctor | idem | idem | idem | 4 |
| | Harriet H. Cox | 24 | | | | | | | | |
| | Sitio No. 6 west of the Colorado below League's land | | | | | | | | | |
| 270 | Abraham Bowman | 44 | Single | | | Farmer | idem | idem | idem | 1 |
| 271 | Thomas Cayce | 34 | Married | 5 | 3 | idem | idem | idem | idem | 15 |
| | Hannah his wife | 34 | | | | | | | | |
| | Sitio No. 1 north of the Colorado adjoining League | | | | | | | | | |
| 272 | Mary Corner | 53 | Widow | 3 | | idem | Louisiana | Dec 1829 | 19 Mar | 4 |
| 273 | Benjamin Rigby | 26 | Married | 1 | | idem | idem | idem | idem | 3 |
| | Catharine his wife | 19 | | | | | | | | |
| | No. 23 on Bedi Creek north of Landrum | | | | | | | | | |
| 274 | Alexander McCulloch | 30 | Married | 3 | 2 | idem | idem | idem | idem | 7 |
| | Mariam his wife | 32 | | | | | | | | |
| 275 | Mastin Holden | 22 | Single | annulled | | idem | idem | idem | idem | 1 |
| 276 | Horace Gorden | 22 | single | | | idem | Mississippi | Aug 1829 | idem | 1 |
| 277 | William Isaacs | 35 | idem | | | idem | Tennessee | 1829 | idem | 1 |

| No. | Name | Age | Status | | | | Occupation | Origin | Date | Reg. | # |
|---|---|---|---|---|---|---|---|---|---|---|---|
| 278 | George M. Cash | 29 | idem | | | | Tanner | Pennsylvania | 1829 | 24 Mar | 1 |
| 279 | Abraham Dillard | 25 | idem | | | | Farmer | Missouri | 1827 | 24 Mar | 1 |
| | Wants his land adjoining Byrd and Sam Gates | | | | | | | | | | |
| 280 | Charles Gates | 34 | Married | 1 | | | idem | Arkansas | 1822 | | 3 |
| | Minerva his wife | 25 | | | | | | | | | |
| | Asks for land of C. Williams on Three Palms if it vacant | | | | | | | | | | |
| 281 | S. Rhoads Fisher | 35 | Married | 2 | 1 | | Trader | Phila | Feb 1830 | 26 Mar | 5 |
| | Anne his wife | | | | | | | | | | |
| | Wants his land adjoining Payton on the south, to adjoin Payton's full length | | | | | | | | | | |
| 282 | Robt Wilson | 36 | Widower | 2 | | | Artisan | Louisiana | Jan '30 | 26 Mar | 3 |
| 283 | James Braberry | 27 | Single | | | | Farmer | idem | Jan 1829 | 26 Mar | 1 |
| 284 | Robert Clokey | 25 | Married | | | | idem | Pennsyla | Mar 1830 | 26 id | 2 |
| | Anne his wife | 22 | | | | | | | | | |
| | He wants land at the headwaters of Palmito Creek on both sides of the | | | | | | | | | | |
| | Bahia Road, 24 miles from the Brazos by road | | | | | | | | | | |
| 285 | Tomas Moore | 25 | Married | | | | idem | Arkansas | Oct 1829 | 27 id | 2 |
| | Nancy his wife | 20 | | | | | | | | | |
| 286 | Benjn F. Jaques | 33 | idem | 1 | 2 | 1 | idem | Missouri | Mar 1830 | 27 id | 6 |
| | Adeline his wife | | | | | | | | | | |
| | Wants his land adjoining land below Fisher's or opposite Fisher's on Flat Creek | | | | | | | | | | |
| 287 | Alexr Farmer | 32 | Single | | | | Artisan | Louisiana | 1829 | 27 id | 1 |
| 288 | Stephen Jones | 53 | Married | 3 | 2 | | Farmer | Arkansas | Dec 1828 | 27 id | 7 |
| | Susannah his wife | 53 | | | | | | | | | |
| | The sitio adjoining Paulo de Bravo measured from that of James White on the Bejar Road | | | | | | | | | | |
| 289 | James McCain | 35 | Married | 2 | | | idem | Tennessee | Dec 1828 | 28 id | 4 |
| | Sarah his wife | 27 | | | | | | | | | |
| 290 | Moses A. Foster | 31 | Single | 2 | | | idem | Louisiana | Mar 1830 | 28 id | 3 |
| (67)(68) | | | | | | | | | | | |
| 291 | Nathl Lewis | 23 | Single | | | | Mariner | Massachusetts | Aug 1839 | 28 Mar | 1 |
| 292 | Henry Tierwester | 33 | idem | | | | Farmer | Ohio | 1828 | 28 Mar | 1 |
| 293 | Noah Griffeth | 44 | Married | 4 | 1 | | idem | N York | Jan 1829 | 29 id | 7 |
| | Ester his wife | 42 | | | | | | | | | |

| No. | Name | Age | State | Children | Other dep. | Profession | Origin | Arrived | Took Oath | Total 52 Souls |
|---|---|---|---|---|---|---|---|---|---|---|
| 294 | Levina Hubbs | 25 | Single [female?] | | | | Mississippi | 1825 | 14 id | 1 |
| 295 | Demis Maria Pierce | 19 | Single [female?] | | | | N York | Jan 1829 | 14 id | 1 |
| 296 | Edward S. Carrell | 23 | Single | | | Farmer | Luisiana | Jan 1830 | 14 id | 1 |
| 297 | Alfonse Courseaux | 26 | Single | | | idem | idem | Jan 1830 | 14 id | 1 |
| 298 | Benjn C. Reeder | 45 | Married | 2 | 1 | Farmer | Mississippi | 1827 | 18 id | 5 |
|  | Mary his wife | 45 | | | | | | | | |
| 299 | Joseph D. Harrison | 50 | Married | 4 | 3 | idem | Alabama | Jan 1830 | 21 id | 9 |
|  | Rachael F his wife | 46 | | | | | | | | |
| 300 | Eliza Hubbs | 23 | Single [female?] | | | | | 1825 | | 1 |
| 301 | Samuel B. Ormsbee | 21 | Single | | | Trader | Vermont | Feb 1830 | 30 Mar | 1 |
| 302 | Matthew Moss | 24 | Single | | | Farmer | Arkansas | Nov 1829 | 30 Mar | 1 |
| 301 | Louis C. Moore | 21 | Single | | | idem | Luisiana | Mar 1830 | 31 Mar | 1 |
| 304 | Lewis L. Veeder | 38 | idem | | | idem | Missouri | Feb 1830 | 31 id | 1 |
| 305 | Robert Matthews | 32 | idem | | | id | Luisiana | id | id | 1 |
|  | Between 5 and 6 east of Carancahua and west of --- Creek | | | | | | | | | |
| 306 | John Cole | 25 | Married | 1 | 2 | id | Missouri | Jan id | 1 Apr | 5 |
|  | Polly his wife | 25 | | | | | | | | |
| 307 | Albert Cone | 30 | Single | | | Trader | Connct | Feb id | 1 id | 1 |
| 308 | John G. King | 36 | Married | 3 | 4 | Farmer | Louisiana | Apr id | 3 id | 9 |
|  | Pamelia his wife | 28 | Annulled and the documentation has been returned to the petitioner | | | | | | | |
| 309 | Richard Allen | 37 | Single | | | id | id | Dec 1827 | 5 id | 1 |
|  | Void. Turned over certificate | | | | | | | | | |
| 310 | Cornelius H. Vandewier | 31 | Married | 3 | | Carpenter | id | Feb 1830 | 5 id | 5 |
|  | Anne his wife | 21 | | | | | | | | |
| 311 | Samuel Hinch | 26 | Married | | | Farmer | Kentu | Feb 1827 | 6 id | 2 |
|  | Leah Anne his wife | 18 | | | | | | | | |
| 312 | Laurence Martin | 25 | Single | | | id | Alabama | 31 Mar | 6 id | 1 |
|  | Wants his land on the west bank of the Colorado opposite the point of Barton's Prairie. 1st July 1830 | | | | | | | | | |
| 313 | Wm E. Dundass | 39 | Single | | | id | Mississippi | 31 Mar | 7 id | 1 |

| # / Name | Age | Status | | | Occupation | Origin | Date | | Count |
|---|---|---|---|---|---|---|---|---|---|
| 314 Wm J. Russell | 28 | id | | | Mariner | Louisiana | 1828 | 7 id | 1 |
| 315 Alexr Bailey | 30 | id | | | Farmer | Ohio | 1827 | 8 id | 1 |
| 316 Arabella Harrington | 58 | Widow | | | | Arkansas | 1826 | 9 id | 1 |
| 317 Nancy Frailey | 32 | | 2 | 2 | | Alabama | 1824 | 10 id | 5 |
| Wants her land together with J.D. Morris on the Colorado | | | | | | | | | |
| 318 Emilius Savage | 38 | Married | 1 | | Farmer | N York | 1829 | | |
| Mary his wife | 30 | | | | | | | | |
| 319 John Shaw | | id | 2 | 2 | id | Arkansas | 1828 | 10 id | 6 |
| Polly his wife | | | | | | | | | |
| (69)(70) | | | | | | | | | |
| 320 William Wroe | 40 | Married | | 2 | Farmer | Louisiana | 1825 | 12 Apr | 4 |
| Nancy his wife | | | | | | | | | |
| 321 Caleb Kemp | 38 | Widower | 4 | 3 | id | | Mar 1829 | id | 8 |
| East of the Colorado below the 1/2 sitio of J.H. Moore below the Bahia Road | | | | | | | | | |
| 322 Patrick Dolan | 41 | Married | 2 | | Tailor | id | Feb 1830 | id | 4 |
| Anne his wife | 45. | | | | | | | | |
| 323 R.L. Dunn | 30 | id | 1 | 7 | Farmer | id | Apr 1830 | id | 10 |
| Eliza his wife | 30 | | | | | | | | |
| 324 Rhody Kennedy | | | | | id | Missouri | 1828 | id | 1 |
| [Written over] Returned the note | | | | | | | | | |
| 325 Francis Adams | 38 | Single | | | id | S Carolina | 1822 | | 1 |
| 326 William Spence | 32 | id | | | id | Louisiana | 1824 | 14 Apr | 1 |
| 327 Elliot M. Millican | 23 | Married | | | id | Arkansas | 1822 | 14 id | 2 |
| Elizabeth his wife | 18 | | | | | | | | |
| A sitio adjoining and north of that of his father Robert Millican | | | | | | | | | |
| 328 Leroy Stafford | 47 | id | 5 | 2 | 80 id | Louisiana | Apl 1830 | 14 id | 89 |
| Elizabeth his wife | 30 | | | | | | | | |
| 329 Hugh McDonald | 50 | id | 4 | 5 | 28 id | Mississippi | 1830 | 14 id | 39 |
| Catharine his wife | 44 | | | | | | | | |
| 330 Dennis Sullivan | 21 | Single | | | | Louisiana | Feb 1830 | 14 id | 1 |
| Wants his land next to that of Bell --- on Dry Creek | | | | | 8 | | | | |
| 331 James E. Phillips | 26 | id | | | id | Alabama | 1828 | 14 id | 9  53 |

| No. | Name | Age | State | Children | Other dep. | Profession | Origin | Arrived | Took Oath | Total 54 Souls |
|---|---|---|---|---|---|---|---|---|---|---|
| 332 | Elizabeth Gordon | 46 | Widow | 1 | 1 | | Louisiana | Aug 1829 | 14 id | 3 |
| | 3/4 that were surveyed for Litle and another quarter adjoining to complete one sitio | | | | | | | | | |
| 333 | Jesse Grimes | 42 | Married | 5 | 2 | Farmer | Alabama | 1827 | 19 id | 9 |
| | Rosanna his wife | 28 | | | | | | | | |
| 334 | William McIntire | 23 | Single | | | id | Luisiana | 1825 | 19 id | 1 |
| 335 | Margaret McIntire | 38 | Widow | 1 | | id | id | id | 19 id | 2 |
| 336 | Mary Caruthers | 50 | id | | | id | Alabama | Jan 1830 | 19 id | 1 |
| 337 | John M. Burton | 24 | Single | | | id | Georgia | Mar 1830 | 20 id | 1 |
| 338 | Jn W. Mayo | 28 | id | | | id | Luisiana | Feb 1830 | 21 id | 1 |
| 339 | Mark McCausland | 23 | id | | | id | Luisiana | Mar 1830 | 22 id | 1 |
| 340 | Charles Edwards | 25 | Married | 1 | | id | N York | Jan 1829 | 26 id | 3 |
| | Polly Anne his wife | 18 | | | | | | | | |
| 341 | Daniel Yeamans | 22 | Single | | | id | id | id | 26 id | 1 |
| 342 | Joseph Yeamans | 21 | id | | | id | id | id | 26 id | 1 |
| 343 | Jeremiah J.Robinson | 23 | id | | | id | Mississippi | 1830 | 26 id | 1 |
| | He wants his land on the east bank of the Navidad below Hardy | | | | | | | | | |
| 344 | Bartholmew McClure | 24 | id | | | id | Kentucky | 1830 | 26 id | 2 |
| | Sarah Anne his wife | 18 | | | | | | | | |
| 345 | James Lindsey | 30 | Single | | | id | Kentucky | Dec 1827 | 26 id | 1 |
| 346 | William Burnett | 28 | Married | 2 | 3 | id | Louisiana | Mar 1830 | 29 id | 7 |
| | Nancy his wife | 28 | | | | | | | | |
| | The No. 3 sitio on Palmito Creek above Delaney | | | | | | | | | |
| 347 | Josiah Lester | 37 | Married | 4 | | id | id | Dec 1829 | 29 id | 6 |
| | Solita his wife | 33 | | | | | | | | |
| | He takes the sitio chosen earlier by Robert Ray on Mill Creek | | | | | | | | | |
| (71)(72) | | | | | | | | | | |
| 348 | William Fitzgibbons | 46 | Married | 2 | 1 | Farmer | Louisiana | 1822 | [1830] | 5 |
| | Nancy his wife | 50 | | | | | | | | |
| | West of the Brazos on 8 mile Creek about 1 mile from Jno Whiteside | | | | | | | | | |
| 349 | William Whitaker | 28 | Married | 2 | | id | id | 1822 | | 4 |
| | Nancy his wife | 24 | | | | | | | | |

| No. | Name | Age | Status | | | | Occupation | Native of | Date | Date | No. |
|---|---|---|---|---|---|---|---|---|---|---|---|
| 350 | John Cartwright | 43 | Married | 5 | 2 | 11 | id | Mississippi | 1830 | 3 May | 18 |
| | Mary his wife | 42 | | | | | | | | | |
| 351 | John Marshall | 48 | idem | 5 | | 1 | id | Arkansas | Jan 1830 | 4 May | 8 |
| | Leah his wife | | | | | | | | | | |
| | In case Elisha Roberts does not should be his plot or No. 3 above on the same creek | | | | | | | | | | |
| 352 | Jesse Clifft | 31 | idem | | | | Blacksmith | Louisiana | Feb 1830 | 2 May | 2 |
| | Mary his wife | 16 | | | | | | | | | |
| 353 | Francis G. Keller | 29 | id | | | | Farmer | Mississippi | 1825 | 8 May | 3 |
| | Levina his wife | 23 | | | | | | | | | |
| 354 | Gross Welsh | | [Written over]: Annulled | | | | id | Louisiana | May 1830 | 11 May | 1 |
| | Sandy Prairie beginning 4000 varas below the lake and above | | | | | | | | | | |
| | his other quantity of a quarter of a sitio west of the Colorado | | | | | | | | | | |
| 355 | Jesse Leftwich | 55 | Married | 3 | 6 | | id | Tennessee | Apr 1830 | 13 May | 11 |
| | Sarah his wife | | | | | | | | | | |
| 356 | E.M. Connelly | 34 | Single | | | | Mariner | La | id | 13 id | 1 |
| 357 | Wm Sutherland | 30 | Married | | | | Farmer | La | id | 15 id | 2 |
| | Susan his wife | 30 | | | | | | | | | |
| | Sitio No. 4 west bank west branch of Palmito Creek | | | | | | | | | | |
| 358 | Asa Yeamans | 57 | Married | 3 | 1 | | id | N York | Jan 1829 | 15 id | 6 |
| | Jerusha his wife | 52 | | | | | | | | | |
| 359 | Margaret Kennedy | 37 | Widow | 1 | 1 | | id | La | 1824 | | 3 |
| 360 | [Entry not legible. Written over]: Annulled | | | | | | | | | | |
| 361 | Wm H. Taylor | 41 | Widower | 1 | 4 | | id | La | 1829 | | 6 |
| 362 | Henry Morse | 34 | Married | 2 | 1 | 3 | id | Mississippi | Apr 1830 | 17 May | 8 |
| | Eliza his wife | 28 | | | | | | | | | |
| | Wants his land adjacent to George Duty left bank of the Colorado | | | | | | | | | | |
| 363 | Phinneas Jones | 23 | Single | | | | id | Tennessee | Mar 1830 | 17 May | 1 |
| 364 | S.J. Moseley | 27 | id | | | | Doctor | Tennessee | Mar 1830 | 17 id | 1 |
| 365 | Theophalus Eddings | 56 | Married | 4 | 3 | | Farmer | Alaa | April | 17 id | 9 |
| | Nancy his wife | 40 | | | | | | | | | |
| 366 | Henry Q. Wright | 40 | idem | 1 | 4 | | id | Ohio | April | 17 id | 7 |
| | Anne his wife | 39 | | | | | | | | | |

| No. | Name | Age | State | Children | Other dep. | Profession | Origin | Arrived | Took Oath | Total 56 Souls |
|---|---|---|---|---|---|---|---|---|---|---|
| 367 | John Sullivan | 38 | idem | 3 | | id | Ohio | Feb 1830 | | 7 |
| | Eunice his wife | 37 | | 2 | | | | | | |
| 368 | Harlem Hatch | 23 | Married | 1 | | id | Ohio | Feb 1830 | | 3 |
| | Mary his wife | 19 | | | | | | | | |
| 369 | Robert J. Moseley | 24 | Single | | | id | Tennessee | March | | 2 |
| 370 | Hugh McDonald Jr | 28 | Married | | 1 | id | Mississippi | March | | 2 |
| | Mary his wife | 22 | | | | | | | | |
| | (73)(74) | | | | | | | | | |
| 371 | Daniel McDonald | 32 | Married | 2 | | Farmer | Mississippi | March | | 5 |
| | Mary Ann his wife | 29 | | | | | | | | |
| 372 | Roderick Nicholson | 28 | id | 1 | | id | id | id | | 4 |
| | Mary Anne his wife | 18 | | | | | | | | |
| 373 | James Norton | 38 | Single | 1 | | id | Luisiana | 1826 | | 1 |
| 374 | Dugald McFarlane | 33 | Married | 1 | | | Alabama | April | | 4 |
| | Eliza his wife | 27 | | | | | | | | |
| 375 | Norman Woods | 25 | Single | | | Farmer | Missouri | 1826 | | 1 |
| 376 | Jorge Fisher | | Married | 3 | 7 | Trader | Mississippi | | | 12 |
| | Elizabeth his wife | | | | | | | | | |
| 377 | J.H. Bostic | 23 | Single | | | Farmer | Tennessee | March | | 1 |
| 378 | Abram Eddings | 22 | idem | | | Farmer | Ala | March | | 1 |
| 379 | William Sexton | 24 | idem | | | idem | Luisia | Jan 1830 | | 1 |
| 380 | Henry K. Lewis | 37 | idem | | | idem | Kentucky | Feb 1829 | | 1 |
| 381 | Isaac Jamieson | 31 | Married | 2 | | idem | Tennessee | April 10 | | 5 |
| | Margaret his wife | 28 | | | | | | | | |
| 382 | Saml P. Browne | 35 | Married | 3 | | idem | Missouri | April 10 | | 6 |
| | Susan his wife | 27 | | | | | | | | |
| 383 | John Jones | 38 | Married | 4 | 6 | idem | Missouri | April 10 | | 13 |
| | Mary his wife | | | | | | | | | |
| 384 | James Stuart | 29 | Married | 2 | | idem | Mississippi | Nov 1829 | | 4 |
| | Zillah Anne his wife | 22 | | | | | | | | |

| # | Name | Age | Marital | | | Occupation | Origin | Date | |
|---|------|-----|---------|---|---|------------|--------|------|---|
| 385 | Levi Killen | 18 | Orphan | | | Farmer | Louisiana | April 2 | 1 |
| | A quarter sitio right bank of the Colorado between Monte Miller and Norman Woods | | | | | | | | |
| 386 | Hughes Witt | 30 | Single | | | idem | Florida | April | 1 |
| 387 | Amos Gates | 29 | Married | | | idem | Arkansas | 1822 | 2 |
| | Lydia his wife | 20 | | | | | | | |
| | Wants his land adjoining with the land of his father and brother Samuel | | | | | | | | |
| 388 | George A. Bell | 47 | Single | | | idem | Louisiana | 1828 | 1 |
| 389 | Archibald S. White | 49 | Married | 4 | 3 | idem | Alabama | Feb 1830 | |
| | Margaret his wife | 53 | | | | | | | |
| | Together with Sutherland above, on Mule Creek west bank | | | | | | | | |
| 390 | Toliver Martin | 36 | Married | | | | Carolina | Feb 1830 | |
| | Elizabeth his wife | 37 | | | | | | | |
| | Wants his land on Big Creek together with B. Wickson above. 26 May 1830 | | | | | | | | |
| 391 | Joshua Nelson | 39 | Single | | | School Master | N York | Jan 1829 | 1 |
| 392 | M. Hubert | 34 | Married | 2 | | Farmer | Alabama | Jan 1830 | 4 |
| | Frances his wife | 32 | | | | | | | |
| 393 | Wm M. Rankin | 43 | Married | 2 | 2 | idem | idem | Jan 1830 | 6 |
| | Sarah his wife | 33 | | | | | | | |
| 394 | Zachariah Landrum | 64 | Married | | | idem | idem | Jan 1830 | 2 |
| | Lettuce his wife | 54 | | | | | | | |
| (75)(76) | | | | | | | | | |
| 395 | William Rankin | 21 | Single | | | Farmer | Alabama | Jan 1830 | 1 |
| 396 | Crawford Burnett | 24 | Married | 1 | 1 | idem | La | Dec 1829 | 4 |
| | Anne his wife | 22 | | | | | | | |
| 397 | James Copeland | 28 | Single | | | idem | Georgia | Aug 1827 | 1 |
| 398 | Thomas Cope | 28 | idem | | | idem | Luisiana | Jul 1829 | 1 |
| 399 | John Owen | 21 | Married | | | idem | idem | 1822 | 1 |
| | Christina his wife | | | | | | | | |
| | On Green Bayou where he has made improvements | | | | | | | | |
| 400 | Elisha Flack | 31 | | | | idem | Kentucky | Feb 1830 | 1 |

| No. | Name | Age | State | Children | Other dep. | Profession | Origin | Arrived | Total Souls |
|---|---|---|---|---|---|---|---|---|---|
| 401 | Reuben Hornsby | 37 | Married | 5 | 1 | Farmer | Mississippi | Feb 1830 | 8 |
| | Sarah his wife | 35 | | | | | | | |
| | Wants his land left bank of the Colorado adjacent and above that chosen by James Gilliland | | | | | | | | |
| 402 | David Kneeland | 45 | Married | 1 | | idem | Luisiana | May 1830 | 3 |
| | Silence his wife | 41 | | | | | | | |
| 403 | James H. Skinner | 35 | Single | | | idem | idem | idem | 1 |
| 404 | Henry Linney | 50 | Widower | 2 | 1 | idem | Kentucky | May 1830 | 1 |
| | Wants his land together with Walker on the south. His children reside in the Aises District, he will bring them. | | | | | | | | |
| 405 | James F. Perry | 39 | Married | 4 | 2 | idem | Missouri | April 1st | 8 |
| | Emily M his wife | 34 | | | | | | | |
| 406 | Alexr H. Morton | 29 | Married | 1 | | idem | N York | May 1st | 3 |
| | Elanor his wife | 25 | | | | | | | |
| 407 | Thomas Gay | 25 | Single | | | idem | Georgia | May 1830 | 1 |
| | At the top end of Sandy Prairie to include the bend of the river, west bank of the Colorado | | | | | | | | |
| 408 | John G. Holtham | 29 | idem | | | Lawyer | Luisiana | Nov 1829 | 1 |
| 409 | Samuel Gordon | 23 | idem | | | Farmer | id | Aug 1827 | 1 |
| 410 | James Smith | 25 | idem | | | id | id | 1826 | 1 |
| 411 | James Rankin | 22 | idem | | | id | id | 1827 | 1 |
| 412 | Mary Smith | | Widow | | | id | id | 1829 | 4 |
| 413 | Augt Hotchkiss | 30 | Married | 2 | 1 | id | id | 1830 | 5 |
| | Anne my wife | | | | | | | | |
| 414 | Talbot Chambers | 35 | Single | | | id | Pennsyla | 1827 | 1 |
| 415 | James Foster | 26 | id | | | id | La | 1830 | 1 |
| 416 | Wm D. Mayes | 24 | id | | | id | Missipi | " | 1 |
| 417 | Lewis Endt | 27 | Married | | | id | id | " | 2 |
| | Mary my wife | 15 | | | | | | | |
| 418 | John Gates | | | | | id | | " | |
| 419 | Edwd Burleson | 33 | Married | 3 | 1 | id | Tennese | " | 6 |
| | Sarah my wife | 35 | | | | | | | |
| | East bank of Greens Bayou together with the land of Reel & --- | | | | | | | | |

Total 58

| No. | Name | Age | Status | | | Occupation | Origin | Date | |
|---|---|---|---|---|---|---|---|---|---|
| 420 | Edw Shipman | 26 | Single | | | | Arkansas | 1823 | 1 |
| 421 | Saml Holt | 44 | Widower | 4 | | | Misipi | 1830 | 5 |
| 422 | John Lawrence | 50 | id | | | | Louisa | 1827 | 1 |
| 423 | D.S. Ford | 26 | Single | | | | Tennessee | Feb 1830 | 1 |

One quarter of a sitio on the Colorado above the road and which was selected
by Gregg in the upper part of Jenkin's Plain west bank Colorado River

(77)(78)

| No. | Name | Age | Status | | | Occupation | Origin | Date | |
|---|---|---|---|---|---|---|---|---|---|
| 424 | Elizabeth Smith | 64 | Widow | 1 | 1 | Farmer | Louisiana | 1 May 1830 | 3 |
| 425 | James North Cross | 28 | Single | | | id | Alabama | Aug 1829 | 1 |

Wants his land adjoining Wilbarger

| 426 | Timothy Davis | 50 | id | | | | N Carolina | 1827 | 1 |

Between the place called Big Creek above Wilbarger east bank of the Colorado
at the head of Windy Prairie    27 June 1830

| 427 | J.C. Tannehill | 32 | Married | 1 | 1 | Farmer | Tennessee | Apr 1828 | 4 |

Jane his wife

| 428 | Heirs of Pace | | | 5 | 3 | | | | 8 |
| 429 | William Smith | 28 | | | | id | Georgia | 1 Apr 1830 | 1 |

Wants his land behind the lot of T.A.L. Phelps

| 430 | Wm H. Jack | 25 | Married | 1 | | id | Alabama | 3 Jun 1830 | |

Laura H his wife    17

The road where Collins used to live on Cummings Creek

| 431 | Richard Andrews | 30 | Single | | | id | Georgia | 1827 | |

At the headwaters of New Year's Creek the same selected by S. Lawrence who abandoned it

| 432 | George Kimball | 22 | id | | | id | Louisiana | 1830 | |

Wants his land on the side and adjacent to the land granted to James Cumming on the Colorado

| 433 | Ira Ingram | 40 | Widower | | | id | id | 1825 | |

On the east side of the land granted to Wightman

| 434 | James Hall | 55 | Married | 2 | 1 | id | Illinois | 3 June | 5 |

Winaford his wife    54

Behind Minser

| 435 | John Moore | 54 | Widower | 1 | 2 | id | Louisiana | Apr 1830 | 4 |
| 436 | L. Smither | 27 | Single | | | | Alabama | Apr 1826 | 1 |

Behind Henry Jones and below John Jones

| No. | Name | Age | State | Children | Other dep. | Profession | Origin | Arrived | Total Souls |
|---|---|---|---|---|---|---|---|---|---|
| | | | | | | | | | 60 |
| 437 | John Smith | 26 | Married | 2 | 2 | id | Ohio | Jan 1830 | 6 |
| | Sarah his wife | 26 | His family is in Ohio | | | | | | |
| 438 | Nichs Lockridge | 53 | Married | 5 | 5 | id | Louisiana | Apr 1830 | 13 |
| | Alsey his wife | 45 | | | | | | | |
| | Wants his land on the right bank of the Colorado below and adjacent to the place of Thomas Crosley | | | | | | | | |
| 439 | Rosalie Hammer | 24 | | 1 | 4 | id | id | Apr 1830 | 6 |
| | Abandoned woman | | | | | | | | |
| 440 | G. Manent | 26 | Single | | | | France | Jun 1830 | 2 |
| 441 | J. Manent | 24 | id | | | | & Luisa | | |
| 442 | Gains Bailey | 25 | " | | | id | Luisiana | 1822 | 1 |
| 443 | John Kincaid | 33 | " | | | id | Kentucky | 1826 | 1 |
| 444 | Noah Smithwick | 22 | id | | | id | Tennessee | 1827 | 1 |
| 445 | V. Pepin | 49 | " | 2 | 2 | id | Luisa | Jun 1830 | 3 |
| 446 | John McClaren | 36 | " | | | id | Virginia | 1825 | 1 |
| 447 | James Cochran | 30 | " | | | id | Alabama | Jul 1829 | 1 |
| 448 | John Dinsmore | 40 | " | | | id | New Hampshire | Jul 1829 | 1 |
| 449 | Saml Lockhart | 45 | Married | 1 | | id | Louisiana | Jun 1830 | 3 |
| | Conicy his wife | 34 | | | | | | | |
| 450 | David Stoddard | 35 | Single | | | id | id | Aug 1829 | 1 |
| 451 | Richard Morris | 39 | Married | 1 | 4 | id | N York | May 1830 | 7 |
| | Cathrine his wife | 34 | | | | | | | |
| (79)(80) | | | | | | | | | |
| 452 | William P. Harris | 31 | Single | | | Artisan | Luisa | Jul 1830 | 1 |
| 453 | Andrew L. Phinney | 30 | id | | | Farmer | id | Nov 1829 | 1 |
| | Top point of Bay Prairie behind Parker and Parke | | | | | | | | |
| 454 | S.W. Peebles | 28 | id | | | Tailor | Alabama | May 1830 | 1 |
| 455 | Alfred Metcalf | 36 | id | | | Farmer | Mississippi | Jul 1830 | 1 |
| 456 | Henry Smith | 40 | Married | 3 | 4 | Farmer | Missouri | Mar 1827 | 9 |
| | Elizabeth his wife | 30 | | | | | | | |
| 457 | S.C. Bundick | 21 | Single | | | id | Louisiana | Jan 1830 | 1 |
| | On the Galveston Bay east of the delta of Highland Creek | | | | | | | | |

| No. | Name | Age | Status | | | Occupation | Origin | Date | |
|---|---|---|---|---|---|---|---|---|---|
| 458 | J.R. Jefferson | 30 | Single | | | Mariner | Rhode Island | Feb 1830 | 1 |
| 460 | Perkins Lovejoy | 38 | Married | | | id | Louisiana | Jul 1830 | 1 |
| | Carolina his wife | 23 | | | | | | | |
| 461 | William Williamson | 42 | Married | | | Carpenter | Ohio | Jul 1830 | 1 |
| | Mary T his wife | 18 | | | | | | | |
| 462 | William Busby | 21 | Single | | | id | Louisiana | Mar 1830 | 1 |
| | On the Matagorda Bay peninsula | | | | | | | | |
| 463 | William Birch | 26 | idem | | | Farmer | Missouri | Jul 1830 | 1 |
| 464 | Antonio Mancha | 48 | Married | 4 | 3 | id | Bexar | | 9 |
| | Maria Canado | 46 | | | | | | | |
| | Wants his land in an existing corner between Esteban Richards and that of Williamson | | | | | | | | |
| 465 | George Tunnell | 58 | Married | 2 | 2 | id | Missouri | 1826 | 6 |
| | Sally his wife | 34 | | | | | | | |
| 466 | William C. Clark | 30 | Married | 3 | | id | Louisiana | Jan 1830 | 6 |
| | Rebecca his wife | 28 | | | | | | | |
| 467 | Nathl Townsend | 26 | id | | | Trader | Mississippi | Jul 1830 | 2 |
| | Maria his wife | 25 | | | | | | | |
| 468 | Daniel E. Colton | 28 | Single | | | id | New York | " " | 1 |
| 469 | Henry T. Walker | 24 | Married | 1 | | Farmer | Alabama | Jun 1830 | |
| | Prudence his wife | 20 | | | | | | | |
| | On the west branch of Middle Creek | | | | | | | | |
| 470 | Thos Choate | 51 | Married | 6 | | id | Louisiana | Jun 1830 | 8 |
| | Jane his wife | 37 | | | | | | | |
| | On a branch of Clear Creek known by the name of Turkey Creek adjoining | | | | | | | | |
| | J.R. Williams to include the corral or horse pen | | | | | | | | |
| 471 | John Anderson | 27 | Married | 1 | | Mariner | Orleans | Aug 1830 | 3 |
| | Anne his wife | 36 | | | | | | | |
| | He wants land on the west branch of Cummins Creek some five miles below Bahia Road. | | | | | | | | |
| | It will not reach Cane Creek nor does it include the headwaters of said branch. | | | | | | | | |
| 472 | Henry Harter | 25 | Single | | | Farmer | Ohio | Jun 1830 | 1 |
| 473 | James Bell | 29 | Married | 1 | 3 | id | Tennessee | Jun 1830 | |
| | Winsey his wife | 29 | | | | | | | |
| | On Davidson's Creek to join above with the Bexar Road and below to complete the amount | | | | | | | | |

| No. | Name | Age | State | Child-ren 1 | 2 | Other dep. | Profes-sion | Origin | Arrived |
|---|---|---|---|---|---|---|---|---|---|
| 474 | Thomas Bird | 25 | Married | 1 | 2 | | Farmer | Tennessee | Jun 1830 |
| | Nancy his wife | 23 | | | | | | | |
| | Sitio No. 20 north of Mare Creek and adjacent to the Bexar Road | | | | | | | | |
| 475 | Ephraim Fuqua | 40 | id | 3 | 2 | | id | Alabama | Apr 1828 |
| | Martha his wife | 36 | | | | | | | |
| (81)(82) | | | | | | | | | |
| 476 | Wily B.D. Smith | 25 | Single | | | | Farmer | Alabama | 1827 |
| 477 | James Day (orphan) | 19 | id | | | | id | Louisiana | Mar 1829 |
| 478 | Humphrey N. Gores | 34 | id | | | | id | id | Apr 1830 |
| | On the Matagorda peninsula | | | | | | | | |
| 479 | Daniel Gilleland | 35 | Married | 2 | 3 | | id | Arkansas | Jul 1830 |
| | Priscilla his wife | 26 | | | | | | | |
| 480 | Michael Scanlon | 21 | Single | | | | Trader | La | Aug 1830 |
| | On the Colorado above Wm Robinson the place chosen by --- | | | | | | | | |
| 481 | John Bowman | 50 | Married | 1 | 1 | | Farmer | Arkansas | Aug 1830 |
| | Margaret his wife | 29 | | | | | | | |
| 482 | Patrick Dunn | 25 | Single | | | | Mariner | La | Aug 1829 |
| | A quarter part of No. 5 on Mill Creek which was surveyed for Shelly | | | | | | | | |
| 483 | B.A. Porter | 25 | id | | | | Farmer | Kentucky | Mar 1830 |
| 484 | Thos H. Mays | 27 | id | | | | id | Tennessee | may 1830 |
| | A quarter of sitio No. 7 forks of the Colorado surveyed for Borden | | | | | | | | |
| 485 | Michael Young | 27 | Married | 2 | | | id | Alabama | Mar 1829 |
| | Rachel his wife | 24 | | | | | | | |
| 486 | A.J. James | 25 | Single | | | | id | id | " 1829 |
| 487 | Jeremiah Dwyer | 42 | Married | 1 | 2 | | id | Tennessee | Jun 1830 |
| | Eliza his wife | 25 | | | | | | | |
| 488 | Jesse Wilson | 39 | id | Free man of color | | | id | Louisiana | May 1830 |
| | Jane his wife | 24 | | | | | | | |
| 489 | Robt Spears | 22 | Orphan | 4 | 1 | | id | Alabama | Mar 1828 |
| 490 | Anne White | 30 | Widow | | | | id | id | Apr 1830 |

| No. | Name | Age | Status | | | | Occupation | Place | Date |
|---|---|---|---|---|---|---|---|---|---|
| 91 | James D. Grey | 30 | Married | 1 | 1 | | | id | Feb 1830 |
| | Levina his wife | 25 | | | | | | | |
| 492 | Daniel McDonald | 31 | id | 2 | 1 | | | Canada | Aug 1830 |
| | Hannah his wife | 28 | | | | | | | |
| 493 | John H. Scott | 34 | Single | | | | | Alabama | 1828 |
| | Wants his land on the west bank of the Navidad where the Gonzales Road crosses | | | | | | | | |
| 494 | Ephraim Anderson | 49 | Widower | 3 | 4 | 1 | | id | Apr 1830 |
| 495 | Milton J. Anderson | 25 | Single | | | | | id | id |
| 496 | Henry Austin | 50 | Married | | | | | | |
| 497 | John H. Connell | 30 | Married | | | | | Pennsylva | Sep 1830 |
| | Matilda his wife | 22 | | | | | | | |
| 498 | Ira Strickland | 30 | Single | | | | | Mississippi | Apr 1830 |
| | Wants his land behind that of Dr. Phelps | | | | | | | | |
| 499 | Abraham Peck | 32 | id | | | | | id | 1828 |
| 500 | Philip Coonce | 24 | id | | | | Blacksmith | Luisiana | 1828 |
| 501 | William Laughlin | | id | | | | | Kentucky | 1824 |
| 502 | John Morris | 40 | Married | | | | Farmer | Tennessee | 1830 |
| | Nancy his wife | 32 | | | | | | | |
| 503 | Franklin J. Greenwood | 26 | Married | | | | Farmer | Arkansas | Oct 1830 |
| | Mary Jane his wife | 22 | | | | | | | |
| (83)(84) | | | | | | | | | |
| 504 | Robert Martin | 40 | Single | | 40 | | Farmer | Louisiana | 1829 |
| 505 | William Burnett | 28 | id | | 5 | | id | Kentucky | 1828 |
| 506 | John Burgess | 37 | Married | | | | id | Scotland | Jul 1830 |
| | Margaret C. his wife | 37 | | | | | | | |
| | Sitio No. 1 between Huisache and Bowling Green. His family in Scotland. Has a year's extension. | | | | | | | | |
| 507 | William Clapp | 27 | Single | | | | | id | Arkansas | Jul 1830 |
| | On Trespalacios Creek above John H. Scott | | | | | | | | |
| 508 | David Grammer | 28 | id | | | | id | Tennessee | Feb 1830 |
| 509 | Chs. S.P. Johnstone | 26 | id | | | | id | Florida | Jan 1830 |
| 510 | Andw Montgomery | 30 | id | | | | id | Alabama | Oct 1830 |
| | Adjoins Jesse Grimes on southeast | | | | | | | | |

| No. | Name | Age | State | Child-ren | Other dep. | Profes-sion | Origin | Arrived | Total Souls |
|---|---|---|---|---|---|---|---|---|---|
| 511 | James Stephenson | 40 | Married | 2 | 1 | Farmer | Canada | Oct 1830 | |
| | Dimanes his wife | 37 | | | | | | | |
| 512 | C.C. Wyatt | 27 | Single | | | id | Luisiana | May 1830 | |
| 512 | C.B. Stewart | 26 | id | | | Trader | S.Carolina | Jun 1830 | |
| 513 | Burrel Perry | 58 | Married | 1 | 4 | Farmer | Luisiana | Nov 1830 | |
| | Jane his wife | 37 | | | | | | | |
| 514 | James Rion | 21 | Single | | | id | | id  id | |
| 515 | Henry Griffith | 40 | Widower | 2 | | id | N York | Dec 1828 | |
| 516 | B.B. Pool | 30 | Married | 2 | 1 | id | Arkansas | Oct 1830 | |
| | Sarah his wife | 31 | His family in Orleans; has nine months to 23 Novr to bring | | | | | | |
| 517 | Michael Gill | 32 | id | 1 | 1 | id | Ireland | Jun 1830 | |
| | Mary his wife | 29 | | | | | | | |
| 518 | Edward Dickenson | 26 | Single | | | id | England | Mar 1824 | |
| 519 | Susan Vince | 33 | Single | | | id | Mississippi | 1822 | |
| 520 | Chs H. Bennet | 23 | id | | | id | N York | Jan 1830 | |
| 521 | Elizabeth Standeford | 35 | Widow | 2 | | id | Ala | Mar 1829 | |
| 522 | James Standeford | 21 | Married | 1 | | id | id | id  id | |
| | Sarah his wife | 19 | | | | | | | |
| 523 | Heirs of Gillet | 4 | | | | | | | |
| | Sitio No. 10 on Lake Creek San Jacinto water | | | | | | | | |
| 524 | John F. Brush | 25 | Single | | | id | N York | Jul 1830 | |
| | At the point where the road crosses kby Jennings Camp, the --- Trespalacios right bank of said creek | | | | | | | | |
| 525 | Charles K. Reese | 20 | id | | | id | Tennessee | Feb 1830 | |
| | On Prairie Creek above --- | | | | | | | | |
| 526 | H.B. Stringer | 39 | Widower | 1 | | id | Virginia | Aug 1830 | |
| 527 | Jabez Barney | 30 | Married | 3 | | id | R. Island | Jul 1830 | |
| | Anne Eliza his wife | 39 | | | | | | | |
| 528 | Howard McElroy | 26 | Married | 1 | 1 | id | Arkansas | Nov 1830 | |
| | Betsey his wife | 20 | | | | | | | |
| 529 | John Smith | 22 | | | | id | | | |

| No. | Name | Age | Status | No. | Occupation | Origin | Date |
|-----|------|-----|--------|-----|------------|--------|------|
| 520 | Samuel Kinman | 34 | Married | 2 | Farmer | Indiana | |
| | Carey his wife | 27 | | 2 | | | |
| | Behind Dottery | | | | | | |
| | (85)(86) | | | | | | |
| 531 | Edwd Hogan | 45 | Married | 2 | Farmer | Louisiana | Dec 1830 |
| | Hannah his wife | 35 | | 2 | | Native of Ireland | |

His family is in Louisiana. He has until June 1, 1831 to bring them here

| No. | Name | Age | Status | No. | Occupation | Origin | Date |
|-----|------|-----|--------|-----|------------|--------|------|
| 532 | Francis Lowen | 25 | Single | | id | Kentucky | id id |
| 533 | John S. Black | 40 | Married | 32 | Farmer | Tennessee | 1830 |
| | Mary his wife | 32 | | | | | |

To adjoin the land surveyed for W.H. Jack to include a spring called Dripping north of Jack

| No. | Name | Age | Status | No. | Occupation | Origin | Date |
|-----|------|-----|--------|-----|------------|--------|------|
| 534 | Joseph Johnson | 51 | Single | | id | Louisiana | Nov 1830 |

Together with Francis Holland

| No. | Name | Age | Status | No. | Occupation | Origin | Date |
|-----|------|-----|--------|-----|------------|--------|------|
| 535 | John Flanders | 32 | id | | id | N Hampshire | Dec 1830 |

Flanders is to be included as a colonist although he takes no land

| No. | Name | Age | Status | No. | Occupation | Origin | Date |
|-----|------|-----|--------|-----|------------|--------|------|
| 536 | Perry B. Iles | 29 | Married | 1 | id | Kentucky | Aug 1830 |
| | Nancy his wife | | | | | | |
| 537 | Pleasant B. Riggs | 25 | Single | | id | Tennessee | id id |
| 538 | George M. Patrick | 29 | id | | id | Kentucky | Jan 1828 |

One fourth of a sitio on the west bank of Flores Bayou

| No. | Name | Age | Status | No. | Occupation | Origin | Date |
|-----|------|-----|--------|-----|------------|--------|------|
| 539 | James Walker Moore | 33 | Married | 2 | id | Arkansas | Dec 1830 |
| | Matilda his wife | 21 | | | | | |
| 540 | Willis Stanley | 28 | id | 1 | id | id | Dec 1830 |
| | Betsey his wife | 23 | | 1 | | | |

Sitio on Caney Creek adjoining Chandler

| No. | Name | Age | Status | No. | Occupation | Origin | Date |
|-----|------|-----|--------|-----|------------|--------|------|
| 541 | J.W.E. Wallace | 31 | Widower | 1 | id | Louisiana | Feb 1830 |

A quarter sitio north of Trespalacios Creek below and adjoining Johnson

| No. | Name | Age | Status | No. | Occupation | Origin | Date |
|-----|------|-----|--------|-----|------------|--------|------|
| 542 | Francis S. Mayes | 35 | Married | 3 | id | Mississippi | Dec 1830 |
| | Betty his wife | 25 | | | | | |
| 543 | Garret Low | 28 | Single | | id | id | Dec 1830 |
| 544 | Abner Lee | 30 | Widower | 1 | id | Arkansas | Aug 1830 |
| | Jonathan Wodwort | | | | | | |

65

| No. | Name | Age | State | Child-ren | Other dep. | Profes-sion | Origin | Arrived | Total Souls |
|---|---|---|---|---|---|---|---|---|---|
| | John McHenry | 32 | Married | 1 | | id | Luisiana | 1828 | |
| | [Blank] | 28 | | | | | | | |
| 545 | Robert Taylor Jr | 24 | Single | | | id | id | Nov 1830 | |
| 546 | Edmund Andrews | 34 | Married | 1 | | id | Carolina | Dec 1830 | |
| | Isabella his wife | 24 | | | | | | | |
| 547 | A. Brigham | 41 | Married | 2 | | id | Luisiana | Apr 1830 | |
| | Elisabeth S. his wife | 41 | | | | | | | |
| 548 | Samuel H. Barlow | 30 | Married | 2 | | id | Vermont | Dec 1830 | |
| | Rebecca J. his wife | 24 | | | | | | | |
| 549 | James Morgan | 43 | Married | 2 | 2 | id | Carolina | Dec 1830 | |
| | Celia his wife | 30 | | | | | | | |
| 550 | Henry Dibble | 24 | Single | | | id | N York | Dec 1830 | |
| | G.F. Richardson | 26 | id | | | id | Illinois | Mar 1830 | |
| | William Dupuy | 39 | id | | | id | Kentucky | Mar 1830 | |
| 551 | Francis W. Dempsey | 67 | Married | 1 | | id | Ohio | Dec 1830 | |
| | Maria his wife | 45 | | | | | | | |
| (87)(88) | | | | | | | | | |
| 552 | Thos P. Crosby | 26 | Married | 1 | 1 | Farmer | Phila | | |
| | Clementina his wife | 20 | His family is in Philadelphia | | | | | | |
| | Sidney Whitehead | 18 | Orphan | | | | | | |
| 553 | James Perry | 41 | Married | 3 | 3 | id | Mississippi | Dec 1830 | |
| | Elizabeth his wife | 36 | | | | | | | |
| 554 | Joel Wheaton | 42 | Married | 4 | 1 | Blacksmith | id | Dec 1830 | |
| | Elizabeth his wife | 26 | | | | | | | |
| | John T. Vince | 25 | | | | | | 1822 | |
| 555 | Allen T. Milburn | 30 | Single | | | | Louisiana | Dec 1830 | |
| 556 | Phinneas Smith | 45 | Married | 1 | 1 | Farmer | N York | Dec 1830 | |
| | Sophia his wife | 43 | | | | | | | |
| | Colbert Baker | 37 | Married | 1 | 1 | id | Arkansas | Dec 1830 | |
| | Anne his wife | 26 | | | | | | | |

| # | Name | Age | Status | | | Occupation | Origin | Date |
|---|------|-----|--------|---|---|------------|--------|------|
| 557 | Benjamin Bowles | 43 | Married | 2 | 5 | id | Missouri | Mar 1827 |
| | Betsey his wife | 36 | | | | | | |
| | 13th sitio on Lake Creek water of San Jacinto | | | | | | | |
| 558 | Daniel Perry | 39 | Married | 1 | 3 | id | Mississippi | Dec 1830 |
| | Eliza my wife | 26 | | | | | | |
| 559 | Moses H. Boyden | 33 | Married | | 2 | id | id | Dec 1830 |
| | Clarissa W his wife | 19 | | | | | | |
| 560 | Joel Greenwood | 28 | Married | | 1 | id | Arkansas | Nov 1830 |
| | Anne his wife | 18 | | | | | | |
| 561 | John Y. Criswell | 44 | Married | 6 | 2 | id | Kentucky | Jan 1831 |
| | Elenor his wife | 36 | | | | | | |
| 562 | Danl D.D. Baker | 25 | Single | | | | Massachusetts | " |
| 563 | Isaac Maden | 20 | id | | | id | Indiana | 1825 |
| 564 | J. San Pierre | 56 | Married | 2 | | id | id | 1825 |
| | Margaret his wife | 45 | | | | | | |
| 565 | William D. Lacey | 22 | | | | id | Tennessee | |
| | He wants a quarter of a sitio to adjoin with John Ingram land left bank | | | | | | | |
| | of Colorado River if there is available land | | | | | | | |
| 566 | William Hardin | 49 | Married | 2 | 4 | | Kentucky | Dec 1830 |
| | Caroline his wife | 29 | | | | | | |
| 567 | Josiah F. Hamilton | 32 | Married | | 2 | id | Missouri | May 1830 |
| | Fanny his wife | 21 | | | | | | |
| 568 | Daniel Monroe | 27 | Married | 1 | 1 | id | Luisiana | Oct 1830 |
| | Sally his wife | 22 | | | | | | |
| 569 | Samuel Woody | 26 | Married | 1 | | id | Alabama | Jan 1830 |
| | his wife | 26 | | | | | | |
| | John H. Money | 35 | | | | | | |
| (89)(90) | | | | | | | | |
| 571 | George Gailbreth | 30 | Single | | | Farmer | S Carolina | Oct 1830 |
| 572 | James Miles | 31 | Married | 1 | 3 | id | Arkansas | Jan 1830 |
| | Sarah his wife | 30 | | | | | | |

Total Souls 68

| No. | Name | Age | State | Children | Other dep. | Profession | Origin | Arrived | Total Souls |
|---|---|---|---|---|---|---|---|---|---|
| 573 | James Hodge | 28 | Married | 1 | | id | id | in 1824 | |
| | Juliana his wife | 16 | | | | | | | |
| | Sitio No. 3 on the San Jacinto including the mouth of Lake Creek | | | | | | | | |
| 574 | Joseph House | 60 | Married | 1 | 1 | id | Louisiana | Dec 1830 | |
| | Mary his wife | 50 | | | | | | | |
| | Joseph House | 26 | Single | | | | " | " | |
| 575 | Felix D. Earnest | 27 | id | | | id | id | Apr 1827 | |
| 576 | Lyman Conkrite | 26 | Married | 1 | | Doctor | Tennessee | Jan 1831 | |
| | Sarah his wife | 22 | | | | | N York | | |
| | Sitio on the head of M--- Bayou surveyed by Weightman | | | | | | | | |
| 577 | Albert Silsbee | 22 | Single | | | Farmer | id | id | |
| 578 | John Cronkrite | 28 | id | | | id | id | id | |
| 579 | Joshua Hadley | 36 | Married | 3 | 5 | id | Tennessee | Feb 1831 | |
| | Obedience his wife | 31 | | | | | | | |
| | A sitio NE of Black where there is a rock ridge | | | | | | | | |
| 560 | James W. Taylor | 24 | Single | | | id | id | id | |
| 581 | John Laurence | 25 | Married | Cancelled at the request of the interested parties | | | | | |
| | Sally his wife | 16 | | and has returned his obligation | | | | | |
| 582 | Wm Montgomery | 58 | Widower | 1 | | id | id | Sep 1830 | |
| 583 | Elisabeth Hensen | 36 | Widow | 3 | | id | id | id | |
| 584 | Joshua W. Martin | 28 | Single | | | id | Maine | Jan 1830 | |
| 585 | Eli Church | 27 | id | | | id | N York | Feb 1831 | |
| 586 | John Bird | 36 | Married | 2 | 2 | id | Tennessee | Jun 1830 | |
| | Sally his wife | 31 | | | | | | | |
| 587 | Alexr Brown | 32 | Married | 2 | 1 | id | Arkansas | Nov 1830 | |
| | Sally his wife | 24 | | | | | | | |
| 588 | Ashley R. Stevens | 25 | Married | | | id | Tennessee | Feb 1831 | |
| | Sophia his wife | | | | | | | | |
| 589 | Coleman Hays | 22 | [Single] | | | id | id | id | |
| 590 | Levi Taylor | 26 | Married | 1 | | id | id | id | |

[Columns tabulating children seem to be shifted on this page and next]

| No. | Name | Age | Status | | | Occupation | Origin | Date |
|---|---|---|---|---|---|---|---|---|
| 591 | Mary Clarisa | 21 | Single | | | | | |
| 592 | John Harris | 23 | Single | | | Farmer | Tennessee | Feb 1831 |
| | NE of Hadley's land | | | | | | | |
| 593 | Hannah Cornaugh | 62 | Widow | | 3 | id | Missouri | Dec 1829 |
| 594 | James Hollingsworth | 38 | Single | | | id | Arkansas | Jun 1829 |
| 595 | Wm W. Ford | 27 | id | | | id | Alabama | in 1828 |
| | West of Lake Creek south of Rankin and west of Rogers | | | | | | | |
| 596 | James Ford | 54 | Widower | 1 | 2 | id | id | Jan 1831 |
| 597 | Matthew Burnet | 35 | Married | 1 | 4 | id | Arkansas | Jan 1831 |
| | Sally his wife | 33 | | | | | | |
| | (91)(92) | | | | | | | |
| 598 | Frances Simmons | 20 | Orphan | | | Farmer | Pennsyla | Jan 1831 |
| 599 | Thomas McCaslen | 30 | Single | | | Farmer | Georgia | Mar 1830 |
| 600 | Dudley J. White | 27 | Married | | | id | | Feb 1827 |
| | Bethia his wife | 24 | | | | | | |
| 601 | William W. Hunter | 24 | Single | | | Trader | Missouri | 2 Jan 1831 |
| | Matthew J. Grantham | 37 | id | | | Carpenter | Tennessee | Feb 1831 |
| | Head of Lake Creek | | | | | | | |
| 602 | James McLester | 22 | id | | | Farmer | id | id |
| 603 | John Byrne | 37 | Married | | | id | Ireland | Apr 1829 |
| | Pamelia his wife | 30 | | | | | | |
| 604 | Obadiah Pitts | 37 | Married | 3 | 4 | id | Arkansas | |
| | Polly his wife | 28 | | | | | | |
| 605 | Levi B. Jones | 50 | Married | 2 | 1 | id | Mississippi | Dec 1829 |
| | Sarah his wife | 35 | | | | | | |
| | Free man of color. One half sitio on Fish.Pond Creek, to adjoin J.E. Groces's eastern boundary | | | | | | | |
| 606 | Wm Shepherd | 27 | | 1 | 2 | | Alabama | Dec 1830 |
| | Elisa his wife | 23 | | | | | | |
| | Returned to the United States of the North | | | | | | | |
| 607 | John K. Hale | 25 | id | | 2 | id | Maine | Feb 1831 |
| | Janie F. his wife | 23 | | | | | | |

[Columns tabulating children seemed to be shifted on this page. Ed]

| No. | Name | Age | State | Children | Other dep. | Profession | Origin | Arrived |
|---|---|---|---|---|---|---|---|---|
| 608 | John Martin | 35 | Married | 4 | 1 | Farmer | Tennessee | Jan 1831 |
|  | Mary C. His wife | 36 |  |  |  |  |  |  |
| 609 | Charles D. Sayre | 33 | id |  | 1 | Trader | N York | Mar 1831 |
|  | Cathrine his wife | 24 |  |  |  |  |  |  |
| 610 | J.J. Tinsley | 27 |  |  |  |  |  |  |
|  | Joh S. Moore | 29 | Married | 1 | 1 | id | id | Feb 1831 |
|  | Cathrine his wife | 25 |  |  |  |  |  |  |
|  | On Bray's Bayou above Luke Moore and Tierwester and he has until January 1, 1832 to bring his family |  |  |  |  |  |  |  |
| 611 | James OFlaherty | 37 | Single |  |  | id | Ireland | Mar 1831 |
|  | North of Buffalo Bayou to adjoin Hardin |  |  |  |  |  |  |  |
| 612 | Thomas Bray | 43 | Married |  | 1 | Farmer | England | Aug 1830 |
|  | Cynthia Anne | 23 |  |  |  |  |  |  |
|  | Adjoining Bowman |  |  |  |  |  |  |  |
| 613 | James Cox | 26 | Married |  |  | Farmer | Arkansas | id |
|  | Sarah his wife | 20 |  |  |  |  |  |  |
| 614 | William S. Townsend | 24 | Single |  |  | id | S. Carolina | Jan 1831 |
|  | John Townsend | 26 | id |  |  |  |  |  |
| 615 | F.W. Grasmeyer | 30 | id |  |  | Trader | Germany | Mar 1831 |
|  | John A. Schutte | 26 | id |  |  | id | id | Apr 1829 |
| 616 | Thos Barron | 34 | Married | 4 | 2 | Farmer | Arkansas | Jan 1831 |
|  | Elizabeth his wife | 28 |  |  |  |  |  |  |
| 617 | Holdon Evans | 25 | Married |  | 1 | id | Alabama | Feb 1830 |
|  | Charlotte his wife | 25 |  |  |  |  |  |  |
|  | Returned to the United States of the North |  |  |  |  |  |  |  |
| (93)(94) |  |  |  |  |  |  |  |  |
| 618 | Daniel R. Gandy | 20 | Married |  |  | Farmer | Alabama | Jan 1831 |
|  | Nancy his wife | 21 |  |  |  |  |  |  |
|  | Returned to the United States |  |  |  |  |  |  |  |
| 619 | J.J. Evans | 46 | Married | 5 | 4 | id | id | id |
|  | Polley his wife | 16 |  |  |  |  |  |  |
|  | Returned to the United States |  |  |  |  |  |  |  |

| No. | Name | Age | Status | | | Occupation | Origin | Date |
|---|---|---|---|---|---|---|---|---|
| 620 | Benj Fuqua | 36 | Single | | | id | id | Mar 1828 |
| | Adjacent to Judge Tennel and J.B. Austin | | | | | | | |
| 621 | John Shannon | 36 | Married | 5 | 3 | id | Arkansas | Oct 1830 |
| | Charlotte his wife | 30 | | | | | | |
| | First sitio above the tributaries on the San Jacinto | | | | | | | |
| 622 | Owen Shannon | 70 | Married | | | id | id | id |
| | Margaret his wife | 60 | | | | | | |
| | On the San Jacinto | | | | | | | |
| 623 | Thos Decrow | 28 | Single | | | id | Maine | Jan 1831 |
| | East of the Colorado | | | | | | | |
| 624 | Matthew Boren | 28 | Married | 3 | | id | Arkansas | Dec 1830 |
| | Nancy his wife | 20 | | | | | | |
| 625 | A.C. Reynolds | 45 | Married | 1 | 3 | id | New York | Feb 1830 |
| | Harriet his wife | 40 | | | | | | |
| 626 | William R. Hunt | 50 | Married | 3 | 1 | id | Alabama | id |
| | Rhody his wife | 49 | | | | | | |
| 627 | Thomas Hanson | 40 | Single | | | id | Louisiana | id |
| 628 | Lydia Allen | 26 | Widow | 1 | 1 | id | Missouri | May 1830 |
| 629 | Charles Fordhran | 29 | Single | | | Trader | Germany | Apr 1831 |
| 630 | James Hislop | 33 | " | | | Farmer | Scotland | Oct 1829 |
| | Left the Country | | | | | | | |
| 631 | John Brown | 21 | " | | | id | New Orleans | Mar 1830 |
| 632 | George M.Collingsworth | 21 | " | | | id | Mississippi | Feb 1831 |
| 633 | John Aitken | 26 | " | | | Printer | Pensacola | " |
| | Annulled | | | | | | | |
| 634 | David Hanson | 29 | " | | | Farmer | Louisiana | Jun 1830 |
| 635 | Marcus L. Black | 26 | " | | | " | Alabama | Dec id |
| 636 | Gabriel Eagan | 37 | " | | | " | Tennessee | Apr 1831 |
| 637 | John Hall | 24 | " | | | " | Illinois | Jun 1830 |
| | Behind Mouser | | | | | | | |
| 638 | Robert D. Moore | 36 | Married | | | " | Alabama | Apr 1831 |
| | Anne Coleman his wife | 26 | | | | | | |

| No. | Name | Age | State | Children | Other dep. | Profession | Origin | Arrived |
|---|---|---|---|---|---|---|---|---|
| 639 | Abner Phelps | 26 | Single | | | Farmer | Massachusetts | Feb 1831 |
| 640 | William Mackey | 46 | Married | 3 | 5 | Blacksmith | Alabama | " id |
| | Ruth his wife | 35 | | | | | | |
| 641 | Richard Smith | 65 | | 2 | 4 | Farmer | id | Mar id |
| | Margaret his wife | | | | | | | |
| | William R. Clements | 45 | Married | 4 | | id | id | Feb id |
| | Letis his wife | 47 | | | | | | |

(95)(96)

[There is an overlap of numbering at this point and the reason is not apparent. Ed]

| No. | Name | Age | State | Children | Other dep. | Profession | Origin | Arrived |
|---|---|---|---|---|---|---|---|---|
| 543 | John Caldwell | 28 | Married | 1 | 5 | Farmer | Alabama | Feb 1831 |
| | Lucinda W. his wife | 21 | | | | | | |
| 544 | Thomas Winston | 26 | id | 3 | 7 | id | id | id id |
| | Eliza C. his wife | 23 | | | | | | |
| 545 | John Matthews | 33 | Single | | 20 | id | id | Dec 1830 |
| 546 | Joseph Rector | 28 | Married | | 4 | id | id | Apr 1831 |
| | Harriet his wife | 23 | | | | | | |
| 547 | Raleigh Rogers | 37 | id | 1 | | id | Louisiana | Dec 1830 |
| | Polly Anne his wife | 24 | | | | | | |
| 548 | Frederick Ernst | 35 | id | 3 | 2 | id | Germany | Apr 1831 |
| | Louisa Augusta his wife | 30 | | | | | | |
| | James M. Royster | 30 | id | | | id | Tennessee | Feb id |
| | Sarah his wife | 25 | | | | | | |
| 549 | Abraham M. Clare | 29 | id | | | id | Missouri | 1822 |
| | Sarah his wife | 16 | | | | | | |
| 550 | Stephen G. Letcher | 39 | Widower | 1 | | id | Alabama | Dec 1830 |
| 551 | George L. Bellows | 33 | Married | 1 | 1 | Trader | New York | Apr 1831 |
| | Charlotte L. his wife | 22 | | | | | | |
| 552 | Edwin Waller | 31 | id | 3 | 7 | id | Missouri | id id |
| | Julieta M. his wife | 23 | | | | | | |
| 553 | Francis Courteaux | 37 | Widower | 2 | | Farmer | id | id 1830 |

| No. | Name | Age | Status | | | Occupation | Place | Date |
|---|---|---|---|---|---|---|---|---|
| 554 | B.M. Foley | 28 | Single | | | Trader | Luisiana | Feb 1831 |
| | Quarter No. 10 on Chocolate Bayou | | | | | | | |
| 555 | J.S. O'Connor | 69 | Married | 4 | | Farmer | id | May id |
| | Mary Frances his wife | 69 | | | | | | |
| 556 | Samuel Kennelly | 36 | Married | 1 | | id | England | Apr 1829 |
| | Jane his wife | 36 | | | | | | |
| 557 | De La F. Raysden | 27 | id | 2 | | Lawyer | Mississippi | May 1831 |
| | Nancy Adeline his wife | 19 | | | | | | |
| 558 | Patrick C. Jack | 24 | Single | | | id | Alabama | Apr id |
| 559 | John Logan | 26 | id | | | Farmer | Virginia | Jul 1830 |
| 560 | Jasper Seargeant | 33 | Married | 1 | 2 | id | Alabama | Jan 1831 |
| | Jane Maria his wife | 27 | | | | | | |
| 561 | A.W. Breedlove | 32 | id | | | | New Orleans | Feb id |
| | Susan J. his wife | 19 | | | | | | |
| 562 | Edward Jeffery | 28 | Single | | | | Mississippi | Apr id |
| 563 | James Rogers | 26 | Married | 1 | 3 | id | Tennessee | id |
| | Racheal his wife | 28 | | | | | | |
| | **(97)(98)** | | | | | | | |
| | John S. Cox | 44 | Single | | | Farmer | Tennessee | Apr 1831 |
| | Andrew Ray | 50 | id | | | id | Aises | Feb 1830 |
| 564 | William Waters | 44 | Widower | 1 | | id | Virginia | Apr 1831 |
| 565 | Tandy Walker | 62 | Married | 2 | 6 | id | Palogacho | Jun 1830 |
| | Mary his wife | 55 | | | | | | |
| | Joseph Rogers | 28 | id | 1 | 3 | id | Tennessee | Apr 1831 |
| | Nancy his wife | 28 | | | | | | |
| 566 | Abraham Zuber | 50 | id | 1 | 4 | id | Aises | Feb id |
| | Mary Anne his wife | 37 | | | | | | |
| 567 | Thomas Polk | 38 | id | 2 | 3 | id | Arkansas | May id |
| | Sally his wife | 37 | | | | | | |
| 568 | Edward Dwyer | 23 | Single | | | id | Ireland | Dec 1830 |
| 569 | Abner Kuykendall | 24 | Married | 1 | | id | Tennessee | May 1831 |
| | Maria his wife | 19 | | | | | | |
| | League No. 7 north of the Yegua | | | | | | | |

73

| No. | Name | Age | State | Child-ren | Other dep. | Profes-sion | Origin | Arrived |
|---|---|---|---|---|---|---|---|---|
| 570 | Joseph Powell | 25 | Single | | | Farmer | New Orleans | Dec 1830 |
| 571 | Jacob Reed | 49 | Married | 5 | 3 | id | Tennessee | May 1831 |
| | Matilda his wife | 49 | | | | | | |
| 572 | John Crownover | 56 | id | | | id | Arkansas | 1830 |
| | Elizabeth his wife | 52 | | | | | | |
| 573 | John Iiams | 23 | Single | | | id | Luisiana | 1831 |
| 574 | Archolaus Dodson | 23 | id | | | id | Missouri | 1827 |
| 575 | James Murphy | 32 | id | | | id | Ireland | 1830 |
| 576 | Joseph Scott | 48 | Married | 8 | 1 | id | Alabama | Apr 1831 |
| | Betsy his wife | 42 | | | | | | |
| 577 | James W. Scott | 27 | id | 3 | 1 | id | Tennessee | id |
| | Patsey his wife | 30 | | | | | | |
| 578 | William B. Travis | 22 | Single | | | Lawyer | Alabama | May id |

A quarter sitio adjoining William Price and below

| No. | Name | Age | State | Child-ren | Other dep. | Profes-sion | Origin | Arrived |
|---|---|---|---|---|---|---|---|---|
| 579 | Charles S. Wilson | 39 | id | | | Farmer | Virginia | id id |
| 580 | Joseph E. Scott | 24 | Married | | | id | Alabama | Apr id |
| | Lucy his wife | 20 | | | | | | |
| 581 | Samuel McCarley | 55 | id | 5 | 5 | id | Nacogdoches | Dec 1830 |
| | Celia his wife | 32 | | | | | | |
| 582 | Jacob Walker | 31 | id | 1 | | id | Luisiana | id id |
| | Sarah Ann his wife | 19 | | | | | | |
| 583 | John M. Heard | 26 | id | 1 | 1 | id | Alabama | Feb 1831 |
| | Maria his wife | 23 | | | | | | |
| 584 | Samuel C.A. Rogers | 21 | id | 1 | | id | id | id id |
| | Mary his wife | | | | | | | |

(99)(100)

| 585 | Richard Carter | 41 | Married | 5 | 3 | Farmer | Alabama | Apr 1831 |
| | Elizabeth his wife | 38 | | | | | | |

The league of land entered by McTavish on the Colorado

| No. | Name | Age | Status | | | Place | Occupation | Date |
|---|---|---|---|---|---|---|---|---|
| 586 | Thomas J. Reed | 21 | Married | | 1 | Alabama | Farmer | Dec 1830 |
| | Martha his wife | 18 | | | | | | |
| 587 | Thomas H.P. Heard | 25 | id | | 1 | id | id | Apr 1831 |
| | Nancy his wife | 21 | | | | | | |
| 588 | William C. Manifee | 35 | id | 4 | 2 | id | id | id 1830 |
| | Agnes his wife | 36 | | | | | | |
| 589 | David Clarke | 35 | id | | 1 | Luisiana | id | Dec id |
| | Bershela his wife | 26 | | | | | | |
| 590 | William Truit | 53 | id | | 1 | Tennessee | id | Apr 1831 |
| | Elizabeth his wife | 51 | | | | | | |
| 591 | Margaret Jordan | 58 | Widow | | 1 | | | May id |
| 592 | Charles Donoho | 35 | Married | | 2 | Mississippi | id | Apr id |
| | Maria his wife | 24 | | | | | | |
| 593 | James McLaughlin | 32 | Widower | 4 | 1 | Luisiana | id | Mar 1829 |
| 594 | Thomas Taylor | 42 | Married | | 4 | Tennessee | id | Apr 1831 |
| | Sarah H. his wife | 35 | | | | | | |
| 595 | Hamilton L. Cooke | 31 | Single | | | Florida | id | Feb id |
| 596 | Jacob Long | 35 | Married | 3 | 1 | Tennessee | id | id id |
| | Nancy his wife | 22 | | | | | | |
| 597 | Francis Christie | 55 | Single | | 1 | | id | Nov 1830 |
| 598 | John Tumlinson | 26 | Married | | 1 | id | id | 1821 |
| | Laura his wife | 20 | | | | | | |
| 599 | Kesiah Crier | 33 | Widow | 21 | | Arkansas | id | Dec 1830 |
| 600 | Richard Marsh | 24 | Single | | | New York | Doctor | May 1831 |
| 601 | William M. Lloyd | 24 | id | | | Ayesh Bayou | Farmer | Feb 1831 |
| 602 | William Bridge | 23 | id | | | Arkansas | id | Apr id |
| | Wiley Parker | 28 | Married | 3 | | Luisiana | id | |
| | Lucinda his wife | 24 | | | | | | |
| 604 | James Price | 41 | id | 3 | 3 | Arkansas | id | Aug 1830 |
| | Margaret his wife | 41 | | | | | | |
| | Wants his land to adjoin Groce's Retreat and Stevens | | | | | | | |
| 605 | Joseph Smith | 23 | Single | | | New York | id | Apr 1829 |

| No. | Name | Age | State | Children | Other dep. | Profession | Origin | Arrived |
|---|---|---|---|---|---|---|---|---|
| 606 | Ephraim Roddy | 38 | Married | 2 | | Farmer | Tennessee | Apr 1831 |
| | Harriet his wife | 28 | | 3 | | | | |
| (101)(102) | | | | | | | | |
| 607 | Thomas Caruthers | 32 | Married | 2 | | Farmer | Alabama | Apr 1831 |
| | Elizabeth his wife | 28 | | | | | | |
| 608 | William G. Evans | 28 | Married | | | id | Tennessee | id id |
| | Martha his wife | 22 | | | | | | |
| 609 | Pendleton Rector | 25 | Single | | | id | Alabama | Jan 1830 |
| 610 | Claiborne Rector | 27 | id | | | id | id | id id |
| 611 | Morgan Rector | 50 | Married | 1 | | id | id | Apr 1831 |
| | Amelia his wife | 51 | | 7 | | | | |
| 612 | William Heard | 30 | id | 2 | | id | id | Dec 1830 |
| | America his wife | 21 | | | | | | |
| 613 | Thomas Manifee | 51 | Widower | 4 | | id | id | id id |
| 614 | Benjamin J. White | 37 | Married | 3 | | id | id | Feb 1831 |
| | Polly his wife | 29 | | 1 | | | | |
| 615 | John Davis | 33 | id | 2 | | id | id | id id |
| | Louisiana his wife | 33 | | | | | | |
| 616 | Lydia Glasgow | 70 | Widow | 6 | | id | id | id id |
| 617 | Frances Manifee | | id | 1 | 5 | id | id | Dec id |
| 618 | Elizabeth Devers | | id | 5 | | id | id | Feb id |
| 619 | Moses Baine | 27 | Married | 1 | | id | Ireland | Apr id |
| | Cecelia his wife | 18 | | | | | | |
| 620 | Elisha Mather | 35 | id | | | id | Mississippi | May id |
| | Nancy his wife | 25 | | | | | | |
| 621 | Alexander J. Stanford | 22 | Single | | | id | Ohio | id id |
| 622 | Mills McDowell | 21 | id | | | id | Luisiana | Dec 1829 |
| 623 | Scott Gerard | 22 | id | | | id | Canada | May 1831 |
| 624 | Chs Ed Thonke | 28 | id | | | id | Germany | Jan id |

| No. | Name | Age | Status | | | Occupation | Place | Date |
|---|---|---|---|---|---|---|---|---|
| 625 | James C. Neill | 42 | Married | 2 | 7 | Farmer | Alabama | Feb 1831 |
| | Harriet his wife | 34 | | | | | | |
| 626 | Jacob Shannon | 28 | id | 2 | 2 | id | Arkansas | Nov 1831 |
| 627 | Catherene his wife | 28 | id | 2 | 3 | id | Alabama | Jan id |
| | Kincheon W. Davis | 39 | | | | | | |
| | Fanny his wife | 30 | | | | | | |
| 628 | James C. Carr | 32 | id | 1 | 1 | id | Tennessee | May 1831 |
| | Harriet his wife | 30 | | | | | | |
| 629 | Samuel Sawyer | 32 | id | | | Trader | New York | Apr id |
| | Elizabeth | 19 | | | | | | |

(103)(104)

| No. | Name | Age | Status | | | Occupation | Place | Date |
|---|---|---|---|---|---|---|---|---|
| 630 | Burk Trammell | 26 | Single | | | Farmer | Alabama | Jan 1828 |
| 631 | John Eblen | 34 | Married | | | id | Tennessee | May 1831 |
| | Elizabeth his wife | 26 | | | | | | |

Upper league or league below Tannehill's selection

| No. | Name | Age | Status | | | Occupation | Place | Date |
|---|---|---|---|---|---|---|---|---|
| 632 | R.M. Coleman | 33 | id | 2 | 2 | id | Kentucky | id id |
| | Elizabeth his wife | 27 | | | | | | |

First league above lower Moseley quarter and above Webber

| No. | Name | Age | Status | | | Occupation | Place | Date |
|---|---|---|---|---|---|---|---|---|
| 633 | Lewis Barksdale | 26 | Single | | | id | Tennessee | Feb 1828 |
| 634 | Philip Coe | 31 | Married | 1 | 3 | id | Alabama | Dec 1831 |
| | Elizabeth his wife | 18 | | | | | | |
| 635 | Nathaniel Moore | 53 | id | | | id | Arkansas | Nov 1830 |
| | Rebecca his wife | 43 | | | | | | |
| 636 | Elizabeth McConnell | 21 | Widow | | | | | Oct 1828 |

In case there is a place he wants a quarter of a sitio below Luke Ingram, Colorado

| No. | Name | Age | Status | | | Occupation | Place | Date |
|---|---|---|---|---|---|---|---|---|
| 637 | Augustus Williams | 21 | Married | | | id | Mississippi | 1825 |
| | Love his wife | | | | | | | |
| 638 | John F. Martin | 27 | Single | | | id | Alabama | May 1831 |
| 639 | John P. Gill | 28 | id | | | id | id | id id |
| 640 | William S. Martin | 27 | id | | | id | id | id id |
| 641 | George W. Brooks | 23 | Married | | | id | Mississippi | id id |
| | Eliza Anne his wife | 16 | | | | | | |

| No. | Name | Age | State | Child-ren | Other dep. | Profes-sion | Origin | Arrived |
|-----|------|-----|-------|-----------|------------|-------------|--------|---------|
| 642 | Charles W. L'Hommedieu | 28 | Single | | | | Ohio | Jun 1831 |
| 643 | Ira R. Lewis | 30 | Married | 4 | | Farmer | Louisiana | Apr id |
| | Eliza his wife | 27 | | | | Lawyer | | |
| 644 | John H. Pickens | 23 | id | 4 | | Farmer | Kentucky | Mar id |
| | Elizabeth his wife | 27 | | | | | | |
| | Head of Cow Creek | | | | | | | |
| 645 | Stephen Burnham | 23 | Single | | | id | Arkansas | 1822 |
| 646 | John M. Allen | 25 | id | | | id | Mississippi | Feb 1830 |
| (105)(106) | | | | | | | | |
| | John Woodruff | 41 | Married | 2 | 4 | Farmer | Tennessee | Jan 1831 |
| | Rhody his wife | 40 | id | 3 | | | | |
| | Dennis Harril | 36 | id | 3 | | id | id | May id |
| | Nancy his wife | 30 | | | | | | |
| | Samuel Young | 40 | Single | | | id | Pennsyla | id id |
| | Samuel Fuller | 37 | Married | 1 | 2 | id | Massas | Oct 1830 |
| | Hannah his wife | 39 | | | | | | |
| | J.S. Counsel | 33 | Single | | | Doctor | Louisiana | Mar 1831 |
| | James G. Wright | 29 | Married | 1 | | id | Tennessee | id id |
| | Sarah his wife | 18 | | | | | | |
| | Greenbury Logan | 33 | id | 2 | 3 | Blacksmith | Missouri | Feb id |
| | Judah Duncan his wife | 25 | | | 8 | | | |
| | John D. Newell | 23 | Single | | | Farmer | Mississippi | May id |
| | Erasmus D. Downer | 32 | id | 3 | | Doctor | New York | id id |
| | John C. Cunningham | 31 | Married | 1 | | Farmer | Ohio | id id |
| | Susan his wife | 34 | | | | | | |
| | William T. Austin | 22 | id | 1 | | id | Connect | Nov 1830 |
| | Joanna his wife | 20 | | | | | | |
| | Henry Louis | 43 | id | 6 | | id | Alabama | Jan id |
| | Sarah his wife | 34 | | 1 | | | | |
| | Abijah L. Burnap | 35 | id | 1 | | id | Massacus | Jun 1831 |
| | Sarah his wife | 34 | | | | | | |

| Name | Age | Condition | | | | Occupation | Residence | Date |
|---|---|---|---|---|---|---|---|---|
| A.C. Taylor | 32 | Single | | | | Doctor | Illinois | May 1831 |
| George W. Hall | 31 | id | | | | Artisan | Luisiana | Mar id |
| Joshua Abbott | 51 | Married | 2 | 3 | | Farmer | Arkansas | Dec 1830 |
| Elizabeth his wife | 37 | | | | | | | |
| William Bard | 42 | Married | 5 | 2 | | id | id | Apr 1831 |
| Martha his wife | 38 | | | | | | | |
| Braxton Mullins | 30 | Single | | | | id | Virginia | May id |
| Mandred Wood | 22 | id | | | | id | Penna | id id |
| Silas Dinsmore jr | 34 | Married | 1 | 1 | | id | Mobile | id id |
| Amanda F. his wife | 30 | | | | | | | |
| Henry Husted | 33 | Single | | | | Hatter | New York | id id |
| Solomon Lapham | 34 | Married | | 3 | | Farmer | id | Nov id |
| Lovicy his wife | 28 | | | | | | | |
| John E. Finch | 24 | Single | | | | id | Virginia | May id |
| Joseph T. Bell | 31 | Married | 2 | 2 | 1 | id | Tennessee | Jan 1830 |
| Jane his wife | 24 | | | | | | | |
| **(107)(108)** | | | | | | | | |
| Winston S. McDaniel | 28 | Married | | 1 | | Farmer | Tennessee | Nov 1830 |
| Lydia his wife | 24 | id | | | | | | |
| J.F.D. Byrom | 33 | id | | | | id | Alabama | Feb 1831 |
| Mary Anne his wife | 17 | id | | | | | | |
| Joseph Urban | 35 | id | | | | Trader | Francisco | Jan 1826 |
| Uabetia fite | 36 | | | | | | | |
| Richard Lawrence | 22 | Single | | | | Farmer | Philadela | Dec 1831 |
| William Scott | 23 | id | 3 | | | id | Alabama | Mar 1831 |
| James Taylor | 37 | Married | 4 | 2 | | id | New York | Jun 1830 |
| Rachael his wife | 29 | id | | | 15 | | | |
| James Routh | 30 | Single | | | | id | Louisiana | Feb 1831 |
| Samuel B. Watts | 23 | id | | | | Doctor | Alabama | |
| Branch T. Archer | 43 | Widower | 3 | 3 | | id | Virginia | Jun id |
| Green H. Coleman | 30 | Married | 2 | 1 | | Farmer | Louisiana | id id |
| Sarah H. his wife | 25 | id | | | | | | |
| John A. Thompson | 22 | Single | | | | id | New York | May id |

| No. | Name | Age | State | Children | Other dep. | Profession | Origin | Arrived |
|---|---|---|---|---|---|---|---|---|
| | Francis Henderson | 50 | Married | 2 | | id | Louisiana | Jun id |
| | Martha Kirk his wife | 50 | | | | | | |
| | Thomas McQueen | 35 | Single | 3 | | Trader | id | Jan 1830 |
| | W.W. Thompson | 31 | Married | 2 | | Farmer | Alabama | Jun id |
| | Fanny Nixon his wife | 27 | | | | | | |
| | Benjamin Jewell | 32 | Single | | | id | Louisiana | id id |
| | William Malcolm | 30 | id | | | id | id | Jul id |
| | Silas Jones | 40 | Married | 2 | | id | Alabama | Mar 1829 |
| | Milly his wife | 28 | | 1 | | | | |
| | Derrel H.M. Hunter | 21 | Single | 2 | | id | Louisiana | Feb 1831 |
| | James Burlerson | 57 | Widower | | 4 | id | Tennessee | Apr id |
| | Thomas Husham | 27 | Single | | | id | Ireland | Jan id |
| | Spencer A. Pugh | 36 | Married | 3 | | id | Virginia | May 1830 |
| | Susan his wife | 36 | | | | | | |
| | Mathew T. Hines | 31 | Single | 1 | | id | id | Jul 1829 |
| | M.H. Tennille | | id | | | id | Louisiana | id 1831 |
| | J.W. Mason | 27 | Married | 3 | 10 | id | id | Jan id |
| | Malinda his wife | | | | | | | |
| | Benjamin T. Hughes | | Single | | | id | id | id id |
| | Jane Hughes | | Widow | 3 | 55 | id | id | |
| | Peggy Frazier | 30 | id | 1 | | id | id | Nov 1831 |
| | John McClinton | 25 | Single | 2 | | id | Arkansas | Dec id |
| (109)(110) | | | | | | | | |
| | Robert Karr | 44 | Single | | | Farmer | Tennessee | Mar 1831 |
| | John Nicholls | 33 | Married | 2 | 1 | id | Sabine | 1827 |
| | Fanny his wife | 31 | | 2 | | | | |
| | Henry Klonne | 58 | Single | | | id | Germany | Jul 1829 |
| | John H. Jones | 28 | id | | | id | Mississippi | Feb id |
| | Daniel Smith | 44 | Married | 2 | | id | New York | Sep 1831 |
| | Alona his wife | 44 | | 2 | | | | |

[Entries that follow are in a different hand]

    John H. Wade    22  Single  S.Carolina
        Land on Trespalacios No. 38, west side
    William Parks  24    do    N.York
        Land on Trespalacios No. 38, west side
    John Wharton   24    do
        Coast. Applied for 1/4 League of land
        below M. Henry

(111)(112)   [These two pages contain a list and
description of premium lands reserved by S.F.
Austin under terms of his contract with the Gov-
ernent as Empresario]

(113)   [This page is blank]

(114)   [This page has 3 slips of paper]

[1]   Jesse Denson --- on Spring Creek beginning
    at Samuel McCarleys NW corner & running N & S.
    2 Labors on N Fork of Cyprus Creek.
    16th May 1831

[2]   Isaac Casner from Alabama, wife and five
    children arrived in June 1831. Is to be
    admitted if there is room after the 15 Decr.
    Lived with John Castleman.

    John Israel Waters, single, came in 1828, is
    to be admitted if there is room.

    Michael Castleman, same --- that Andrew
    entered.

[3]   Francis Henderson, came in last July a year
    ago, gets a certificate for the Colorado
    Colony wants to be included in the 500 family
    Colony. Also his son-in-law, Green H. Coleman,
    in the same situation, both have large
    families.

    These to be included in the 500 colony if
    possible. October 18, 1832.

Nov. 12 Elemeleck Swearingen, wife & one child, came in 2 years ago, is to be recd if there is room.

Hugh M. Childers, wife & child, lives near --- came in here in 1831.

(116)

Thomas F. Fay two brothers and mother, have one year after 2 Dec_r_ 1830, is of Virginia.

Samuel Williams   8 Febry    British Subject

(118)(120

[More notes on premium land for Austin]

[121]

[Memoranda on certificates and passports issued.  No names]

VOLUME 2

The section that follows is the second volume of the Register as it was written, but it has been bound as "Volume A". The dividing date was about April 1833.

The bound manuscripts in the General Land Office are now in two volumes called 2 and A. They are in reverse from the order of writing. The numbers 1 and 2 used here are in order of the date of writing.

The manuscript page numbers have been retained and placed in parentheses (XX) in the text.

In the Personal Names Index that appears at the end, the volume number is given, and then the manuscript page. Regular page numbers that appear in this book are used only in the Index of Contents.

The user should be aware that Samuel May Williams and perhaps others added notes at dates later than the original entry.

Volume 2 has a final section called "Remembrances" that appear to be reminder notes. They are indexed as R-xx.

There are references to a "Remembrances" section for Volume 1 but such a section does not now exist.

84
(1)
Henry Fanthorpe born in Lincolnshire, England, 42 years of age, widower and has a son who resides in England. Wants to choose land in the Contract of Empresarios Austin & Williams. Is a farmer.
[Margin]  Little Colony

John P. Phelan 27 years of age, born in Ireland, entered the country on the 2d of Decr of 1831.

Kemeys Lacy 31 years of age native of Yorkshire, England, came in this colony on the 1st day of May in 1832. Has returned to Missouri to return in the fall.

Joseph Biegel 29 years of age, married.  Margaret 34 years of age, do not have children.  20 June 1832. Given a certificate in writing.

Christian Wertzner 32 years of age, native of Germany, single.  24 of Novr of 1832. Given a certificate in writing.

John Quinn 29 years of age, native of Ireland where his family resides, bears a certificate of the British Consul in Mexico, the Sr. O'Gorman. Wants land in our Contract. 8 Decr 1832.

George B. Wilson, 34 years of age, native of England. Elizabeth his wife 28 years, one male, one female, has two years to return to the country, wants land in our contract.

(2)
Pedro Salinas, Mexican living in Tenoxtitlan, wants to establish himself in the Colony.
2 January 1833.

Anselmo Patineo 21 years of age
Maria Catarina, his ---
Mexican, has arrived in Tenoxtitlan.

[In the margin across the two names above]:
22 Feb 1833 given orders for survey.

Francisco Cruz 35 years  )  Living in
Maria Gertrudes Gonsales )  Labahia

Neales Peterson, native of Switzerland, 60 years of age.  Nancy his wife. 2 Children, has been given a certificate and leave to select his land.

Joh Dud George Varrelman 45 years of age
Catr Henr his wife 40 years of age
5 Female and one male, 6 children
Natives of Germany, arrived in in Febr of this
year, wants his land on Cummings Creek.

Adolphus Sterne native of Germany, 33 years of
age, married.
Maria Rosa his wife 22 years of age.
One male, two female, 3 children. Has 8 years of
residence. Issued certificate of reception
11 April 1833.

Charles S. Taylor, 22 years of age, native of Eng-
land. Ana Maria his wife, 17 years of age.
Has five years of residence, and one child.
Issued certificate of reception 11 April 1833.

John George Enderle, 25 years of age. Native of
Germany. Mariana his wife, 23 years of age.
His family is in the state of Pennsylvania.

(3)
John Burdgess wants a quarter of a league of land
to join S.S. Haddy. 19 Novr 1833.

1834      Leeman Kelcey, 24 years of age
Jany 23   Elizabeth      16  do      do
          Native of the State of New York
          Wants his land adjoining with that of
          Madam Powell a sitio on Snake Creek.
          Took the oath.

23d       Thomas Gilmore 27 years of age
          Caroline       24  do      do      Alabama
          2 Female children
          Wants his land joining & North of 1/2
          League of A. Vince on Lake Creek

          Obedience Hill 48 years of age. Widow.
          1 Male, 3 female minor children.
          One league adjoining Thos Gilmore.

Mairad Stiffler 35 years of age, native of Swit-
zerland. Single man. Land adjoining Alexander
Thompson surveyed by Brown. Plot given to Mr.
Borden. [Margin]: Land

Charles Gieske 23 years of age, native of Germany.
Single man.

Henry Bruning 27 years of age, native of Germany.
Married. Adilaide his wife.

John Daley single man, native of Ireland.
27 years of age.

(4)
Frederick Adolph Zimmerschmitt native of Germany,
49 years of age. Married, wife in this Country.

Frank Vander Hoya native of Germany, 29 years of
age. Amelia Arlmut 22 years of age, wife in Germany. Gave him a certificate.

Joseph Rittery 24 years of age, native of Germany.
Wants his land adjoining with land given Vance
where Mr. G.B. McKinstry lives. The entrant is
single and lives with Hodge. Wants land adjoining
Vance Gr where McKinstry lives 3 miles above Mound
League. Claiborn Wright, Agent.

George M. Patrick 3/4 part of his sitio at point
on Buffalo Bayou below a sitio for Robert Wilson.

Louis Von Roeder 27 years of age
Ottilie Ploger    22    do      do
From Germany. Wants a place about 12 miles from
Dottery.

Thomas Drummond married a native of Scotland.
Family resides in Scotland. A Botanist.
Wants land on Dry Creek.

James Seymour family in New York and one other
family to be brot by him to have land if here by
1st Octr 1835.

John H. Estes from Tennessee family in U.S.
Intends moving this winter.

(5)
Archibald McDonald widower from the State of
Alabama.

James Cole 40 years of age  single man
Land 1/4 League next to Joseph Powell.
Entered 29" Octr 1834.

Daniel McKay 21 years of age from the State of
Main has been living with John Cummings at the
Mill. Wants the place back of Chriesman & Ken-
nedy's labors on Dry Creek.  21 Novr 1834.
Trade Boot Maker. [Added note]: Relinquished &
deeded to Sixto Dominges.

John W. Kenney 34 years of age
Maria E. his wife 30 years of age
Moved from Kentucky & arrived 23 Decr 1833.
2 Male 1 female children
[Added]: Mill Creek W. fork W. side back of
Bostick.

Wingfield Alford 30 years of age      From State of
Eliza his wife 25 years of age        Illinois
1 Male 1 female children
Occupation farming. Arrived 15 June 1832.

Britton Capel married, his family is in the State
of Alabama.
Jabez Britton Capel son of the above also from the
State of Alabama.
Profession of both farmers. Nov. 25th 1834.

Jas Robertson single man, native of Scotland.
Wants land on Buckners Creek. 1/4 League No. 4
marked "Garrison". Dec 4" 1834.

(6)  1834
William B. Aldridge single man from the State of
Virginia. Wants land on the head waters of SW
branch of Mill Creek.

Wade Elkins single man 21 years old from the State
of Alabama. Occupation farming. Applies for 1/4
League No. 26 & 27 on Lake Creek.

H.C.C. Lotze single man from Germany, 23 years of
age. Dec 12.

13th Jesse McCrabb aged 27 years from the State of
Tennessee. Joanna his wife aged 35 years. Family
Mrs. Dunlavy. Wants land between Lavaca and
Navidad high up.

James S. Goodman single man 22 years of age.
Lives with his father in the Fort Settlement.
Wants land. Dec 16".

David R. Nash from the State of Massachusetts, 27
years old. C.M. his wife 24 years.
1 Female child 6 months old.
Profession, Merchant. Has selected the 17 Sitio
on Matagorda Bay, Half Moon Point.
Written application dated 1st Dec 1833.

Charles Dale from the State of Massachusetts 29
years of age. His wife Isabella P. aged 21 years.
Application Dec 1st 1833.

Joseph E. Field from Massachusetts aged 33 years.
Single man. Profession a Phisician. Wants the 1/4
sitio north of Margaret Wightman on ---.

(7)    1834
M.B. & S.T. Foley single man (brothers) from the
State of Alabama.   Dec 27th.

Jany 3d.   Edwd E. Este single man from New Jersey.
The land to join D.G. Burnet.

Jany 5th Stephen Best wants the tract of land
formerly granted to Blufad Brooks, if forfited.

Jan 13.   Thomas Chatham from the State of Alabama.
33 years old. Ditha his wife 23 years old.
1 Male child 3 female do.
Occupation farming. Applied for 4 quarters of
league in Lake Creek settlement, marked J.M.
Springer who relinquishes in favor of Chatham.
[Later note]: Relinquishes his --- and vacates and
applies for vacant land between Austin & Greenwood.

Amziah E. Baker 31 years of age. Trader arrived
July 1834. Written application dated Brazoria
1 Nov 1834.

Robert Eden Handy 27 years of age. Merchant arrived
July 1834. Written application dated Brazoria
1st November 1834.

1835 Jan 17th
Daniel Harmon 30 years of age from the State of
Louisiana. Arrived in Texas 1st March 1831.
His wife Mahala 32 years old, 4 Male children.
Wants land on Cl--- or Dickinsons. Mr. Harmon is a
farmer & stock raiser.

(8)    1835
Henry James Leach from Wales his family now on
their way to this Country. Wants land.
Occupation a farmer.

Wm Cave 48 years of age from Indiana. Arrived last
Oct. Applies for land on the waters of Buffalo
Bayou or San Jacinto 4 miles more or less from
Burnets.   [Note]:   C.C.

1st May 1834 )
Certificate  )  Hance Baker has a family. His
              wife's name is Ann, has two child-
              ren. Is a farmer. From Alabama.

23 Feby 1835   Edwin Henderson 29 year of age mar-
              ried. Elvira 27 years of age.
              Children 1 male 2 female.
              Farmer from Kentucky.

26 Feby John Y. Wallace 34 years of age married.
              Eliza T. 27. Has 2 females.
              Physition from Pennsylvania.

"   "   Michael Minch 41 years of age married.
              Mary W. 36. Farmer from Alabama, has
              four children 1 male 3 female.

27  "   S.D. Gervais 56 married.
              Catherine O. 52. Four children 1 male
              3 female. Lawyer from Mississippi.

"   "   William Kannon 40, married.
              Agnes K. 42. Two children.
              Farmer from Alabama.

"   "   F.B. Jackson 32 single farmer from
              Missouri.

2d March Moseley Baker married.
              Eliza W.   1 female.
              Lawyer from Alabama.

3d May   Richard Allen 42 applies for 1/4 L on
              Donoho's Creek above Donoho's if vacant.
              (Was permitted) to change location. Selects
              new 1/4 White Milford Springs.
              Vide P.15 in Remembrances.

(9)(10)

## Memorandum of Applications for Land in Austin's Colony

| Names of Apl | Where From | Date of Arrival | Date of Application | Family & Age | Children | Occupation |
|---|---|---|---|---|---|---|
| Joseph Baker | Maine US | 7 Dec 1831 | 1st Feb 1835 | Single man | | Instructor of youth |
| Wants land North of McKinney & W of 1/4 League surveyed for Isaac Donoho | | | | | | |
| Lancelot Abbots | England | 4 Jany 1835 | 1sr " | do | | Printer |
| Wants land east of Oakes and south of J. Hall | | | | | | |
| Alonzo Wood his wife Sarah | Indiana | 15 Dec 1834 | 17 " | Married 40 years 37 years | 2 Male 2 Female | Farmer |
| Locates Lea. No. 32 on San Anto | | | | | | |
| D.S. Southmayd Joana his wife | Vermont | 14 Jan 1835 | 18 " | 33 years 34 " | 3 Female | Farmer |
| Locates above Wheaton  Buffalo B | | | | | | |
| E.D. Harmon | | 15 Dec 1834 | 23 " | Married | | Phys & Mercht |
| Locates back of Barton Jenkins and E. White west side Colorado | | | | | | |
| Abner Woolsey | Alabama | March 1st 1835 | 23 Feb " | Single 21 years | | Farmer |
| Applies for 1/4 League No. 4 on Buckners Creek | | | | | | |
| Richard Duty | Resident Citizen | | 23 Feb 1835 | Single | | Farmer |
| Applies for a quarter back of M.Duty's 1/4 Sitio. | | | | | | |
| Isaac Decker Deborah his wife | Michigan | Dec 15, 1834 | 28 " | Married 38 years 34 years | 3 Male 2 Female | Boot & Shoe Maker |
| Upper Colony. Applies for a League back of Hornsby, Duty & Gilleland. | | | | | | |

| Name | Origin | Date | Status | M/F | Occupation |
|---|---|---|---|---|---|
| Col. Pettus for Mrs. Bell | | 2d Mar 1835 | Widow with family | 5 Male 1 Female | Carries on a farm |
| Thos Bell son of the above | | Jan 1834 | 2d " " Married | | Farmer |
| Stewart for Evans Corner | | About 4 years ago " " " Married | | | Farmer |
| Francis Messoner | Maryland | Dec 1834 | | | |
| (11)(12) Jas. Burleson Jr. | Tennessee | 20 Feb 1834  3d Mar 1835 | Widower | 1 Male | Farmer |
| Burleson Gage Malinda his wife | " | " | Married 25 years 20 years | 1 Male 1 Female | Farmer |
| Alex. Ewing | Pennsylvania | 15 Mar 1833  Apl 1833 | Single | | Phisician |
| Chs. Howard Ann Waldin his wife | New Hampshire | Dec 15, 1834  Mar 12, 1835 | Married 33 yrs 25 yrs | 1 Female | Merchant |
| Anthony B. Fleury | N. York | 15 Dec 1834  12 Mar 1835 | Single | | Merchant |

Col. Pettus for Mrs. Bell — Husband died here. Wants a league south east of O. Pettus league & joining ----.

Thos Bell son of the above — Wants land as is stated for Mrs. Bell, as above. Applies for P. Pipers --- if he has not come forward in time.

Stewart for Evans Corner — Wants land in Groce's neighborhood, a League selected by Rumfield.

Francis Messoner — Written Apl dated 14 Febr 1835.

Jas. Burleson Jr. — Applies for League No. 4 Pin O[ak] br Colorado

Burleson Gage — Applies for Lea. No. 3 north of No. 2 on Pin O Creek

Alex. Ewing — Applies for a quarter of a league of land between Leas. No. 4 & 13 Cum. Creek if forfeited by 1st applicant

Chs. Howard — Wants land. If he likes will take a league back of Lea No. 6 above Cayce on the west side Colorado. He paid $4. See memorandum.

Anthony B. Fleury — By Mr. Chs. Howard. Wants land near the same place.

| Names of Apl | Where From | Date of Arrival | Date of Application | Family & Age | Children | Occupation |
|---|---|---|---|---|---|---|
| Fisher<br>Wants land. | N. York<br>Is now doing business for Howard Flewry. Matagorda. | 15 Dec 1834 | 12 March by the same | Single | | |
| Jas. A. Prest<br>Written application dated 10 -- 1835. Family in New Orleans.<br>Wants land, will bring his family when assured of a prospect of land. | England | 1 Jan 1835 | | Married | | Instructor<br>of youth |
| His son Jas Prest<br>Will also be on as soon as he can. | In New Orleans | | | Has a family | | |
| Chas Kneass<br>Wants land. Lives at present in Brazoria.<br>Upper 1/4 League joining Cummins --- applied for by Drummond & --- have if Drummond does not come. | Maryland | 1 Jan 1835 | 14 Mar 1835 | Single | | Miniature & Portrait Painter<br>and house painter |
| Wm L. Cazneau<br>Has a certificate dated some time ago. Applies wants on island in the Colorado<br>gully Cane Island above the Raft. | Boston | | 17 Mar 1835 | Single | | Merchant |
| Saml D. Denison<br>Written application 20 Nov 1833. Wants land. | New York | | | Married | One child | Merchant |
| Thos Bridges<br>Written application dated 1st Dec 1833. Wants land. | Massachusetts | | | Married, wife, one child | | Mariner |
| (13)(14)<br>Js L. Hill<br>Wants land | Georgia | 28 Nov 1834 | 20 Mar 1835 | Single | | Instructor of youth |
| J.B. Cahill<br>Wants land near Groces. Joins Bracey. | Ireland | June 1834 | 23 " " | Single | | Instructor |

Kuykendall Abrm L   Tennessee        1834           23 Mar 1835   Married age 22 yrs   1 Female   Farmer
Eliza Ann his wife                                                age 18 yrs
Per John M. Shipman.  Applies for a league granted to Williams on Clear Creek if forfeited.

Norris Philbrick   New York City   19 Jan 1835   25 Mar 1835   Married   Family in New York
Wants the league on Cummings Creek (No. 3) granted to Daniel E. Colton if forfeited.

Thos Cochrane      New Hampshire   Apl 1834      "    "        Married   Family in New Hampshire
Wants land.  Applies for Lawrence 1/4 L on Cr. if forfeited.
Per Bro James on premises.

Jno. Clay          Alabama         Jan 1835      "    "        Married   Has a large family   Blacksmith
Per S.H. Jack.  Wants land.

J.W. Fanning       Georgia         Jan 1835      Mar 25        Married
Per S.H. Jack.  Family in Georgia but will bring them on immediately.

J.G. Reinerman     Germany         Dec 1835      March 20      Married 55 years   2 Male     Farmer
A.A. Strodman his wife                                         52 years           27 & 24 years
Wants to live about 11 miles below Wheatons on Buffalo Bayou near John Austin's
two leagues on N. side of Bayou.

S. Darling                                        March 26      Married                       Farmer
H. Manton                                            "          Married                       do
Moses S. Hornsby                                     "          Single                        do
Malcolm Hornsby                                      "          do                            do
Wm Hornsby                                           "          do                            do
Per their agent Reuben Hornsby.  Wants land back of 11 league grant in Little Colony as per plat.

(15)(16)
William Goodman    Resident Citizen              April 12, 1835 Single                        Farmer
Lives at Fort Bend.  Wants a qr. of a league of land.

| Names of Apl | Where From | Date of Arrival | Date of Application | Family & Age | Children | Occupation |
|---|---|---|---|---|---|---|
| Jas. Cochran<br>Emaline his wife<br>Wants 3/4 league. | Resident Citizen<br>San Felipe | | Apl 2d 1835 | Married 33 yrs<br>26 yrs | None | Merchant |
| John Mall<br>Wants land on waters of Cypress Creek. | Louisiana | 1st Jan 1835 | " " | Single | | Carpenter |
| Jas. Allen<br>Lives with his father. Applies for the upper part of Leag. No. 6 on the W. side Brazos below. | Resident Citizen | | " " " | Single | | Farmer |
| Robert W. Atkinson<br>Wants land. | New York | Jan 4, 1835 | Apr 3, 1835 | Single | | Machinist |
| Garding C. Jennings<br>Katherine is wife<br>Wants land in Austin's Little Colony or A & W's Upper Colony | Missouri | Dec 4, 1833 | Apr 4, 1835 | Married 56 years old<br>45 years old | 2 Male<br>2 Female | Farmer |
| S.T. Whatley<br>Mahala his wife<br>Wants land in Austin's Little Colony or A & W's Upper Colony. | Alabama | Feb 1835 | " " " | Married 42 years old<br>31 years old | 1 Female | Farmer |
| Abner B. Speir<br>Betsey Ann his wife 9pe Whatley)<br>Wants land in like manner as the two last. | Alabama | Feb 1835 | " " " | Married 26 years old<br>19 years old | 1 Male<br>1 Female | Farmer |
| Asahel C. Holmes<br>Applies for 1/4 league of land, dont intend to bring his family. Wants land between the Brazos & Bernard surveys above Bell. | Georgia | Apl 1824 | Apl 5, 1835 | His family in Geo. Wants land | | Merchant |
| Amos Pollard<br>By Asahel C. Holmes. Applies as above for 1/4 league. | New York | Dec 23, 1833 | Apl 6, 1835 | His family in N.Y. | | Phisician |

Jesse Stockwell    Illinois    29 Jan 1834    Apl 7    "    Married 30 years    2 Females    Farmer
Elizabeth his wife    19 years
Applied to Mr. Williams for League No. 3 on San Jacinto.

Andrew M. Clopper    Resident Citizens    April 7, 1835    Single    Farmer & Grazing
by his father Andrew N. Clopper. Applies for one fourth league back of
Battle, Cartwright & Jane Wilkins.

John Burgess    Scotland    1832    "    "    Single    Farmer & Grazing
Applies for a quarter at the mouth of Cedar Creek.

(17)(18)
Solomon Rumpfeld    Pennsylvania    Apl 1831    5 Apl 1835    Married 50 years old    2 Male    Farmer
                                                    Widower                4 Females
by Mr. Fleury to pay fees
agent for R. Mills. Wants land on the north and adjoining Durnahoe on the east side of the Brazos River.
[Later note]: Evans Corner    page 9    will take this.

James Duncan    Tennessee    2 Mar 1835    5 Apl 1835    Married 50 years    3 Females    Farmer
his wife    44 years
By his agent S.R. Lewis. Wants a league of land on the --- between --- and the Heirs of Wighman.

J.B. Johnson    Alabama    Oct 1834    8 Apl 1835    Married. Has wife    Farmer
by S.R. Lewis agent. Applies for two half leagues.

Ignasia Sartuche    Resident Citizen    9 April    "    Boy
heirs of.    By J. Cochran. Wants a league back of Bowls on the E side Colorado above.

John Cheven    Alabama    Feb 1830    9 Apl    "    Single    Farmer
by W. Seale. Wants land.

Alx Blair    Louisiana    9 Apr 1835    Single 26 years of age
by S.H. Jack. Applies for 1/4 league No. 5 north of Yeagua east of Davidson Creek.

| Names of Apl | Where From | Date of Arrival | Date of Application | Family & Age | Children | Occupation |
|---|---|---|---|---|---|---|
| Wm Huff | Resident Citizen | | 9 Apl 1835 | Married 24 years | | Merchant |
| Mary his wife | | | | 22 years | | |
| by S.H. Jack. Applies for League No 6 north of Yegua east of Davidson's Creek. | | | | | | |
| Ammon Underwood | Massachusetts | Apl 1834 | 10 Apl 1835 | 25 Single | | Farmer & Grazer |
| Applies for 1/4 league No. 2 north of Yegua east of Davidson's Cr New Survey. | | | | | | |
| McHenry Winburn | Alabama | Dec 15, 1834 | Apl 11, 1835 | Single | | Farmer & Grazer |
| Wants land. | | | | | | |
| Chambers | | | | | | |
| Ths Sothers | | | | | | |
| Foster | [Line through these 5 names] | | | | | |
| Smith | | | | | | |
| Roberts | | | | | | |
| (19)(20) | | | | | | |
| Rufus Wright | New York | 11 Jul 1834 | 11 Apr 1835 | Single | | Farmer |
| Applies for 1/4 league of land below Harden on north side Buffalo Bayou. | | | | | | |
| Gleason Wallace | New York | 11 Jul 1834 | 11 Apl 1835 | Widower his family on way | | Farmer |
| Applies for --- of land on the E side of Colorado back of Austin and the Bastrop league. | | | | | | |
| Danl M. Frazer | do | 10 Mar 1835 | " " | Married 38 years | 2 Male | do |
| Sally N. his wife | do | | | 37 years | 2 Female | |
| back of Bowls, Highsmith & Cottle. | | | | | | |
| Edmund Ellis | do | " | " | Married has family on way | | " |
| back of one quarter league No. 14, 15 & 16 & part of League No. 20. | | | | | | |
| Alpheus Rice | do | 20 Jan 1835 | " ' | Married family here | | " |
| west side back of League No. 12 & 11 and Austin's quarter. | | | | | | |

Cyrus Gleason          do                          Single
          do          same place as above.

By their Agent Danl M. Frazer [His list begins with Gleason Wallace].
     These persons are now erecting a steam mill on the Highsmith League, for the
     purpose of sawing lumber, grinding corn and ginning cotton.

Thos Whittington    Kentucky         12 Apl 1835   Married           1 Male    Carpenter
Rosa his wife                                                        1 Female

Wm R. Bowen         Tennessee       5 Apl 1835    12 Apl 1835    Family in Ten.          Farmer
     Wants land for himself and these following his move in this Colony, or Austin & Williams,
     Upper Colony.  He applies as agent for
Gideon Walker       Alabama          5 Apl 1835
Gideon Townsend        do               do
     Their families large and in Matagorda awaiting selections.
     Mr. Bowen has moved Walker & Townsend to this Country at his individual expense
     and he has agreed to pay fees on their land shares.

Wm G. Roulhac       Tenn            4 Apl 1835    12 Apl 1835    Family in Tenn
     Wants land as above.

(21)(22)               Memorandum of Applications for Land

Dan Etherton    England    some 8 or 10 years ago  12 Apl 1835   Family            Farmer
     per S.R. Fisher. Applies for League No. 3 on Trespalacios side.

Isham Thompson  S.R. Fisher agent  Wants land on the Colton League.

Duncan          Tenn    About two years ago   12 Apl 1835    Married    Wants land

Hammelton L. Cook per Howard      1831        12 Apl 1835    37 years                Farmer
Mary his wife                                                18 years
     Wants land on Jones Cr or Navidad Lea. No. 31 E. side. Has a Certificate dated 28th May 1831.

| Names of Apl | Where From | Date of Arrival | Date of Application | Family & Age | Children | Occupation |
|---|---|---|---|---|---|---|
| B.L. Hanks | Tennessee | | 15 Apl 1835 | Has a family | | Farmer |

By his agent David Ayres. Has been here some time. Applied for a league No. 16 on the Yea. [Struck out and note added]: Has a deed.

| L.B. Franks | | | 15 Apl 1835 | Family | | |

By his agent D. Ayres. Has been in the Country some time. Applied some time ago for a league on the Yegua joining Campbell near F---. Paid on said league by --- as per receipt shown.

| Benj Grenville | Michigan | 1 Dec 1834 | 15 Apl 1835 | Married 45 years | 1 Male | Farmer |
| Mary his wife | | | | 24 years | 4 Females | |

T.H. Borden agent. Mr. Grenville applies for a league on the west side Cummins Creek NE of Dr. Peebles and between No. 3 and Thos Gay.

| Wells | Alabama | | 15 Apl 1835 | Unmarried | | Teacher |

Applies for 1/4 L. granted to Smith on Jacksons Creek if forfeited. Relinquishes in favor of Sanders.

| Anderson Estis | Mississippi | 1 Mar 1834 | 16 Apr 1835 | Married | 1 Male | Farmer |
| Elizabeth his wife | | | | | 1 Female | |

Applies for a League M on Yeagua.

| Timothy Jones | Kentucky | | 16 April 1835 | Married | 3 Males | Farmer |
| Gennet his wife | | | | | 1 Female | |

League No. 6 E. of Brazos.

| Alvin Woodward | Resident Citizen | | 17 Apl 1835 | Single | | Farmer & Grazer |

Applies for 1/4 Lea. No. 3 --- side of Cany near the mouth --- [if not] taken.

Memorandum of Applications for land in Austin's Colony

| Name | State | Date | Date | Status | Family | Occupation |
|---|---|---|---|---|---|---|
| Steward Keass | Maryland | Feb 10, 1835 | 17 Apl 1835 | Single | | Carpenter |
| By his brother Chs Keuass. Applies for land 5 miles above the Germans on road to Buttery's. | | | | | | |
| William Baxter | England | May 1831 | 20 Apl 1835 | Married 26 years 22 years | 1 Female | Farmer & Grazer |
| --- W. his wife | | | | | | |
| Applies for land. | | | | | | |
| [Henry] Baxter | England | Dec 1834 | 20 Apl 1835 | Single | | Hatter [?] |
| by his brother William. Applies for land. | | | | | | |
| John W. Buckner | Missouri | Dec 1832 | 20 Apl 1835 | 47 years old 33 " " | 2 Males 3 Females | Farmer & Grazer |
| Elizabeth his wife | | | | | | |
| Has got a certificate dated December 1832. Applies for a league on the head of Prairy Creek Bay --- joining Vaders Survey. | | | | | | |
| Isaac Votaw | Missouri | 1 Apl 1835 | 21 Apl 1835 | 13 Male & Female | | Farmer |
| Liza his wife | | | | | | |
| by John Whiteside. Applies for the league on the San Anton Road E of Navasota & where Danl Parker was camped when they first came. | | | | | | |
| John Votaw | Missouri | 1 Apl 1835 | 21 Apl' 1835 | Single | | Farmer |
| by Mr. Whiteside. Applies for a quarter between T. Walker and McNeely. | | | | | | |
| Relinquishes in favor of Henry Wingfield. | | | | | | |
| Paschal Borden | Resident Citizen | | " Apl 1835 | Married 29 years old | | |
| Frances his wife | | | | | | |
| Applies for land. One labor formerly granted to Mr. Andrus situated in Fort Bend on the Brazos which for some time has been subject to forfeiture. | | | | | | |
| A.G. Moore | Dist of Columbia | Jany 1835 | 24 Apl 1835 | Single | | Carpenter |

| Names of Apl | Where From | Date of Arrival | Date of Application | Family & Age | Children | Occupation |
|---|---|---|---|---|---|---|
| Jamres Green | Kentucky | Feb 1834 | 23d Apl 1835 | 28 years old | | Farmer |
| --- his wife | | | | 26 " | 3 Females | |
| Applies for land on the waters of Rocky Creek Navidad at a place where meeting place has been made. They having surveyed ---. | | | | | | |
| Benjamin Green [with the above, same petition]. | | | | 24 Widower | 2 Females | Farmer |
| Abijah L. Burnap | Massachusetts | 9 Apl 1835 | 24 Apl 1835 | 39 years old | 1 Male | Farmer |
| ---h his wife | | | | 39 " " | 2 Female | |
| Applies for land. | | | | | | |
| Mr. L. Burnap | Family not yet arrived. | | | | | |

(25)(26)

Memorandum for Applications for land in New Contract

| Names of Apl | Where From | Date of Arrival | Date of Application | Family & Age | Children | Occupation |
|---|---|---|---|---|---|---|
| Joseph A. Parker | Illinois | March 1833 | 24 Apl 1835 | 40 years old | 3 Male | Farmer |
| Lucinda his wife | | | | 31 " " | 2 Female | |
| Applies for a League in the forks of the San Jacinto & Spring Creek at their junction. Mr. Parker came here this day ready to receive the title for his land to comply with the law in every respect. But intends to start on the 11th instant for the American camp to fignt on common enemy & etc | | | | | | |
| Octavius A. Cook | Florida | Jan 1, 1832 | 27 Apl 1835 | Single 28 years old | | Farmer |
| Applies for 1/4 league above League No. 29 on the E. side Navidad. | | | | | | |
| Jesse Franco Mancha | Mexican Citizen | | 27 Apl 1835 | 24 years old | | |
| Malina his wife | | | | | | |
| Authorized to select land. Mr. John W. Alcorn did so, paid Commissioner as per receipt. | | | | | | |
| Jas. D. Allcorn | Resident Citizen | " " " | " " " | 32 years old | 1 Female | Farmer |
| Lydia his wife | | | | 27 " " | | |
| Tho. J. Allcorn | Resident Citizen | " ", " | " " " | 24 years old | | Farmer |

Steward, heirs of Steward from Misdissippi [arrived] 1830. Died in this Colony.
Petitioner J.D. Allcorn Step Father. 2 Males 1 Female

| | | | | | | |
|---|---|---|---|---|---|---|
| Thos. Chambers | Tenn | Dec 1833 | " " | 22 years old | 2 Males | Farmer |
| Isabella his wife | | | | 25 " | 1 Female | |
| Thos. Houston | Tenn | Dec 1833 | " " | 28 years old | 1 Male | Farmer |
| Emily his wife | | | | 18 " " | | |
| David Houston | Tenn | Dec 1833 | " " | 30 years old | 2 Males | Farmer |
| Harriet his wife | | | | 26 " " | 1 Female | |
| Davis Moore | Tenn Resident Citizen | | " " | 23 years old | | |
| Martha his wife | | | | 18 " " | | |
| Green Webb | Tenn | 1829 | " " | 22 years old | | |
| his wife | | | | 19 " " | | |

[The following was written across the margin beginning with Jas. D. Allcorn]:
Wants land between San Antonio Road and the Labahia Road east of the Navasota on the waters of Reedy
& Cainy, including selections made by Crist & Brown on the Parkes Road leading from Mrs. Andersons
to San Antonio Road.

| | | | | | | |
|---|---|---|---|---|---|---|
| Wm Barnhill | Tenn | Dec 1833 | " " | 76 years | 1 Male | Farmer |
| Cinthia his wife | | | | 58 " | 1 Female | |

Applied for land in the A & W Upper Colony, received certificates from Mr. Jack and contracted
with F--- to select his land. Land on Sabine. Title issued by G.W. Smyth.

(27)(28)                    Applications for Land in New Contract 1835

| | | | | | |
|---|---|---|---|---|---|
| Chs. S. Jones | Alabama | Jan 1835 | Apl 27, 1835 | Single | Farmer |
| Applies | | | | | |

| Names of Apl | Where From | Date of Arrival | Date of Application | Family & Age | Children | Occupation |
|---|---|---|---|---|---|---|
| Wyly B.D. Smith | Alabama Resident Citizen | | Apl 27, 1835 | 29 years | | Farmer |
| Loretta his wife | | | | 19 " | | |
| Has drawn his quarter. Applies for 3/4 league. | | | | | | |
| John Smith | Resident Citizen | | Apl 27, 1835 | 22 years Single | | Farmer |
| Applies. | | | | | | |
| Joseph Burleson Jr | Tenn | Apl 1834 | Apl 27 [1835] | 26 years | 2 Male | Farmer |
| Ally his wife | | | | 27 | 1 Female | |
| Applies for League No. 26 joining DeWits Colony. Survey by B. Sims. | | | | | | |
| [Written over]: Relinquishes in favor of Moses Gage vide Page 73. | | | | | | |
| Joseph Burleson Sen | Alabama | Apl 1834 | Apl 27 [1835] | 65 years | 2 Female | Farmer |
| Elizabeth his wife | | | | 37 " | | |
| applies for League No. 13 Sims new survey. | | | | | | |
| Nancy Kenner a Widow Tennessee | | Mar 1832 | Apl 29, 1835 | 46 years | | |
| By Mr. H. Chriesman. Applies for a league on the divide between Buckners Creek | | | | | | |
| and the Labahia Road on a road leading to Hopkins Mustang Pen. | | | | | | |
| Noah Scott | Resident Citizen | | Apl 29 [1835] | 25 years | | Farmer |
| Phebe his wife | | | | 22 " | | |
| Apply for a league on Cummins Creek surveyed for Peter Pieper. | | | | | | |
| Henry Parker | S.Carolina | 1 Jul 1833 | | 45 years old | 2 Male | Farmer |
| Henrietta his wife | | | | 30 " | 1 Female | |
| Application same summer [1833]. Selects part of League No. 31 E. side Trespalacios | | | | | | |
| and 1/4 Lea. No. 34 on W. side stream. | | | | | | |

| | | | | | |
|---|---|---|---|---|---|
| David Willmans | S.Carolina | 1 Apl 1835 | 30 Apl 1835 | Single | Farmer |
| Fayette Copeland | Miss. | 25 Mar 1835 | " " | 36 years old | Teacher of Youth   2 Females |
| Sally his wife | | | | 30 " | |
| Claiborne Wright | Resident Citizen | | 2 May 1835 | 26 years Single | |

(29)(30)

Memorandum of Appalications for Land in Austin's Colony

| | | | | | |
|---|---|---|---|---|---|
| Wm Simpson | Missouri | Feb 1833 | 4 May 1835 | 35 years | Silversmith & Watch Maker |
| Pamela his wife | | | | 31 " | |

by J.R. Lewis. Applies for League No. 13 E. side Colorado on Matagorda Bay.

| | | | | |
|---|---|---|---|---|
| Wm Bridges | by J.R. Lewis | | 4 May 1835 | Single |

Applies for 1/4 League on the W. side Trespalacios Bay near the mouth (unsurveyed).

| | | | | | |
|---|---|---|---|---|---|
| Humphrey Best | Resident Citizen | | 4 May 1835 | 22 years old | Farmer |
| Elizabeth his wife | | | | 21 " | |

Applies for League L on Yeagua.

| | | | | | |
|---|---|---|---|---|---|
| Jas Tyley | New York | Dec 1834 | 4 May 1835 | 41 years aold | Farmer |
| Matilda his wife | | | | 24 " | |

| | | | | | |
|---|---|---|---|---|---|
| Moses A. Foster | Resident Citizen | | 4 May 1835 | Single | Farmer |

Application for 1/4 League back of Isaacs & Knight & White on East side Brazos below.
[Added]: Since applied for by Whitehead see 53.   See Remembrances p 14.

| | | | | | |
|---|---|---|---|---|---|
| A.C. Ainsworth | R.I. | 4 Feb 1833 | 11 May 1835 | Single man | Lawyer |

Applies for land between the Brazos & Bernard surveys above Bells.

| | | | | | |
|---|---|---|---|---|---|
| Matthew Boren | Has a Certificate | Apl 1831 | 13 May 1835 | Married | Farmer |

Applies for League O, east of Brazos between San Antonio & Labahia Roads on Bidai Bayou.

| Names of Apt | Where From | Date of Arrival | Date of Application | Family & Age | Children | Occupation |
|---|---|---|---|---|---|---|
| Matthew Sparks by their Agt. Jas. Hughs | | | 13 May 1835 | Married | | |

Applies for League E east side of Brazos between Labahia & San Antonio R on waters of Bidai Bayou.
[Added]: This league was granted to Simon Jones. Sparks took a league on Yegua.

| Names of Apt | Where From | Date of Arrival | Date of Application | Family & Age | Children | Occupation |
|---|---|---|---|---|---|---|
| L.T. Pease | Conn | 1 Mar 1835 | 13 May [1835] | 48 years | 2 Males | Farmer |
| S.M. his wife | | | | 40 " | 2 Females | |

Applies for League No. 5 back of T.J. Gazley, Sims Survey

| E.M. Pease | Conn. | 1st March 1835 | 13 May [1835] | 23 years old Single | | Farmer |
|---|---|---|---|---|---|---|

Applies for 1/4 League No. 18 East of No. 13 (Thompson)

| D.C. Barret | Penn. | | Applies for No. 37 Plum & Pinto Cr | | | |
|---|---|---|---|---|---|---|
| G. Overton | | | Applies for Lea. No. 1 do | | | |
| Labbe Laeverens | | | Applies for No. 2 San A. Road | | | |
| G. Merrill | | | Appliesfor League No. 41 same place, all Sims Surveys | | | |

(31)(32)

Memorandum of Applications & Entries

| R.O. Hulbart | | | May 13, 1835 | | | |
|---|---|---|---|---|---|---|

Applies for League No. 52 East of No. 51 and South of No. 9.

| Thos O. Berry | Tennessee | 1828 | 15 May 1835 | 30 years old | 1 Male | Farmer |
|---|---|---|---|---|---|---|
| Lucinda his wife | | | | 18 " | | |

Applies for a League of land on the divide between Buckners Creek and the
Labahia Road on a road leading to Hopkins mustang pens.

| Noah Carns | Tenn | 1830 | 15 May 1835 | 34 " | 3 Males | Farmer |
|---|---|---|---|---|---|---|
| his wife | | | | 25 " | 2 Females | |

Wants land in the same place. This is where Greens have taken land, all unsurveyed.

| Name | Origin | Date | Age / Status | Family | Occupation |
|---|---|---|---|---|---|
| Gonsolvo D. Salvado Woods | Resident Citizen | 15 " | Single | | Farmer |
| Wants land in same place if any left. | | | | | |
| John Adkinson | Alabama | Feb 1835 | 42 years old | 3 Males | Farmer |
| Mariah his wife | | 16 May " | 32 " | 5 Females | |
| Wants his land 7 miles above Hardys on West side of Navidad. | | | | | |
| Samuel Damon | Resident Citizen | | 28 years old | | Farmer |
| Lorena his wife | | 18 May | 24 " | | |
| Wants land below the Darst league and to embrace the heirs of Vandercamp. | | | | | |
| James Parky | Tenn | Long time ago | 53 years | 1 Male | Farmer |
| Mary is wife | | 13 May 1835 | 40 " | 3 Female | |
| A.L. Clements | Ala. | 20 Apl 1835 | 24 years Single | | Merchant |
| Conrad Jurgens | Germa. | Last year | 40 years | 2 Males | Farmer |
| Heneike his wife | | 16 May 1835 | 25 " | | |
| William Lewis | Tenn | 1830 | 30 | | Farmer |
| | | 18 May 1835 | | | |
| Applies for League 3 on west side Colorado below. | | | | | |
| Nancy Farley | Miss. | 1831 | 30 years | 1 Female | |
| Widow | | " " | Widow | | |
| Burnett Matthew | | | 33 years  Widower | | |
| Wm Ward | Indiana | see Remembrances p 14 | | | |
| Applies for League No. 25 on E. side Tresps if forfeit. | | | | | |
| [J.E. Robinson was Agent for the three names above] | | | | | |
| J.E. Robinson | | do [1831]          do | | | |
| Applies for Dempsey's league if forfeited. Found not vacant 28th Sept 1835. | | | | | |

(33)(34)

## Memorandum of Applications for land in Austin's Colony

| Names of Apl | Where From | Date of Arrival | Date of Application | Family & Age | Children | Occupation |
|---|---|---|---|---|---|---|
| Packson Ward | Indiana | | 18 May 1835 | Single | | Farmer |
| Per J.E. Robinson. Applies for 1/4 league on W. Fork Carancahua if forfeited by Aldridge. | | | | | | |
| Danl Perry | Has certificate 20 Jan 1831 | | | Married | | Farmer |
| Chriesman & Capt Austin to select his land League H Yegua. | | | | | | |
| Lawrence W. Perry | Alabama | 1 Feb 1835 | 19 May 1835 | Single | | Farmer |
| Applies for a gr. of a league NE of McKenney & Donahoe on the head of Fish Pond Creek. | | | | | | |
| [Added note]: Married 1 child | | | | | | |
| David Wade | Ken | May 1833 | 19 May 1835 | 40 years old | 2 Males | Farmer |
| Nancy his wife | | | | 44  " | 2 Females | |
| Applies for [blank] | | | | | | |
| Jacob Walters | Germany | 7 May 1835 | 20 May 1835 | 38 years old | 3 Male | Farmer |
| Gerdraut his wife | | | | 36  " | 1 Female | |
| Applies for land on Cummins Creek takes No. 3 on San Jacinto Road. | | | | | | |
| George Green | Maryland | 7 may 1835 | 20 May 1835 | Single | | Farmer |
| Johann Oetkins | German | May 1835 | 20 May 1835 | Single | | Farmer |
| Isaac S. Addison | Maryland | 7 May 1835 | 21 May  " | 46 years old | 5 Males | Carpenter |
| Sarah his wife | | | | 40  " | 4 Females | |
| Applies for land to be selected by the surveyor. | | | | | | |
| Joseph J. Addison | Maryland | " | " | Single | | Carpenter |
| son of the above | | | | | | |

Joseph Thompson   Georgia       6 Mar 1835    21 May 1835   42 years old   2 Males    Farmer
Martha his wife                                             33 "           4 Female
Applies for League No. 2 or a League marqued q in Chriesman's new surveys.

Wily Harrison     Georgia                                   23             Farmer
Mary Ann his wife                                           17
Wants land some place. Has taken a league NW of Cox's on the Yeagua surveyed for --- or Luster.

John Sap                        Feb 1835                    40 years old   2 Males    Farmer
his wife                                                    30 "           3 Females
Wants land in same place. Agent Joseph Thompson [for last two names]

(35)(36)          Memorandum of Applications for Land

Franklin Sanders  Kentucky      1 May 1835    18 May 1835   Single                    Merchant
Applies for 1/4 league on Jackson's Creek granted to Joseph Smith if "Wills" does not apply in time.

Isaac Millsaps    Mississippi   Mar 10 1835   20 May 1835   33 years       3 Male     Farmer
Mary his wife                                               25 "           3 Female
Wants land north of the Yeagua.

Abner Echols      Tenn          31 May 1831   22 May 1835   33 years       3 Female   Farmer
Sarah his wife                                              25 "
Applies for League No. 16 on Walnut Creek. Sims Surveys.

Joseph Yeomans    New York      Has certificate  22 May 1835  27 years                Farmer
Mary his wife                                               20 "
Applies for land by his agent Nelson and Tone in Bay Prairie above V---.

John Goodman      Tenn          31 Mar 1831   22 May 1835   55 years       7 Male     Farmer
Rebecca his wife                                            48 "           4 Female
Applies for the league granted to Rosseau on the Colorado & Road.

| Names of Apl | Where From | Date of Arrival | Date of Application | Family & Age | Children | Occupation |
|---|---|---|---|---|---|---|
| Meredith Tongate | Missouri | Spring of 1834 | 22 May 1835 | Single | | Farmer |
| Applies for 1/4 League No. 2 on Walnut Creek Sims Survey. | | | | | | |
| Mary Reeder | Widow | | 22 May 1835 | | | |
| by Nelson & Tone. Applies for No. 14 in the same survey as above. | | | | | | |
| Mortimer Donoho | Missouri | Feb 18 1830 | 23 May 1835 | Single | | Brickman |
| Applies for one fourth league on land joining T. Stevens, Bell & Bracy East of ---. | | | | | | |
| David Fowler | Maryland | Apl 20 1835 | 23 May 1835 | Married 50 years / 49 " | 3 M / 2 Fm. | Rigger of V. |
| Catharene his w. | | | | | | |
| John Bartlett | New York | 3 May 1835 | 23 May 1835 | Single | | Farmer |
| Applies for a quarter of a league on a little branch running into Clear Creek in between Ruths and Sims. | | | | | | |
| Fabricius Reynolds | Louisiana | 3 May 1835 | 25 May 1835 | 33 years / 30 " | 1 Male | Farmer |
| Elizabeth Ann his wife | | | | | | |
| Applies for land on Riddle Creek. | | | | | | |
| (37)(38) | Memorandum of Applications for Land in Austin & Williams Colony | | | | | |
| John Crownover | Arkansas | 1830 | 25 May 1835 | 69 years / 58 " | 1 Female | Farmer |
| his wife | | | | | | |
| D.S. Richardson [Agent]. Applies for League H Navasota new survey. | | | | | | |
| Roberts | Resident Citizen | | | 24 years | | |
| Applies for land on [blank] | | | | | | |
| John Woods | Ohio | 23 Jan 1835 | 25 May 1835 | Single | | Merchant |
| Wants land. | | | | | | |

Francis Hollgreen Germany   Dec 1834   15 May 1835   Single             Farmer
Applies for 1/4 League on E. side Cummins Creek joining League No. 6 above.

James Lastly Arkansas   Jan 1834   23 May 1835   34 years old   2 Male   Farmer
Katharine his wife                           25 "
Applies for League No. 6 on big dry Creek head waters.

Turner Amacy Illinois   May 18 1835   25 May "   34 years   2 Male   Farmer
Julian M. his wife                                 children
Applies for league No. 29 surveys Bartlett Simms.

W. Frampton S.Carolina   June 1833   26 May 1835   48 years   1 Son   Farmer
Eliza S.                                   32
Wants land in New Surveys on the waters of the Yeagua & Navasota.

Robt J. Moseley Tennessee   1830   26 May 1835   29 years   1 Son   Farmer
Susan Ann his wife                            21
Applies for a league of land unsurveyed on the west Bernard in the road leading from this place
to Moseleys including a Spring on the road. Land to run northerly and westerly.

Jared E. Groce Jr. Applies for land (1 League) west of McKinney's & Charles Donoho north of
the Barnard tract & Whiteside's league East of C----.

John T. Edwards Resident Citizen   26 May 1835   27 years   3 Boys   Farmer
Martha his wife                              22
Applies for 3/4 league.

(39)(40)    Memorandum of Applications for Land in Austin & Williams Colony

William Walker Miss   Febr 1835   28 May 1835   35 years old   3 Male   Farmer
Mary his wife                           32 "      3 Female
Applies for 1 League above John Austin on the north fork of Buffalo Bayou

| Names of Apl | Where From | Date of Arrival | Date of Application | Family & Age | Children | Occupation |
|---|---|---|---|---|---|---|
| James Tuttle | N. York | 1831 | 28 May 1835 | Single | | Farmer |
| Elbert G. Head<br>Maria his wife | Miss. | Oct 1833 | | 42 years<br>36 " | | Planter |
| Certificate dated 27 May 1835. Applies for League No. O in the C's New Survey on Yeagua. | | | | | | |
| Benj Head | Miss | | | | | |
| Wyly M. Head | Miss. | May 1833 | 29 May 1835 | Single | | Planter |
| Applies for one quarter league on C's new survey No. 1. | | | | | | |
| Jas. Daughtery | Tenn | Oct 1832 | " " " | Single | | Carpenter |
| 1/4 League same place No. 3. | | | | | | |
| Thos McDugal | " | 1833 | " " " | Single | | Farmer |
| 1/4 [League same place] No. 4. The above person applies as their agent E.G. Head who has paid surveying fees. | | | | | | |
| Wm Allen | | 1831 | 29 May 1835 | Single | | Farmer |
| By his agent W. Walker. Applies for 1/4 league of land on the west fork of Buffalo Bayou at the place known as Cain Island. Declined taking. Entered to Latham. Vide 69 | | | | | | |
| Worthly AL. | Alabama | Feb 24 1835 | 30 May 1835 | | | Farmer |
| Applies for land. | | | | | | |
| Francis M. Nash<br>Martha his wife | Ala. | Feb 1835 | 30 May 1835 | 42 years old<br>35 " | 4 Male | Farmer |
| William Countryman<br>Jane his wife | Ala.<br>By his agent F.M. Nash | " 1835 | 20 " " | 32 years<br>28 " | 1 Male | Farmer |
| Robt Carlisl | Ala. | " 1835 | | Single | | |
| Applies for 1/4 of a league. | | | | | | |

(41)(42)

Kuykendall R.H.    Resident Citizen    1 Jun 1835    Farmer
Electra his wife
Wants land on Buffalo Bayou next above Reinermann.

Morton W.P.    Resident Citizen    1 Jun 1835    Single    Farmer
Wants land adjoining Kuykendall next above on Buffalo Bayou.

Powell John    Resident Citizen    1 Jun 1835    4 Children    Farmer
Dorcas his wife                                   2 male 2 female
Per his agent J. Hunt.  Wants land on Buffalo Bayou next above W.P. Morton.

D.S. Richardson    Alabama    Feb 1835    2 male children    Farmer
Sarah Ann his wife
Wants land taken by his friends selection No. U in the New Surveys. Navasota,
and League U entered by Epps Despain.
Not entitled to land.  His family not here.

David Hanson    Has a certificate    2 Jun 1835    Single    Farmer
Wants land on the north fork of Buffalo Bayou joining Powell.

Eli Fenn    Mississippi    Jul 5 1834    2 Jun 1835    2 child    Farmer
Sarah his wife                                               2 males
Wants land.

Peter T. Duncan    Ala.    May 11 1835    3 Jun 1835    48[?] years old    1 Male    Farmer
Sally his wife                                             35     "          2 Females
Applies for land on W side San Jacinto between White, Harris, Carpenter and joining Hirams.

William Beasley    Louisa.    Oct 1834    4 Jun 1835    64 years    1 Female    Farmer
Rachel his wife                                          61    "
Baker & Jack to select and clear out.

| Names of Apl | Where From | Date of Arrival | Date of Application | Family & Age | Children | Occupation |
|---|---|---|---|---|---|---|
| Charles Edwards | Ala | Dec 1834 | 4 Jun 1835 | Single | | Farmer |
| by his agent J. Dzioskoski. Applies for 1/4 League. | | | | | | |
| Jesse Sutton | Miss | May 1832 | 6 Jun 1835 | Single | | Farmer |
| Applies for quarter league north of the Colorado above S.F. Austin's grant east of the Heirs of --- League Mo. 12. | | | | | | |
| Joseph Bartlett | Resident Citizen | | 6 Jun 1835 | Single | | Farmer |
| Applies for 1/4 league east of Best's League and south of Stevem's. | | | | | | |
| Geo. W. Brooks | Mississ | May 1831 | 6 Jun 1835 | 25 years | 1 Female | Farmer |
| his wife | | | | | | |
| Has old certificate. Applies for land in Chriesman's new survey Yeagua. | | | | | | |
| Wm G. Evans | 1831 | 6 Jun 1835 | 30 years | | | |
| his wife | | | | | | |
| Has a certificate. B. Travis his agent and will pay fees. | | | | | | |

(43)(44)                    Memorandum of Applications

| Names of Apl | Where From | Date of Arrival | Date of Application | Family & Age | Children | Occupation |
|---|---|---|---|---|---|---|
| Dr. Archer Agent [for the 3 names below] | | | | | | |
| Hays G. Gilly | Alabama | | 6 Jun 1835 | 28 years old | 2 females | Farmer |
| His wife | | | | | | |
| Wants land between Clear Creek and Dickensons Creek. | | | | | | |
| Tallcut Patching | N. York | | 6 " " | 43 years old | 2 male 2 female | Farmer & Mill [?] |
| his wife | | | | | | |
| [Wants land] same place. | | | | | | |
| Eli Noland | Ohio | | 6 " " | 31 years | 2 Male | Farmer |
| West side Navidad above Hardy's. See map. | | | | | | |

| Name | Origin/Status | Date | Date | Age/Status | Count | Occupation |
|---|---|---|---|---|---|---|
| B.M. Hatfield | Ken. | | 6 Jun 1835 | 25 years old | | Farmer |
| Caroline his wife | | | | 22 " | | |

Applies for land in Groces neighborhood. Takes the league west of Neals Yeagua.

| Name | Origin/Status | Date | Date | Count | | Occupation |
|---|---|---|---|---|---|---|
| Mrs. Phelps | Widow | 1 Mar 1835 | 6 Jun 1835 | 2 children | | |

C. Stewart Agent.

| Name | Status | Date | Age/Status | Occupation |
|---|---|---|---|---|
| John M. Stephen Jr | Resident Citizen | 6 Jun 1835 | 21 single | |

Son of Jas Stephen Applies for 1/4 league.

| Name | Origin | Date | Date | Age | Gender | Occupation |
|---|---|---|---|---|---|---|
| Alexander Vernon | S.Car. | Feb 1835 | 6 Jun 1835 | 36 years old | 3 Male | Farmer |
| Ann his wife | | | | 36 " | 2 Female | |
| Wm Roberts | " | " | " " | 21 years | | |
| Elizabeth his wife | | | | 18 " | | |

| Name | Date | Date |
|---|---|---|
| William Atwell | May 1835 | 8 Jun 1835 |

Applies for a quartr league on top of Clear Creek Swamp.

| Name | Origin | Date | Date | Status | Occupation |
|---|---|---|---|---|---|
| Saml A. Maverick | S.Car. | 25 Apl 1835 | 9 Jun 1835 | Single | Attorney |

Applies for 1/4 league.

| Name | Origin | Date | Date | Status | Occupation |
|---|---|---|---|---|---|
| James Cunningham | England | Feb 1835 | 10 Jun 1835 | Single | Farmer |
| Joshua Williams | Resident Citizen | | 10 Jun 1835 | Single | Farmer |

Land on the west side of Sandy above the mouth of Golden Rod Creek.

(45)(46)     Memorandum of Applications for land in Austin's & Williams Colony

| Name | Status | Date | Age | Occupation |
|---|---|---|---|---|
| Francis White | Resident Citizen | 10 Jun 1835 | 25 years | Farmer |
| Rosa his wife | | | 16 " | |
| James Dever | Resident " | " " " | 24 " | Farmer |
| Martha his wife | | | 16 " | |

| Names of Apl | Where From | Date of Arrival | Date of Application | Family & Age | Children | Occupation |
|---|---|---|---|---|---|---|
| John S. Menefee | Resident Citizen | | | Single | | Farmer |
| George Menefee | Resident Citizen | | 10 Jun 1835 | Single | | Farmer |
| W. Sutherland | do | | " " " | Single | | Farmer |
| [On the margin across five names above]: George Sutherland | | | | | | |
| James Foster Jr | Resident Citizen | | 10 Jun 1835 | Single | | Farmer |
| 1/4 South by J.E.G. Jrs land. North by Hall & West by C---. | | | | | | |
| Stoddard | Louisiana | Nov 1834 | " " " | 31 years | 1 Male | Farmer |
| his wife | | | | | 1 Female | |
| [Margin across two names above]: J.E. Groce Jr. | | | | | | |
| James Kincade | Missouri | Mar 1835 | 10 Jun 1835 | 41 years | 1 Male | Farmer |
| Jane his wife | | | | 40 years | 1 Female | |
| [Written across]: Error. See Jesse Richards p 63 | | | | | | |
| Michael Kinnard | Resident Citizen | | 11 Jun 1835 | 25 Single | | Farmer |
| Wants a quarter of a league of land on the south-east corner of --- league. | | | | | | |
| (Relinquished by Kinnard in favor of R. Allen. Vide p 8). | | | | | | |
| He selects a quarter if vacant. S.E. Cor A.Brown, Holland's neighbors. | | | | | | |
| James Robinson | Missouri | Febr 1832 | 12 Jun " | 39 years | 1 Son | Farmer |
| Tuba his wife | | | | 44 | 12 years old | |
| Applies for League No. 5 New Survey between Buckner's Creek & Navidad | | | | | | |
| James Cooper | Virginia | 1 Mar 1835 | 13 Jun 1835 | 35 years | | Farmer |
| Hannah his wife | | | | 40 " | | |
| Applies for land on Spring Creek. | | | | | | |

| Name | Origin | Arrived | Date | Age | Family | Occupation |
|---|---|---|---|---|---|---|
| Robinson | Missouri | 1833 | 13 Jun 1835 | 35 years | | Farmer |
| his wife | | | | | | |
| Faris | Alabama | 1833 | " " " | | 2 children | Farmer |
| his wife | | | | | | |

[Margin across two names above]: T. Borden, Agent. Apply and settling Leagues No. 7 & No. 8 between Navidad & Labaca, T. Borden New Survey.

(47)(48)  Memorandum of Application for land in Austin's & Williams Colony

| Name | Origin | Arrived | Date | Age | Family | Occupation |
|---|---|---|---|---|---|---|
| Pleasant B. Cocke | Louisiana | 25 Apl 1835 | 13 Jun 1835 | Single | | Planter |

Applies for one quarter of a league.

| Name | Origin | Arrived | Date | Age | Family | Occupation |
|---|---|---|---|---|---|---|
| Wm Little | Tennessee | 1832 | 14 Jun 1835 | 30 years | 1 Male | Farmer |
| Matilda his wife | | | | 28 " | 1 Female | |

Capt. Martin Agent. Applies for No. 2 New Survey of Sims on San Antonio Road.

| Name | Origin | Arrived | Date | Age | Family | Occupation |
|---|---|---|---|---|---|---|
| Basil G. Ijams | Alabama | 8 Feb 1835 | 16 Jun 1835 | Single | | Farmer |
| Reddin Andrews | Ala | do | | do | | do |
| Leroy Wilkinson | Georgia | 4 Mar 1835 | | do | | do |
| Joseph Hylan | New York | Jun 1831 | | do | | do |

Apply for land between Navidad and Skull Creek adjoining a five league tract belonging to S.F. Austin. Surveyed for Anne Powell.

| Name | Origin | Arrived | Date | Age | Family | Occupation |
|---|---|---|---|---|---|---|
| Henry Baze | Resident Citizen | | 17 Jun 1835 | 28 years | 1 Male | Farmer |
| his wife | | | | 25 " | 2 Females | |

Jesse Sutton   [No entry]

| Name | Origin | Arrived | Date | Age | Family | Occupation |
|---|---|---|---|---|---|---|
| Abraham Alley | Missouri | Resident | 17 Jun 1835 | 31 married | | Farmer |
| Nancy his wife | | | | 17 years | | |

Applies for land north of the Colorado and back of the league granted to Ranson Alley

| Names of Apl | Where From | Date of Arrival | Date of Application | Family & Age | Children | Occupation |
|---|---|---|---|---|---|---|
| James O'Connor | Dr. Archer Agent | | 16 Jun 1835 | Widower | | |
| Applies for a league of land on the Navidad above Harden. | | | | | | |
| Milton H. Har[din] | Resident Citizen | | 19 Jun 1835 | 19 [or 69] years | | Farmer |
| Applies for land | | | | | | |
| Thos Osborne | S.R. Fisher Agent | | 23 Jun " | 25 years | | |
| Wants the quarter deeded to Williams. | | | | | | |
| Thomas Shadoin | Tennessee arrived in 1829 | | 24 Jun [1835] | Married | 3 children | Farmer |
| Mahely (Chadoin) | | | | | | |
| Wants one of the leagues of land on Labacca surveyed by Hensley below the | | | | | | |
| Gonzales Road the north league. | | | | | | |
| James Lyones | Indiana | in 1832 | 24 June | id | 6 children | do |
| Martha | | | | | | |
| Wants the south league surveyed by the same. | | | | | | |
| (49)(50) | Memorandums for Application for land in Austin's & Williams Colony | | | | | |
| Eliza Perry | Alabama | Feb 1834 | June 26, 1835 | 34 years | 2 Male 1 Female | |
| widow | Applies for land on the LaBaca above Keller. | | | | | |
| Geo C. Kuhn | N. York | Jun 1834 | " 1835 | 29 years | 1 Male | Farmer |
| Sarah Emile | | | | 18 " | | |
| Peter Kinzy | Resident | 1830 | " | 35 years | 1 Female | Carpenter |
| Married. Sarah former wife of Robt Kuykendall. | | | | | | |
| No. 16 on Matagorda Bay West side of Colorado. | | | | | | |

| Name | Origin | Dates | Status/Age | Family | Occupation |
|---|---|---|---|---|---|
| Wm DeMoss — Resident Citizen / his wife / No. 15 west Colorado on Bay. | | | 28 years / 25 " | 1 [child] | Blacksmith |
| George Elliot / his wife | Eng. | 1831 | 30 " / 28 " | 1 Male | Blacksmith |
| Henry Tanner | N. York | May 1835 | Widower 45 years | 1 Male | Farmer |
| D.C. Cady / 1/4 No. 35 on the Trespalacios west side. | Rhode Island | Nov 1831   June 26, 1835 | Single | | Merchant |
| John Redman / 1/4 No. 12 west Colorado. | Boston, Mass | Nov 1833   " " " | Single | | do |
| Jas. C. Ragsdale / Rebecca his wife | Arkan. | Jan 1834   27 Jun 1835 | 33 years old / 23 " | 1 Male / 1 Female | Farmer |
| Benj Page / Ludia his wife / Applies for land on Buffalo Bayou. | Boston | Oct 1834   3 Jul 1835 | 50 years old / 41 " | 1 Female | Farmer |
| Nathan Finney / Applies for land same place. | Boston | " "   3 " " | Single | | Farmer |
| William Brown / Applies for 1/4 forfeited by R.J. Mosely. | | 4 Jul 1835 | Single | | |
| Joshua James Hall | Louis. | 6 Jul 1835   9 Jul 1835 | 42 Widower | 2 Male | Merchant |
| John L. Hall | " | "   " | 25 Single | | Printer |

[For the three names above]: June 26, 1835 Wm L. Cazneau, Agent.

117

| Names of Apl | Where From | Date of Arrival | Date of Application | Family & Age | Children | Occupation |
|---|---|---|---|---|---|---|
| Steel Brown widower | Louis. | 4 Jul 1835 | 14 Jul 1835 | 35 years | | 1 Male Attorney 2 Females |

Applies for land by their agent E. Hall, a league next above Hall quarter on Chocolate Bayou.

| Solomon Griffin heirs of | Missouri | came 1825 | 15 Jul 1835 | 1 Female | | |

| John Ham | Mass. | Jan 1835 | 15 Jul 1835 | 30 years of age | | Farmer |

Applies for 1/4 League a part of No. 1 between Cox's & Keller's Creek on the Bay.

| Severen Lorche his wife | Louisiana | 19 Oct 1831 | 16 Jul " | 32 years 25 " | | Farmer |

Has certificate. A.L. Phinney, Agent. Applies for League No. 7 head of Bay Prairy.

| Hugh Grant | Scotland | | 16 Jul 1835 | 28 [years] Married | | |
| John Alex. Newland | Scotland | | | 25 " Single | | |
| Edward Hurry | England | | | 35 " Single | | |

| Arthur Crownover | Arkansas | | 19 Jul [1835] | 25 years | | 1 Male Farmer 2 Female |
| Lavina his wife | | | | 23 " | | |

Has a certificate. Applies for land. Had made arrangements with Mr. Chriesman to pay out & if a deed has issued wants to know. If not Thos. E. Borden will select for him. Selects League No. 5 E of Brazos Mrs A. Neighborhood.

Louis Neal
Applies for land between the Colorado & Trespalacios say between No. 12 & 21.

| Name | Origin / Residence | Date | Date | Age | Status | Household | Occupation |
|---|---|---|---|---|---|---|---|
| Spirse Dooley | Tenn | March 1832 | 24 Jul 1835 | 25 years | | 2 Male | Farmer |
| his wife | | | | 20 " | | 1 Female | |
| I. Philips, Agent. Applies for a league adjoining Cedar Isl Bay Prairy. | | | | | | | |
| Jefferson George | Resident Citizen | " " " | | 25 years | Single | | Farmer |
| Applies for a quarter between Geo. Williams on Trespalacios. | | | | | | | |
| Holman George | do | " " " | | | | | |
| Applies for 1/4 League. | | | | | | | |

(53)(54)    Memorandum of Applications for Land in Austin's & Williams Colony

| Name | Origin / Residence | Date | Date | Age | Status | Household | Occupation |
|---|---|---|---|---|---|---|---|
| John C. Hunt | Alabama | 1 Jun 1835 | 24 Jul 1835 | 23 years | Single | | Farmer |
| Applies for 1/4 No. 1 Davidson's Creek. | | | | | | | |
| Edward P. Whitehead | Mississippi | 1831 | 25 Jul 1835 | 21 years | Single | | Farmer |
| Applies for 1/4 league back of Knight & White & Isaacs. | | | | | | | |
| Applied for by Foster p 29. See Remembrances 14. | | | | | | | |
| Randolph Lehmkuhl | Germany | Febr 1835 | 21 Jul 1835 | | Single | | Farmer |
| Applies for 1/4 league. | | | | | | | |
| Thos. M. Blake | Kentucky | 6 Aug 1830 | 28 Jul 1835 | 25 years | Single | | Blacksmith |
| Applies for 1/4 League No. 3 head of Bay Prairy. | | | | | | | |
| Jonathan Kemp | Louisiana | 1830 | | 22 years | | | Farmer |
| Charlotte his wife | | | | 18 " | | 1 Female | |
| J. George, Agent. Applies for a league of land in Bay Prairy back of Bowman. | | | | | | | |
| N.B. Williams | Resident Citizen | 12 Apr 1835 | | 26 years | | | Farmer |
| Levina his wife | | | | 27 " | | 1 Male | |
| This name was first entered on page 21 on the 12th day of Apl 1835. Applies for a league of land on head of Bay Prairy being part of 1/4 League Nos. 4 & 4. | | | | | | | |

| Names of Apl | Where From | Date of Arrival | Date of Application | Family & Age | Children | Occupation |
|---|---|---|---|---|---|---|
| Charles Balkman<br>Applies for 1/4 league. | Alabama | Febr 1835 | August 3d | 28 years old Single | | Farmer |
| Chs Messer<br>Applies for 1/4 league. | | 1831 | August 3d | 35 " | | Farmer |
| Thos. J. Williams<br>his wife<br>Jefferson George [Agent]. Applies by his Agent J. George for a league. | Resident Citizen | | August 3 | 28 years<br>19 " | 2 children | Farmer |
| Isam G. Webb<br>Sarah his wife<br>Applies for a league of land. See page 25. | Resident Citizen | | 4th August | 22 years<br>21 years | | Farmer |
| Thos. W. Bundick<br>Applies for 1/4 league. | Resident Citizen | | 4 August | 22 " | | Farmer |
| (55)(56)<br>John L. Sleight<br>Has a certificate (old). Applies for a quarter on Dry Creek NW --- Nicholas. | N. York | 25 Dec 1830 | 4 August | 26 Single | | Merchant |
| John Burdgess   Applies for Caleb Tenan<br>Caleb Tenan      Resident Citizen<br>Applies for a Quarter on the west side Navasota which Gleason applied for some<br>time ago. [Added later]: Gleason & Tinnin both dead. Granted to Holcomb. | | | " " | 21 Single | | Farmer |
| Benj Cochrane by Mr. Burgess<br>his wife<br>Applies for League No. 31 on Sn Antonio Road E side B---. | | 1834 | 4 August [1835] | 30 | 1 Male<br>3 Females | Farmer |

Enoch Latham      Tennessee      Febr 1831      6 August [1835]      52 years      5 Male / 7 Female      Farmer
  widower
John L. Sleight, Agent.   Applies for a league joining --- Kiney & Donoho.

Thos. Hancock      Illinois      Dec 1833      6 August      50 years      8 Females      Farmer
Patsy his wife                                              42 "
  Applies for land No. 6 Big Dry Creek.

Polly Bird widow      Illinois      Dec 1833      6 August      33 years old      1 Male / 2 Female
  Applies for land

Elijah Votaw      Arkansas      Apl 1835      6 August      21 Single                              Farmer
Francis Votaw      "             "            6 August      23 single                              do

William McCoy                                  6 August      Single                                 Farmer
  Applies for 1/4 Sitio 6 & adjoining league in which is White S. Springs (not surveyed).

Peaks      Alabama      January 1835      6 August      25      3 Males      Farmer
Eliza his wife                                            35
  Applies for a league above the Labahia Road on Labacca.

Wm Medford      Illinois      Jan 1832      7 August      50 years      1 Male / 3 Female      Farmer
  his wife                                     35 "
  Applies for League No. 51 Sims New Surveys.   S. Bacon [Agent].

Hall Roddy      Tennessee      April 1831      10 August      Single 34                           Farmer
  Applies for 1/4 League lying between Saml Gates and Andrew Miller.
  Applied for by Early. Roddy sold his right.

(57)(58)      Memorandum of Applications for Land in Austin's & Williams Colony

Isaac Gorham      Mississippi      Feb 1835      Aug 17, 1835      44 years
  Applies for 1/4 League of land.

| Names of Apl | Where From | Date of Arrival | Date of Application | Family & Age | Children | Occupation |
|---|---|---|---|---|---|---|
| Andrew Northington Jr. | Kentucky | April 1833 | Aug 22, 1835 | 24 years 15 | | Farmer |
| Eliza his wife | | | | | | |
| A. Worthington, Agent. Applies for League on the west side of West Bernard adjoining Jackson. | | | | | | |
| W.P. Scott | | | Aug 22, 1835 | | | |
| Applies for 1 League adjoining S. Hardin 3/4 of which having been surveyed for above. | | | | | | |
| Thomas Isaacs | Missouri | Nov 1833 | Sept 2, 1835 | 32 years 22 " | | Farmer |
| Harriet his wife | | | | | | |
| Applies for League No. 2 to the N.E. and joining Mr. Guffies Black Settlement. | | | | | | |
| Richd Dowdy | Georgia | 1 Feb 1835 | Sep 5, 1835 | 28 years 19 " | | Farmer |
| Mary his wife | | | | | | |
| Applies for a league on Scull Creek. | | | | | | |
| Alfred Kelso | Alabama | Feb 1835 | Sep 3, 1835 | 27 years 23 " | | Farmer |
| Martha his wife | | | | | | |
| Applies for a league on the waters of Navidad or San Celes. | | | | | | |
| John Chaney | Geo | Feb 1835 | Sep 4, 1835 | 39 years 37 " | 5 Males 1 Female | Farmer |
| Lucy his wife | | | | | | |
| Applies for a league on the waters of Navidad. | | | | | | |
| George E. Looney | Tenn | Dec 1833 | Sept 5 " | 30 years Single | | Farmer |
| Applies for 1/4 league. | | | | | | |
| Micah Andrews | Alabama | Feb 1835 | " 7 " | 26 " Single --- | | Farmer |
| Applies for one fourth of the 13th league on the Colorado above --- | | | | | | |

| Name | Origin/Status | Date | Date | Age | Persons | Occupation |
|---|---|---|---|---|---|---|
| Wm H. Toy | Penn | Aug 4, 1835 | " 7 " | 26 " | 1 Male | Printer |
| Elizabeth S. his wife | | | | 21 " | | |
| Applies for land. | | | | | | |
| Ehlinger | France | Jun 1835 | " 11 " | 43 years | 2 Males | Carpenter |
| Mary Ann is wife | | | | 32 " | 1 Female | |
| Applies for a league on Cummins Creek if any vacant land. | | | | | | |
| Jacob Thomas | Resident Citizen | | " " " | 35 | 1 Female | |
| Nancy his wife | | | | 22 | | |
| Applies for an augmentation of 3/4 league on Sims Bayou adjoining his quarter and Luke Moore. | | | | | | |
| Saml Hayslett | Resident Citizen | | " " " | 35 years | 1 Male | Farmer |
| Betsey his wife | | | | 25 " | | |
| Applies for League No. 27. | | | | | | |
| (59)(60) | | | | | | |
| John M. Shreave | Kentucky | July 1835 | 14 Sep 1835 | 24 yrs | | Clerk |
| Wesley Pace | Resident | | 14 Sep " | | | |
| Benjn F. Grayson | U.States | | 14 Sep " | 22 yrs | | Engineer |
| Robert Atkinson | England | Jany 1835 | 14 Sep " | 24 yrs vide p 15 | | Mechanic |
| Geo W. Poe | Alabama | 1834 | 14 Sep " | Married | | |
| Wm P. Smith | Tennessee | 15 Jan 1835 | 14 Sep " | | 4 ch | Farmer |
| Sarah | | | | | | |
| DeWitt C. Harris | | | 14 Sep " | | | |
| First 1/4 L above J. [or I.] Batterson on Brays Bayou. | | | | | | |
| Stephen Prather | A resident citizen | | 14 Sep " | 21 years | | |
| Peter Langlaw | Louisiana | 1833 | 14 Sep " | Single | | |
| Applies for land on the Labaca | | | | | | |

| Names of Apl | Where From | Date of Arrival | Date of Application | Family & Age | Children | Occupation |
|---|---|---|---|---|---|---|
| John a Dutchman at Hatches | | | 14 Sep [1835] | 25 years Single | | Farmer |
| Applies for land | | | | | | |
| Richd Smith | Alabama | March 1830 | 15 Sep " | 70 years / 53 | 2 Males / 4 Female | Farmer |
| Margaret his wife | | | | | | |
| Applies for land. | | | | | | |
| Pascal B. Hamlen | U.States | | 15 Sep " | Married several chil[dren] | | |
| Wm Duty    Resident Citizen | | | 16 Sep 1835 | 26 Single | | Farmer |
| Applies for P league in Sims Survey being the East qr. of 3 surveys on ---. | | | | | | |
| Cyrus Campbell | Arkansas T. | | 16 Sep | 25 / 17 | | Blacksmith |
| Rebecca his wife | | | | | | |
| Heirs of Jos. Campbell Arkansas | | | 16 Sep | | | |
| Thornton Kuykendall  Resident Citizen | | | 21 Sep | 26 Single | | Farmer |
| Applies for one fourth league on St Road, Johnson Survey. | | | | | | |
| (61)(62)     Memorandum of Applications for Land in Austin's & Williams Colony | | | | | | |
| Daniel Nowlan | Washington D.C. | Apr 1835 | Sep 21, 1835 | 21 Single | | Clerk |
| H.O. Campbell | | | Sep 21, 1835 | Mar'd | | |
| Lucinda his wife | | | | | | |
| One league on Neil's Creek marked --- P & is now Neil's league. | | | | | | |
| Wm Baird | | | Sep 21, 1835 | Married | | |
| One league E of Brazos on the waters of Bidai Bayou. | | | | | | |

| Name | Description | Date | | Status |
|---|---|---|---|---|
| Alford | 1/4 League same survey No. 3 | | | Single |
| Burt Kendrick | 1/4 do do No. 1 | | | single |
| Harvey Kendrick | One league marked P same survey | | | Married |
| Wm C.J. Hill | Chriesman Agt | Sep 22 | 1835 | Married |
| Elizabeth his wife | | | | |
| One league I E. of Brazos on waters of Bidais Bayou. | | | | |
| Samuel Bowman | Chriesman Agt | Sep 22 | " | Married |
| League East of Brazos on Bidais Bayou on Labahia R. adjoining Sims Survey south of Sims old survey. | | | | |
| M. McDowel | Chriesman Agt | Sep 22 | " | married |
| League S same survey. | | | | |
| Antonio Rios | | Sep 22 | " | married |
| Same place League C. | | | | |
| Edwardo Arriola | | Sep 22 | " | married |
| League B same place. | | | | |
| Daniel McMahan | | Sep 22 | " | married |
| League T Bidais Cr. | | | | |
| Isaah Curd | | Sep 22 | " | married |
| League No. 18, E. Brazos, N. Navasota. | | | | |
| Fitzgerald | | Sep 22 | " | married |
| League No. 4 head waters of San Jacinto, in Kinnard's neigh. | | | | |
| Peter H. Fulenwider | | | | married |
| League W E. of Brazos, S. of Navasota. | | | | |
| John Dorsey    Ala. | | Sep 23 | " | Single |

| Names of Apl | Where From | Date of Arrival | Date of Application | Family & Age | Children | Occupation |
|---|---|---|---|---|---|---|
| M.L. Fulton | Louis. | Dec 1833 | Sept 23 1835 | 23 Single | | |
| Title made over. | | | | | | |
| John Guild Jr | Boston | 1 Sep 1835 | Sep 24 " | 30 Single | | Farming |
| Applies for 1/4 Leag No. 2 New Survey E. of Davidson's Cr (this quarter previously taken by Underwood). | | | | | | |
| Wm C. Willard | N.Caro. | Jan 1835 | Sept 24 " | | | |
| 1/4 League same place. | | | | | | |

(63)(64)     Memorandum of Applications for Land in Austin & Williams Colony

| Names of Apl | Where From | Date of Arrival | Date of Application | Family & Age | Children | Occupation |
|---|---|---|---|---|---|---|
| Eli Fann | Miss. | 1833 | 24 Sep 1835 | 40 years | 1 Male child | Farmer |
| Applies for League No. 1 E. Nav. | | | | | | |
| Wm Barnett | Ken. | | | | | |
| Benjn Babbit | Has received land but since married. Selects supplement. | | | | | |
| James Scott | Illinois | 1833 | 25 Sep 1835 | Has a family | | |
| HArrison McClain | Abraham Williston | | 25 Sep 1835 | Single | | |
| John Chevers | Saml Highlands | | | | | |
| Apply for land on Cypress Bayou. | | | | | | |
| Swearingen Saml | Tennessee | 1834 | 25 Sep 1835 | 50 years | Applies for league | |
| Wm N. Mack | Alabama | Jan 1835 | 28 Sep 1835 | 29 years | 1 Male child | |
| Ann M. his wife | | | | 25 " | 1 Female " | |
| Applies for a league. | | | | | | |

| Name | Origin | Date | Recorded | Age | Family/Status | Notes | Occupation |
|---|---|---|---|---|---|---|---|
| Thos. McDonald | Mass. | May 1835 | 26 Sep 1835 | 42 | " | 2 Male children | Farmer |
| May his wife |  |  |  |  |  |  |  |
| L. Richardson Agent. Applies for League No. 4 near Mrs. Andersons, Navasota. |  |  |  |  |  |  |  |
| Dolores Arrista | Mexican |  | " | " | Family |  |  |
| Applies for League No. G. |  |  |  |  |  |  |  |
| Jesse Richards | Penn | 1825 | " | " | Family | See p. 45 |  |
| Applies for a league on Pin O. Cr. No. 3 previously applied for by Gage. |  |  |  |  |  |  |  |
| James C. Duff | Tenn | Jan 1834 | " | " | Family | Applies. |  |
| John Cherney | Missouri | 1830 | 28 Sep | " | Family | Applies |  |
| Fondervert | Germany | 1833 | " | " | Family |  |  |
| Applies for land on head waters of Cummins C. League T, E. side. |  |  |  |  |  |  |  |
| Yeagans | Germany | 1834 | " | " | Family |  |  |
| Applies for land head waters of Cummins Creek. League A, W. side. |  |  |  |  |  |  |  |
| John Peske | Germany | 1833 | " | " | Single | Applies for land |  |
| (65)(66) | Memorandums for Applications for Land in Austin & Williams Colony |  |  |  |  |  |  |
| Wm Haddon | Resident Citizen |  | 29 Sep 1835 | 25 y | Single |  | Farmer |
| Applies for 1/4 League No. 33 on Tres. |  |  |  |  |  |  |  |
| Jackson Haddon | same |  | " | 21 y | " |  |  |
| [Applies] for a quarter adjoining and above. |  |  |  |  |  |  |  |
| Charles H. Fenton | N. York | 1834 | " | " | Single |  |  |
| Applies for a quarter. |  |  |  |  |  |  |  |

| Names of Apl | Where From | Date of Arrival | Date of Application | Family & Age | Children | Occupation |
|---|---|---|---|---|---|---|
| Phinneas Smith | N. York | 1830 | | Family | | |
| Certificate 556. H. Austin Agent. Application made 1st May 1835. | | | | | | |
| Selects League I on Yegua. C's New Survey. | | | | | | |
| Matthew Sparks | Arkansas | | 27 Sep 1835 | Family | | |
| Betsey his wife | | | | | | |
| Patrick Dunn | | 1829 | 29 Sep " | Single | See Remembrances | |
| Lorenzo de Zavalla | Mexico | 1834 | 29 Sep 1835 | 46 years | 3 children | |
| Applies for land opposite Carpenter --- South side Buff Bayou. | | | | | | |
| S.Y. Reams | Tenn | 1833 | 30 Sep 1835 | 23 years | Single | |
| Applies for a quarter. | | | | | | |
| Pleasant W. Rose | Missouri | 1833 | " " | 55 years | 4 chil [dren] | |
| Applies for land. | | | | | | |
| James Wells | Missouri | 1833 | " " | Single | Applies | |
| James Buckhannon | Alabama | 1834 | " " ' | 23 yrs | 1 Male | Farmer |
| Mary his wife | | | | 19 " | child | |
| Applies for land League F on Yegua. | | | | | | |
| Robert S. Armistead | Alabama | 1835 | " " | | | |
| Pedro (Peter) Queros | Mexican Citizen | | " " | 28 yrs | Family | |
| Melena his wife | Applies for a league. | | | | | |
| Wm D. Lacy | Resident Citizen | | 2 Oct 1835 | Family | | |
| Applies for an augmentation of 3/4 league on Scull Creek adjoining N. Osborn. | | | | | | |

Robt G. Baugh    Alabama    1833    " Oct    "    Single
Applies for land Chriesmans Survey on the head waters of Cummins Creek.

(67)(68)
Thos J. Adams    Miss    1834    2 Oct 1835    24 years    Single
Applies for a quarter on Rabbs Creek adjoining their mill tract.

John D. Holcomb    N. Carolina    1834    "    "    42    Single
1/4 No. 6 San Antonio & Navasota.

Mrs. Sawyer    N. York    1833

Horatio N. Cleveland    Alabama    1835    3d Oct    "    35 years    4 Males Widower
Applies for tract formerly selected by K--- and will get it if K--- does not come.

John Huffman    Tenn    March 1832    "    "    35 years    Single
Applies for a quarter (Dr Ewing Agent)

Russel Ward    Resident Citizen    "    "    "    23    "
Applies for 3/4 on the Sandy as an augmentation - has a deed from Durst for 1/4 of a league.

Margaret Davis    4 Oct 1835    20 years
Orphan child of Lucinda Davis, a widow who emigrated to the Colony in 1822 &
died in the First Settlement that same year & without drawing her portion of land.

N.C. Moffitt    N. Carolina    1832    4 Oct 1835    27 years    1 Male    Farmer
Applies for a league Spring Cr. near Prichards.
Now 30th Oct for No. 35 Sims Survey.

Wingfield heirs of    6 Oct 1835    1 Male 5 female children
Now the wife of John R. Stevens. Applies for land north of McCearly 8 miles more
or less on the road leading to Lake Creek from McCearlys.

| Names of Apl | Where From | Date of Arrival | Date of Application | Family & Age | Children | Occupation |
|---|---|---|---|---|---|---|
| Jas R. Stephen<br>Says he is willing to bear arms and his father says he has given him his time. | Resident Citizen | | 6 Oct 1835 | 18 years | | |
| John L. Marshall<br>Eliza his wife<br>Applies for No. 14 on Lake Creek. | Arkansas | 1830 | " " | 24 years<br>20 | 2 Female children | Blacksmith |
| James N. House<br>By his agent Jas. Stephen | 1832 | | | Family | | |
| (69)(70)<br>John Davis | Resident Citizen | | 6 Oct 1835 | 25 years  Single | | Farmer |
| Enoch Latham Jr<br>Has selected the 1/4 league resigned to him by William Allen. Vide 32. | Resident " | | 6 Oct " | 23 years  Single | | Farmer |
| Robt Armour<br>Nancy<br>Applies for League No. 5 near Mrs. Andersons Navasota. | Tenn | May 1835 | 7 Oct " | 48 years<br>48  " | 1 Male 4 female children | |
| David Pevehouse<br>Cinthia his wife<br>Preston Pevehouse<br>Applies for League No. B on Navidad. | Arkansas | 1834 | " " | | 3 children | |
| John Tyler<br>Sally his wife<br>Applies for the lower league between --- & Navasota. | Ken | Feb 1835 | " " | 44 years<br>38 [?] | 2 Male  Farmer<br>4 Female children | |
| Wm H. Bryan<br>Applies by his agent A. Zubic for a one fourth league adjoining said Zubic & Gilmore. | Alabama | Feb 1835 | " " | 25 Single | | Carpenter |

Thomas Hablamaha  Germany    Feb 1835    7 Oct 1835    57 years    8 Boys  Farmer
has a wife                                          50 "        2 Girls
Agent J. Cartwright. North of a league granted to Bright to comprehend "the blue ridge".

Stephen Hablamaha  Son of the above    " " "    " " "    25 years  Single
Applies for 1/4 league. At a post on the south side of Buffalo Bayou above
Wheatons and run down for quantity.

Nancy Reavell  Ken.    Feb 1835    " " "    51    2 children
Widow. Applies for a league I promised to give John Tyler League No. 6.

Robert Kleberg  Germany    Decemb 1834    7 October    30    Farmer
Rosalie von Roeder  "    "    21
Applies for a league.

William P. Polke  Resident Citizen    8 Oct    Single
Applies for a quarter adjoining a quarter selected by A. Kuykendall, W. Mill Cr.

C.B. Stewart  Resident Citizen    " "    27

Eliza Peak  Alaba    1835    " "    23    2 Children
Widow  Applies for League A Yegua. See Bowen p 71.

(71)(72)    Memoranda for Applications

Adam Kuykendall  Resident Citizen    8 Oct    22 Single    Farmer
Applies for a quarter of a league adjoining Kuykendall & Hill W. side of Mill Cr.

John S. Taylor  N. York    July 1834    9 Oct    32 years    2 Boys  Farmer
Christiana his wife                                        32 "        1 Girl
Applies for a league of land west side of San Jacinto.

| Names of Apl | Where From | Date of Arrival | Date of Application | Family & Age | Children | Occupation |
|---|---|---|---|---|---|---|
| John & Betsey Jones | Resident Citizens | | 9 Oct 1835 | Family | | |
| Spyars Singleton | Resident Citizen | " " | " " | 24 years Single | | Farmer |
| Mrs. Barrow A. | N.York | 5 Jul 1835 | " " | | | |
| James W. Tuttle | " | 1832 | | | | |
| John Taylor | Scotland | | 9 Oct [1835] | Single | | Ship Carpenter |
| Harrison McClain | Indiana | 1834 | " " | 21 Single | | Farmer |
| Allcorn T.J. | | | | | | |
| Thomas James | Resident Citizen | " " | | Family | | Farmer |
| Alford Gee | | | | Family | Farmer | |
| Bowen | | | | Family | | Farmer |
| Epps D. Paine | | | " " | Family | | Farmer |

John & Betsey Jones — Apply by their agent Wm Scott for a tract of land on W. side of San Jacinto between a five league survey and Amy White.

Spyars Singleton — Applies for a quarter of a league back of Amy White, San Jacinto.

Mrs. Barrow A. — Widow on Trinity. Applies for land.

James W. Tuttle — Applies for Deshienskeys quarter (D. is dead).

John Taylor — Applies for land.

Harrison McClain — Applies for land. See Williston page 63.

Allcorn T.J. — See page 25. Applies for a quarter west of Cox, Yeagua.

Thomas James — Applies for X Yeagua New Survey. [Added note]: 32 on San Antonio Road.

Alford Gee — Applies for League L on Navasota.

Bowen — Relinquishes in favor of Mrs. Peak p 69. Applies for League A on Yeagua.

Epps D. Paine — Applies for League U on Navasota.

Houston                                    "     "            Family                       Farmer

Applies for League T on Navasota.

James Moore                       "     "            Family                       Farmer

Applies for League R on Navasota.

Billings   Applies for League Q on Navasota.

Ponton with wife and family 1834                            Farmer
Applies for a league on West side Navidad next below Mrs. ---.

(73)(74)
John W. Fogg    Alabama   1835 Sept   9 Oct 1935   23 years Single    Teacher of youth
Applies for 3rd tract above Wheatons on Buffalo.

Moses Gage    Tenn     married   9 Oct   "    39 years            Farmer
Elizabeth                                    31  "
Applies for a league west of Colorado relinquished to him by Jo Burleson.

Goacher       Alaba     Jan 1834   10 Oct    Large family         Farmer
   his wife

Samuel Goacher son of the above        "    "    21 Single

Calvin Gage   Gunner at Gonzales                 21 Single
One fourth league on Pin Oak.

David Austin   Tenn    Feb 1835   10 Oct 1835   42 Widower          Farmer
Applies for land on his way to the Battle.

Sterling N. Dobie Virginia   Jan 1835   "  "  "   21 Single          Clerk
Applies for land on his way to the Battle 1/4 league on Buffalo Bayou, joins Earl & W. Vince.

133

| Names of Apl | Where From | Date of Arrival | Date of Application | Family & Age | Children | Occupation |
|---|---|---|---|---|---|---|
| T.J. Robinson | Alabama | Feb 1835 | | 22 yrs Single | | Blacksmith |
| Applies for 1/4 league north and adjoining Mrs. Bowman on Bowmans Creek. | | | | | | |
| Martin B. Lawrence | Arkansas | Jan 1833 | | 41 yrs | 6 children | Farmer |
| Maria his wife | | | | 30 " | | |
| John W. Williamson | Resident Citizen | | 12 Oct [1835] | 35 " Single | | Farmer |
| Applies for land on east side Navidad above Whites survey. | | | | | | |
| Joseph McAllister | Philadel. | July 1835 | | 22 Single | | Carpenter |
| Applies for 1/4 league in League No. 13 Buckners Creek. | | | | | | |
| Mayberry B. Gray | South Car. | Jan 1835 | | 21 Single | | Farmer |
| Applies for a quarter of a league selected by Hall Roddy see 55. | | | | | | |
| Joseh Arenandis | Mexican Citizen | | | | | |
| Anthony D. Kinnard Jr. | Resident Citizen | | 13 Oct 1835 | 21 years Single | | Farmer |
| Applies for a quarter south of his fathers if vacant. | | | | | | |
| W.E. Kinnard | Do | | | 23 " | | Farmer |
| Applies for a quarter nrth Pool. | | | | | | |
| Joseph Ehlenger | See page 57 | Applies for one fourth of a league above the heirs of | | | | |
| Alley if Owen does not come forward. [Added note]: On Cummins Creek. | | | | | | |
| (75)(76) | | | | | | |
| Robt Cochrane | | 1833 | 14 Oct 1835 | Family | | |
| H. Austin, Agent. Applies for League M Chriesmans New Survey. Yegua. | | | | | | |

| Name | Origin | Date | | | Family | Age | | Occupation |
|---|---|---|---|---|---|---|---|---|
| Alex. Edgar | Scotland | Apl 24 1835 | " | " | Family wife 2 children | | | Farmer |
| | | | | | | | | |
| L.C. Manson | N. York | 1832 | 15 " 1835 | | Family 2 children | | | Merchant |
| | | | | | | | | |
| Joshua Abbot | Arkns | 1831 | | | Large family | | | Farmer |
| | | | | | | | | |
| Charles S. Smith | Missouri | 1838 | 16 Oct 1835 | | | 28 years | | Farmer |
| Narcissa his wife | | | | | | 22 " | | |
| | | | | | | | | |
| John H. Callihan | Louisiana | Dec 1833 | " | " | | 21 yrs | | Farmer |
| Malina his wife | | | | | | 20 " | | |
| | | | | | | | | |
| Ann Wooldridge | Missouri | 1834 | " | " | | 40 | | 3 Sons / 2 Daughters |
| | | | | | | | | |
| John Lawrence | | | " | " " | | Family | | |
| | | | | | | | | |
| Alexander Thompson | Resident Citizen | | 17 " 1835 | " | | 37 years | 1 Male | Farmer |
| Sceney his wife | | | | | | 22 " | | |
| | | | | | | | | |
| Dunlavy heirs of | | | | | | | | |
| | | | | | | | | |
| Zoraster Robinson Geo. | | 1835 | 17 " 1835 | | | 27 years | 3 Boys | Farmer |
| Martha his wife | | | | | | 25 " | 1 Girl | |

Applies for League L on Yegua --- Refused it after seeing it.

Applies for a league of land in the Chocolate country.

Applied 3 or 4 years ago for a league of land back of Bolivia league.
Deed promised some time ago. Fees paid by James F. Perry.

Takes League No. 17 east of Col. back of Knight & White new survey.

A league on Cyprus Creek.

Widow. Applies for League E on Yegua.

Applies for League V on the Yegua deeded to Boatwright.

Applies for [blank]

Applies for League T on Yegua.

Applies for League N Navasota.

135

| Names of Apl | Where From | Date of Arrival | Date of Application | Family & Age | Children | Occupation |
|---|---|---|---|---|---|---|
| Holly Arnold | Resident Citizen | | | 30 years | 1 Son | |
| Eunice | | | | 21 " | | |
| Lightfoot [Agent] Applies for a league. | | | | | | |
| (77)(78) | | | | | | |
| Abram M. Wamack | Georgia | 1835 | 17 Oct 1835 | Family | 2 Children | |
| Elizabeth his wife | | | | 22 years | | |
| Applies for a vacant league west & adjoining a league marked Pool. | | | | | | |
| Salathiel F. Knight | Ohio | 1835 | 17 Oct 1835 | 27 yrs | 3 Children | |
| Jane his wife | | | | 31 yrs | | |
| Applies for land. | | | | | | |
| Lewis B. Jones | Carolina | 1831 | " " " | 50 yra | 2 Male | Farmer |
| Sarah | Mississippi | | | 35 " | 1 Female | |
| Applies for a league north of Fulton & west of J. Grimes. | | | | | | |
| Thos. Boatwright | Arkansas | 1833 | 17 Oct 1835 | 27 yrs | 2 Male | Farmer |
| Lydia his wife | | | | 23 " | | |
| Applies for League D on Navasota. | | | | | | |
| Anny Boatwright | Arkansas | 1833 | " " " | 72 " | 1 Male child | |
| Widow. Applies for M same place. | | | | | | |
| Wm Boatwright | | " | " " " | 22 Single | | |
| Applies for 1/4. | | | | | | |
| Richd Boatwright | Arkns | 1833 | " " , " | 24 | 1 Girl | |
| Barbary his wife | | | | 21 | | |
| Applies for League No. 1 on the Middle Barnard. | | | | | | |

| Name | Origin | Date | | Age | Family | Occupation |
|---|---|---|---|---|---|---|
| Friend Boatwright | Arkn | 1833 | " | 32 | 3 Boys | Farmer |
| Lydia his wife | | | " | 25 | 4 Girls | |

Applies for a league.

| John O. Stubbins | | 1831 | " | Family | |
Applies for a league above and adjoining a league selected by Joseph Parkenson
San Jacinto & Spring Creek at the junction.

| Hugh Chandler | Resident Citizen | | " | 21 Single | |
Applies for 1/4 League No. 2 south of No. 2 on San Antonio Road.

| Stephen Miller | New Orleans | 1834 | 19 " | 34 [54?] Single | Carpenter |
Applies for a quarter north and northwest and adjoining Hadys league east of the Brazos.

| Wm Gilmore | Alabama | 1833 | " | 25 Family | Farmer |
League south of Mrs. Hill and west of Vince.

| John M. Springer | Alabama | 1832 | " | 32 | 2 Sons |
| Elizabeth | | | | 25 | 2 Daus |
Applies for League 6 north of John Landrum.

| A.E. Springer | Alabama | 1832 | | 24 Single | |

| John G. Conner | Kentucky | 1832 | | 22 years | 1 Female |
Widower. Cohort Tom Borden. Applies for a league.

(79)(80)                Memorandum of Applications for Land

| Jacob Duckworth | Missis. | March 1835 | 20 Oct 1835 | 50 years | | Farmer |
Widower but no children with him.  Applies for [blank]

| Thos K. Davis | Missouri | Nov 1834 | | 30 years | Family 4 children | Farmer |
Applies for land on Bayou Floris No. 1 west side.

137

| Names of Apl | Where From | Date of Arrival | Date of Application | Family & Age | Children | Occupation |
|---|---|---|---|---|---|---|
| Jesse T. Davis | " | 1828 | | 30 years | Family | |
| Applies for 3/4 league on Bayou Floris No. 1 east side | | | | | | |
| Wm M. Perry | Alabama | Dec 1833 | 21 Oct " | 35 years | 3 Boys | Farmer |
| Ann his wife | | | | 30 " | 1 Girl | |
| Applies for a league. T.Borden, Agent. | | | | | | |
| Clement Allen | Illinois | Apl 1834 | " | 25 | Family | Farmer |
| Artemesia his wife | | | " | 20 | | |
| Applies for a league K Navasota - new survey. | | | | | | |
| Thomas Stephenson Resident Citizen | | | | 17 years | Single | |
| Applies for a quarter of [blank] | | | | | | |
| James Duff | Tenn. | Jan 1834 | " " | 55 years | 2 Sons | Farmer |
| Mary P. his wife | | | | 51 " | 2 Daughters | |
| Applis for League No. One on the coast of Matagorda Bay near Kellers west side of Carancuay. | | | | | | |
| Simon Jones | Ohio | 1832 | " | 42 years | 3 Sons | Farmer |
| Widower | | | | | 3 Daughters | |
| Applies for League E on the Navasota new survey. | | | | | | |
| Elias Gilpin | Kentucky | 1834 | " | 28 " | Family | Farmer |
| John L. Wood & wife | Alabama | 1831 | " | 50 " | 5 Children | |
| John P. House & wife | Alabama | 1831 | " | 20 " | 2 " | id |
| James Walker | Kentucky | 1835 | " | 45 " | 5 " | id |
| Elizabeth Santy widow | Alabama | 1835 | " | 32 " | 1 " | id |
| William J. Smith & wife | Missouri | 1835 | " | 33 " | 2 " | id |

[Note on this list beginning with Gilpin]: Apply for land east of the Brazos between the San Antonio Road and the Labahia Road. Elijah Allcorn Agent.

Blythe   Alabama   1835 [?]   Large family
Enters League L on Yegua. This league previously entered & paid for by H. Best, returned by Chriesman. See p 29 this book. Now takes League --- same place.

Reason Mercer   Resident Citizen   22d Oct 1835   Single   Farmer
Applies for land 1/4 league.

Levi Mercer   id   id   id
Applies for 1/4 League Post Oak Creek Trespalacios.

H.F. Armstrong   id   27 [yrs]   id
Sarah his wife   20
[Applies for] 3/4 league

(81)(82)
Wm Newman & wife   Resident Citizen   22d Oct 1835   26   1 Child
Applies for land.

David Silcriggs & wife   id   "   24   2 Children
Post Oak Creek Trespalacios.

J.D.G. Varrelman   Grman   1832   23   "   Wife   6 children   Physician
Applies for a league.

Ransom House   Louisiana   Dec 1834   24   "   Wife   3 children
C.B. Stewart Agent. Applies for No. 19 Navasota if forfeited by Abner Lee Senr.

R.J.W. Reels   Alabama   1833   26   "   Wife & 1 child
Applies for League I on Yegua.

| Names of Apl | Where From | Date of Arrival | Date of Application | Family & Age | Children | Occupation |
|---|---|---|---|---|---|---|
| S.L. Leonard | Tenn | Oct 1835 | 26 " | 24 Single Applies | | |
| P.F. Fitch | " | " | " | 25 Single Applies | | |
| Henry Wingfield | Resident Citizen | | " | 24 Single | | |
| Applies for 1/4 between Tyler & Walker east of Moore in Hollands Settlement. | | | | | | |
| John Palms | France | 1834 | 28 " | 27 Single | | |
| Applies for 1/4 north of Navasota and north east of Wm Milican. | | | | | | |
| Martin Copeland | Arkansas | 1835 | 29 " | | 6 children | Farmer |
| Susan his wife | | | | | | |
| Applies for 1 league south of S.A. Road and south east of gr. No. 3. | | | | | | |
| Nicholas Copeland | Arkansas | 1835 | 29 Oct 1835 | 55 | 3 children | Farmer |
| Dorcas his wife | | | | | | |
| Applies for 1 league below the above. | | | | | | |
| Anthony Baudrano | France | 12 Oct 1835 | " | 27 / 25 | | Printer |
| Amelia his wife | | | | | | |
| Applies for League No. 36 Sims Survey. | | | | | | |
| Lyman Pease | Massach | 1835 | 30 " | 27 / 23 | | Mechanic |
| Caroline his wife | | | | | | |
| Isaac Betterson | New York | Feb 1834 | " | 43 / 40 | 4 Daughters | Farmer |
| Amelia his wife | | | | | | |
| His application made 12th Feb 1834 by Mr. Williams and selected the league surveyed for John S. Moore on Brays Bayou above and adjoining Tarwesters 1/4. | | | | | | |
| Joseph Callahan | Louisiana | Dec 1833 | ", " | Family 6 children | | Farmer |
| Applies for a league on Cypress Creek or Bayou San Jacinto. | | | | | | |

John S. Coldwell    New York    [blank]    1835    31    "  1835    26    Single    Mechanic
Applies for [blank]

Henry Fried    Indiana    4 Jul 1835    31    "  1835    30    Single    Farmer
Applies for land.

(83)  [These entries are out of chronological order]
10 November 1832    Granted permission to Jorge A. Nixon to locate 11 leagues, date of concession
20 April 1830. Order from the Govt for possession 11 June 1831.

To John A. Sawyer for one league date of concession 26 April 1830.
Order same date as Nixons.

22d Novemr 1832    Josiah F. Harrell this day deposited with me two concessions of 11 leagues and
and for which I gave him a receipt, setting forth that sd Harrell was to
pay 1333 33/100 for location & completion of title.

(84)  [This page is blank]
(85)86)
David Harvey    England    Sept 1834    Nov 2, 1835    Single
Wants 1/4 league east of Wm Millican and above Jno Palms.

John Dorsey    Alabam    Mar 1834    Nov 2, 1835    Single
Applies for 1/4 league on San Jacinto No. 3.

Jesse Clary    Ala    Jan 1835    Nov 2, 1835    30    1 Daughter    Blacksmith
Susanna his wife    18
Applies for land east and adjoining Sam Hardin.    Chs Dunnahoe to see to surveying.

James Seymour    New York    10th Oct    "    "    "    37    1 Son    Farmer
Jane his wife    32    7 Daughters

| Names of Apl | Where From | Date of Arrival | Date of Application | Family & Age | Children | Occupation |
|---|---|---|---|---|---|---|
| Isaac Jaques | New York | 10th Oct 1835 | Nov 2, 1835 | 30 | 2 Daughters | Farmer |
| Mary Ann | | | | 29 | | |
| Wm Day Jr. | | | " " | 22 Single | | |
| Isaac D. Boyce | | | " " | | | Printer |
| George Delesdernier | | | | | | |
| Francis Delesdernier | | | | | | |
| George W. Cartwright | Resident Citizen | | " " | | | |
| Applies for 1/4 league on Buffalo Bayou above a point known as Post Oak Point. | | | | | | |
| Joseph Thompson | Ala | 1833 | " " | | | |
| Applies for 1/4 league on Buffalo Bayou at the forks above Wheatons. | | | | | | |
| David Wade | Resident | 1833 | | | | Farmer |

Volunteer Company of Greys from New Orleans represented by Edw Hall arrived at Velasco on Sunday the 25th Octr 1835 came to Brasoria and immediately took up their line of march for Goliad. Consequently could not appear at the Office in person, the Oath of Citizenship was administered to them by Edmund Andrews one of the Primary Judges and a certificate furnished each member for the purpose of obtaining lands as settlers.

(87)

| | |
|---|---|
| Robert C Morris | Louisiana |
| Wm G. Cook | Virginia |
| Charles B. Bannister | Louisiana |
| Alexander Abrahms | Ohio |
| Amelung, Louis F. | Louisiana |
| Wm Blowne | England |
| William Boyle | Pennsylvania |
| Nathl R. Brister | Virginia |
| John Beldin | N. York |
| Charles S. Curriere | Sth Carolina |
| Seth Carey | Vermont |
| Sydney S. Callender | Mississippi |
| Willard Chamberlain | Ohio |
| Charles M. Conner | Pennsylvania |
| John Cornell | do |
| James M. Case | Connecticut |
| Michael Cronican | Massachusetts |
| Noah Dickerson Junr | Upper Canada |
| Wm D. Durham | England |
| Vincent Drilland | Louisiana |
| George M. Gilland | Pennsylvania |
| Wm Graham | Nova Scotia |
| Francis H. Gray | Scotland |
| George Green | England |
| John L. Hall | Ireland |
| Nicolas Heron | Virginia |
| Stewart C. Hill | |
| Nathl Holbrook | Massachusetts |
| Wm L. Hunter | Virginia |
| Ebenr S. Heath | Masstts |
| Francis Johnson | Maine |
| Allen O. Kinney | Virginia |
| Francis G. Leonard | Louisiana |

| | |
|---|---|
| Albert M. Levy | Virginia |
| Thos S. Lubbock | Sth Carolina |
| Marshall B. McKeever | Kentucky |
| John D. McCloud | England |
| John D. McNeil | Nth Carolina |
| Dennis Mahoney | Ireland |
| Adam Mosher | Kentucky |
| James Nowlin | Ireland |

(88) [This page blank]
(89)(90)

| | |
|---|---|
| Christopher OBrian | Ireland |
| F. Procter Junr | Louisiana |
| Wm G. Preusch | do |
| Jos. P. Riddle | Pennsylvania |
| Richard Ross | Illinois |
| Hiram Russell | Tenne |
| John Rees | Wales |
| Charles Sargent | Masstts |
| Henry S. Smith | New York |
| Martin K. Snell | Penn |
| George Stephens | England |
| Thos R. Stiff | Virginia |
| Edward N. Stringer | Louisiana |
| George Voss | Germany |
| Hartwell Walker | N. Hampshire |
| Thos Wm Ward | Ireland |
| James West | Penna |
| Mandred Wood | do |
| John Wood | Sth Carolina |
| Edwd Wrentmore | England |
| Henry Fisher | Virginia |

Lewis G. Addison                 Maryland
Julian J. Harby                  Sth Carolina
Wm Harper                          Ireland

Also a company of sixty volunteers who embarked on board
the Steam Boat Ouashita for Alexandria, Nachitoches and
Nacogdoches, equally entitled to all the benefits of
settlers but whose names I could not obtain previous to
sailing.

            San Felipe    Novr 4, 1835    Edward Hall

(89)(90)
Shubal Marsh     Resident           Nov 5 [1835]
3/4 L. on Spring Creek joining McKerly and Denson on the N.W.C. of McK.

James Farmer    1831               "  "
  1 L. Br Lake Creek near G--- jopining labor below.

Bernhard Hendrick Beaumer   same as Bohmer
  Applies for No. 4 west of Colorado on the San Antonio Road.

(91)(92)
Anton Hoya     )  Germany           Nov 5  1835    Single
Antony V.D. Hoya )
  Applies for 1/4 league No. 18 Sims New Survey previously applied for by E.M. Pease  Vide page 29.

Gerritt Damken   Germany         "   "      Single
  1/4 No. 12 Sims New Survey W. Colorado.

Robert McLaughlin               Nov 5  1835    Single

Geo E. Dwight   Wants land below Kuykendall on the west side of Mill Creek W. Fork.

| Names of Apl | Where From | Date of Arrival | Date of Application | Family & Age | Children | Occupation |
|---|---|---|---|---|---|---|
| Aaron Burleson | Resident Citizen | | Nov 1835 | 21 yrs Single | | Farmer |
| Ome fourth of League No. 12 in Sims Surveys. | | | | | | |
| Thos J. Hardiman | Tenn | 5th Oct | " " | Family | | |
| Applies for League No. 38 Sims Surveys. | | | | | | |
| David S. Morton | Ala | 20th Oct | 31st Oct | 23 years 17 | | Farmer |
| Mary his wife | | | | | | |
| Martha Standback | Ala | " " | " " | 50 years Widow | 1 Male | |
| Susan Ann Andersn | " | " " | " " | 19 years | | |
| Wm Wright | " | " " | " " | | | |
| wife and family | | | | | | |
| Thos Wright | " | " " | " " | | | |
| wife and family | | | | | | |
| [Note that applies to David Morton through Thos Wright]: These families all came together in company with Wm Heard and are entitled to land. | | | | | | |
| Thos Bertan | Resident Cit. | | | 25 years Single | | |
| 1/4 Lea. WS, W.F. Joins W. Kuykendall on his east line front the creek. | | | | | | |
| Michael R. Goheen | Michigan | 19 Dec 1834 | " | 27 years Single | | |
| Wm Carleton wife & family | G. Sutherland [Agent] | | | | | | |
| John Sutherland | | | | | | |

J. Wright     Applies for a labor formerly granted to Burnham on the Colorado River.

John B. Taylor     Apply for land on Sims Bayou near land granted to J.R. Harris.

Shipman D & J     Resident Citizens     Applied for some time since.

(93)(94)
William Latham     Written appli Dec 26, 1835.  One fourth League No. 8 Sims Survey.

Heirs of David Warren by Jas Rogers & Jas Burleson.  No 15 Sims Surveys.

Delapplan     No 35 [Sims Surveys] applied for previously by Moffet.

L. McNeil     No. 46.

N. Heron     1/2 No. 8 formerly applied for by Latham.

S.W. Sweney     No. 14 applied for by Mrs. Reeder.

For the balance of these selections see (No. 12) Selec

| | | | |
|---|---|---|---|
| Sarah Williams<br>Written application | 1st October 1835   Jan 1, 1836 | Widow | 1 Son<br>1 Daughter |
| Sarah Gleize | | Widow | 1 Daughter |
| Amand De la Croix | | Widow | |
| Thos. M. Whittington  Resident Citizen     [1 Jan 1836]<br>League on Yegua between Cox & Stevens. | | Family | |
| Jack Darwin | | | |
| James C. Duff     Resident Citizen     Jack, Agt | | Family | |

| Names of Apl | Where From | Date of Arrival | Date of Application | Family & Age | Children | Occupation |
|---|---|---|---|---|---|---|
| John Adriance | | | | Single | | |
| Robert Ray | | | | Family | | |
| Has received 1/4 league as a colonist. Applies for supplement 3/4. Chriesman Agt | | | | | | |
| Takes 1/4 league. | | | | | | |
| Herman Holt | N. Hampshire | | 26 Jan 1836 | Single | | |
| Jno G. Robinson | Resident Cit. | | | Family | | |
| Applies for a league of land once grtd to Colton on Cummins Creek. | | | | | | |
| John R.B. Robinson | Louisa Resident Citizen | | | Family | | |
| Applies for land on Scull Creek above League No. 3. | | | | | | |
| Robert Sayers | Kenty. | | | Fam. | | |
| John Sayers | do | Applies for land | | Single | | |
| Mary Ann Frazier | Widow | Applies for land back of S. Snyder. | | | | |
| Freele | Ireland | 1833 | | | | Smith |
| Applies for a league on the head of Eagle Lake. | | | | | | |
| (95)(96) | | | | | | |
| Nicolas Kelly | Louisiana | 1835 | | Single | | Printer |
| Applies for 1/4 of a league No. 2 on Bidais Creek. | | | | | | |
| Danl Gray | | | 2d Feby 1836 | Married | | |
| Sitio 21 on Walnut Creek W.Colorado. | | | | | | |

Thomas Gray                                      "    "    "  Single
    1/4 Sitio No.4 Walnut Creek same place.

Joshua Gray                                      "    "    "  Single
    1/4 Sitio No. 3 same place.

John Birnham Klekamp                                          Married
    Sitio No.41 Sims new surveys W. Colorado.

Micajah L. Brunap ) Deed to be made to Heirs. B. Killed by Indians
Family            ) Sitio No.34 Sims New Survey W. Colorado.

Bernhard Henrich Schneider   1/4 Sitio                        Single
Bernhard Eilers              1/4 Sitio                        do
Anton Lemkuhl                1/4 Sitio                        do

Mariano Cavero                                                do
    1/4 Sitio No. 19 Sims New survey W. Colorado

Solomon Hall      Family Sitio No. 40 same place.

A.C. Hutchins     Mississippi     1835     Wants land

Francis W. Jackson   England            4 Feb 1836   Single

Joshua Canter     S. Carolina           "    "   "   Single

Bennet McNelly    Pen.                  "    "   "     "

Ambrose Gregoire  France                "    "   "   Single

Charles Sage      N. York              6 Feb 1836    Family

Christopher Miller N. York              "    "   "   Family

                                                             149

| Names of Apl | Where From | Date of Arrival | Date of Application | Family & Age | Children | Occupation |
|---|---|---|---|---|---|---|
| Brazilla Kuykendall | Family Has recd 1/4 applies for augmentation. 3/4 on San Antonio road between rivers, adjoining Price's league. | | | | | |
| William Powell | 1/4 immediately above & adjoining a L. of J.A. Powell on S. Jacinto. | | | Single | | |
| Elizabeth Powell | Widow Land not surveyed 1 L. on San Jacinto just above the League of Parker or 1/4 League of Powell. | | 6 Feb 1836 | | | |
| Antonio Trevino | Mexicans F.Adams Agt Applies for a league of land granted to McNeily E. of Brazos below Navasota. | | 6 Feb 1836 | Family | | |
| John Kuykendall | | | | Single | | |
| (97)(98) Thomas William Ward | Ireland U.S. La. 1835 Applies for land. Wants the surveyor to select. | | | Family | | Farmer |
| Ambrose Gregoire | France U.S. La. 1835 Applies for land. Wants same near same. Oath previously taken. | | | Single | | id |
| Isaac B. Shipler | Pennsylvania Applies for land. Took the oath. Quarter No. 7 west Colorado Sims survey. | | Feby 6 [1835] | Single | | Joiner |
| Erastus Litle | Resident Citizen | | " " | 21 Single | | |
| Harvey N. Litle | Resident Citizen Has served in the late campaign. | | " " | Single | | |
| Joseph McLaughlin | Pennsylvania | 15 Jan 1836 | " " | 35 Single | | Saddler |

George Petty    Tennessee    1835    Single    Farmer
Wants land.

Wm Lusk    Cont.    Mar 30    22 Single    Merch.

Chas. S. Davenport    Maine    Oct 25 1834    34 Single    Farmer

Absalom Williams    "    "    1832    Family Wants land    Farmer

Jared E. Groce Jr.
East of Brazos back of a league deeded to the Heirs of Whitesides (title made).

John M. Dillon    Ireland    1832    Wants land

Polly widow of James Day    Resident
Applies for one league on the north side of Buckners Creek, No. 4.

Enos Cooper    Resident    Family

William Roberts    id    id

Jeremiah Cochrane    id    Single
Applies for 1/4 league entered by Thos Cochrane and relinquished to him.

Thomas Cochrane    Resident    Family
Applies for a league between W. Barton & M. Wood west of Colorado.

Josiah Roberts    id    Single

Reuben Fisher    Family Married
Wants a league No. 14 W. side Col. back of Woods & Alley.

| Names of Apl | Where From | Date of Arrival | Date of Application | Family & Age | Children | Occupation |
|---|---|---|---|---|---|---|
| Jackson Hensley | | | | Single | | |
| Applies for 1/4 originally granted to Wm Smithers E. Brazos joining N.F. Roberts. | | | | | | |
| James W. Foster | Applies for 1/4 league entered by J. Cronkwrite. | | | | | |
| Franklin Foster | In league on Caney Creek between Chambers & F. Grimes. | | | | | |
| (99)(100) | | | | | | |
| George W. Speir | Alaba | 1835 Feby | 9 Feb 1836 | Family  Wants land | | Farmer |
| Walter Winn | N. England | 1835 | 9 Feb 1836 | | | Merchant |
| Wants land joining 1/4 league granted to Holcombe. | | | | | | |
| Robt Sellers | | | | Family | | |
| Robt Sellers Jr. | | | | Family | | |
| Wish the Surveyor to make a selection & the Comr to confirm it. | | | | | | |
| Vincent L. Evans | Michigan | 1833 | Feby 1836 | Family | | Farmer |
| Sion R. Bostick | Resident | | | Single | | Farmer |
| Applies for 1/4 league above James H. Bosticks West of Mill Creek. | | | | | | |
| Warner | | | | | | |
| Ezra Hill | Ala | 1833 | Feby 1836 | Family | | Farmer |
| Applies for land. | | | | | | |
| Juan Delgado | Native | Deed issued | | | | |
| Joshua Canter | | | Feb 10 1836 | Wants land | | |

F.O. Jackson                                                    "    "         Wants land

Anthony Houjoa    Germany      1834         Feb 13   "          Single
Applies for 1/4 league No. 2 Sims Survey.

Ths C. Davis      Maryland     1834         "   15   "          Single          Farmer
Applies for 1/4 back of N. Roberts E. of Brazos Bayou.

Wallis Gleason                 1834 Dec     "    "   Family                      Farmer
East of Brazos near Kelly's 8 Mile Creek to be run up and down the creek.

John Fisher       Virginia     1832 Apl     Feb 15 1836   Family in the U.S.
Wants land. Resident of Gonzales.

John Scott        Pennsylvania              "   16   "          Single

Orange Babbit                               "   16   "          Family
Apply for same on Navasota River.

Ephraim Evans                               "    "   "          Family
Apply for same on Navasota River.

Henry Bond                                  "    "   "          Family
Wants land on the River Navasota.

Philip Martingly                            "    "   "          Family
Wants land on the River Navasota.

Eleanor Hayden                              "    "   "          Family
Wants land on the River Navasota.

Joseph T. Killgore                          "    "   "          Family
Wants land on the River Navasota.

| Names of Apl | Where From | Date of Arrival | Date of Application | Family & Age | Children | Occupation |
|---|---|---|---|---|---|---|
| Thos. K. Davis Applies for land north of G. Fennel. | Mo. | 1834 | Oct [1835] | Family | | Farmer |
| John D. Ragsdale On the east side of the Navidad No. 39. | Ken. | 1833 | Dec | do | | Farmer |
| Wm Swenny On the east side of the Navidad No. 38. | Ten | 1835 | Dec 1st | do | | do |
| Amanda McCrackin | Ohio | 1833 | March | Widow Spinster | | |
| Moses Ellison Wants 1/2 of the Thos Powels 1/2 league which is forfeited. | South Car | 1833 | Nov | Single | | Farmer |
| James Ellison Wants the other half. | do | 1833 | Nov | do | | do |
| James Powell Applies for 1/4 No. 1 joining Bowman. | Ala | 1832 | 16 Feb 1836 | Single | | Farmer |
| John Powel Applies for League No. 28 West of Navidad. | Ala | 1832 | 16 Feb 1836 | Family | | Farmer |
| Peter M. Hughes Applied for a league. | Geo | 1832 | Feby 1836 | Family | | Farmer |
| William Fairfax Gray Is an applicant for land as a Colonist. No. 33 East side of the Navidad North of Buck Creek. | Virginia | 1836 | Feb 17 | Family | | |

Amanda McCrackin   Resident Citizen
   Applicant for a league.

(101)(102)
Edward Conrad    Pennsyl_a_    1835    Feb 18 1836    Single    Printer
   Is an applicant.

Rosila Hamer    Resident    Feb 18 1836    Family
   Is an applicant for League No. 8 on waters of the Yegua.

Washington T. Shuff   Resident    Feb 18 1836    Family
   Applies for a league of land on th dividing ridge between Yegua &
   Cummins Creek originally granted to Hinch & forfeited.

Nathan Fike    N.Carolina    1833    Feb 18 1836    Family    Tanner
   B. Sims ·has made his selection.

A. Vanphebber    Mississippi    1835    Feb 18 1836    Single    Gunsmith
   Is an applicant.

Joseph Hopkins    Louisiana    1835    Feb 18 1836    Single    Merchant
   Is an applicant.

Wm P. Dickerman    Louisiana    1835    Feb 18 1836    Single    Saddler
   Is an applicant for 1/4 League No. 3.

H.G. Hudson    Arkansas    1835    Feb 18 1836    Family    Blacksmith
   Is an applicant.

James McDonald    Tennessee    1835    Feb 18 1836    Single    Taylor
   Is an applicant.

| Names of Apl | Where From | Date of Arrival | Date of Application | Family & Age | Children | Occupation |
|---|---|---|---|---|---|---|
| Joel F. Heath Tennessee<br>Is an applicant. | | 1835 | Feb 18 1836 | Single | | Farmer |
| George S. Park Missouri<br>Is an applicant. | | 1835 | Feb 18 1836 | Single | | Farmer |
| J. Vanphebber Mississippi<br>Is an applicant | | 1835 | Feb 18 1836 | Single | | Farmer |
| Jno. F. Beck Tennessee<br>Is an applicant. | | 1835 | Feb 18 1836 | Single | | Taylor |
| Sidney Philips Resident Citizen<br>Applies for 1/4 of league below & joining Silsby. | | | | Single | | |
| John Baker Michigan<br>Wants a league south of D. White & E. of Bartlett's new survey. | | 1835 | Feb 20 1836 | Family | | |
| Theodore Bennet N. York | | 1831 | Feb 20 " | Family | | Merchant |
| Colden Derman Missi | | 1834 | " " | Single | | |
| Cornelius A. Sleight N. York | | 1835 | " " | Single | | |
| John Sharp Scotland<br>Wants Surveyor to make a selection. | | 1833 | " 21 " | Single | | |
| Francis Coaty Tennessee | | 1835 | " 22 " | Family | | Farmer |
| Hugh Killgore Louisiana | | 1833 | " ", " | Family | | Farmer |

| | | | | | |
|---|---|---|---|---|---|
| Ann Bass a widow | Ala | 1833 | " | " | Family | Carpenter |
| Z.B. Outlaw | Tenn | 1832 | " | " | Single | School Teacher |
| Tolbert Wood | Tenn | 1833 | " | " | Single | Farmer |
| Claiborne Lawrence | Resident | | " | " | Family | Farmer |
| Gideon Walker | Alabama | 1835 | " | " | Family | Farmer |
| John Beauchamp | Tennessee | 1833 | " | " | Family | Millwright |
| John Smith | Alab. | 1835 | " | " | Single | Farmer |
| Augustin Santi | " | 1835 | " | " | Single | |

[A note that applies to all names above beginning with Francis Coaty]:
All want land on the Navasota on the west side in the fork. By Special Agent Elijah Allcorn.

| | | | | | |
|---|---|---|---|---|---|
| Hamilton Kiggens | Resident | | | " | Single | Allcorn Agt |

Theodore S. Lee  Vermont  1835  Feb 23 1836  Family
Applies for land.

Jesse Stockwell  Illinois  1833  "  Family
Applies for land and has authorized Elijah Allcorn to select the land for him as agent.

(103)(104)
William McMasters  Louisiana  1834  Feb  1836  Single  Merchant
Applies for land.

Theodore Bennit

Colden Denman  Louisiana  1833  "  Residents
Wants the land in the Upper Colony between Dawson & Galloway.

A. Wickson  )  Ohio  Residents  Family
George Reynolds)  Maine  Single
Want land on Big Creek joining Wickson & Stewart 3/4 & 1/4.

| Names of Apl | Where From | Date of Arrival | Date of Application | Family & Age | Children | Occupation |
|---|---|---|---|---|---|---|
| John Coker<br>Wants land. | Alabama | 1834 | | Single | | Smith |
| Anton Ludwig Siegesmund von Roeder<br>Applies for one Yegua league. | Germany | 1834 | Feb 23 1836 | Family | | Farmer |
| Otto von Roeder<br>Applies for league on Galveston Island near Three Trees. | Germany | 1834 | "  "  " | Family | | Farmer |
| Albrecht von Roeder<br>Applies for league on Galveston Island east of the above. | Germany | 1834 | "  "  " | Family not in Country | | |
| Rudolph von Roeder<br>Applies for league on Galveston Island not selected. | Germany | 1834 | "  " | Family | | Farmer |
| Louis Kleberg<br>Above Coshatte road joining Bostic & Alford. | Germany | 1834 | "  " | Family | | Farmer |
| Louy Knipp<br>Applies for 1/4 league formerly included in Sam Hardin's Survey on which his name is entered. | Germany | 1832 | "  " | Single | | Farmer |
| Hary D. Gary<br>Applies for League No. 34, east side of the River Navidad, south of Buck or Crooked Creek. | Resident Citizen | | Feb 24 1836 | Family | 4 Children | |
| John M. Walker<br>Applies for League No. 35, east side of the River Navidad, north of James Ryon's league. | Resident Citizen | | "  ",  " | Family | Wife & child | |

| Name | Status/Origin | Year | | | Household | | Occupation |
|---|---|---|---|---|---|---|---|
| Sanders Walker | Resident Citizen | | " | " | Single | | Farmer |
| Wants 1/4 league. | | | | | | | |
| Samuel Rickhow | Miss. | 1835 | " 26 | . | Family | | Farmer |
| Applies for League Y on Yegua by H.Austin Agent. | | | | | | | |
| John Foster | Resident Citizen | | " 26 | " | Family | | Farmer |
| Wants land | | | | | | | |
| Fleming T. Wells | Resident Citizen | | " 26 | " | Single | Wants land | |
| John Carlton | Resident Citizen | | " 26 | " | Single | Wants land | |
| Mandred Wood | Louisiana | 1835 | " 26 | " | Single | Wants land | |
| William Attwell | Georgia | 1835 | " 26 | " | Single | Wants land | |
| John Gordon | Resident Citizen | | " 26 | " | Single | Wants land | |
| Charles McCalister | Resident Citizen | | " 26 | " | Single | Wants land | |
| John D.McCalister | Resident Citizen | | " 26 | " | Single | Wants land | |
| Aaron C. Dodd | Resident Citizen | | " 26 | " | Family | Wants land | Farmer |
| James Hayn | Resident Citizen | | " 26 | " | Single | Wants lanfd | Mechanic |
| Lewis H. Peters | Resident Citizen | | " 26 | " | Single | Wants land | |
| Jessee Davis | Resident Citizen | | " 26 | " | Family | Wants land | Farmer |

Fleming T. Wells  Agent [for all the names above, beginning with John Foster].

"REMEMBRANCES"

(1)     Remembrances for Jan & February 1835

Jan  28 Bell James Wants his note,  says he  has
        p̲d̲.
        Ogiest William by John Crier. Applies for
        land in Sims New Surveys west Colorado.

Feb  11 Harris Capt wants to know if the land  on
        Mustang Slough between West Bay & Chocol-
        ate has been selected.

Feb 12 McCune James and 11 others by Mr. Sam̲l̲ A.
        White. Want land on the Sandys above Thos
        Heard not yet surveyed and 2 Leagues at
        Labahia crossing of the Labaca if not
        taken. See Remem - first book of this date
        - 19 p.

 "   18 Bankston Bluford G. Wants a quarter of a
        league of land joining the southeast cor-
        ner of the tract of land at the Sulphur
        Springs.
     25 Grayham Richd̲ by Mr. Bostick for citizn-
        ship and want the upper qr. of the Bostick
        league if Bertrand does not get it. Ber-
        trand relinquishes by his agent Babbett.
(2)
        Remembrances for March & Apl 1835
Mar 17 Mrs. McManns by her agent J.R. Lewis
        Selects the following leagues.
        2 Leagues No. 2 & 3 on Carancahua E. side
        1     "      6    Do  is deeded to Newell
        1     "      5 head of Kellers Bayou
        1     "     29 Prairy Creek Bay Prairy
        1     "     22 Trespalacios E. side
        1     "     20    do          do
        1     "  next west to G--- Peninsula
        1     "     25 on Trespalacios if not
                       deeded in lieu of No. 6

        Curtis J.B. by his agent Maj. Lewis.
        Selected League No. 13 on Matagorda Bay E.
        side Colorado.  Date of his application
        15th Dec 1833. Deeded to Simpson 19 Feb
        1833.  Has cleared out.

(3)          Remembrances for Apl 1835

Apl 15  Ayres David. Says that Hinch drew league
        No. 9 south of Yegua, paid out by Vaden
        wants to know when government fees are to
        be paid & when improved to prevent for-
        feiture.

        Buckner John W. wants copy of deed for two
        labors in Bay Prairy granted to his
        brothers.

        [Pages 4 through 7 were not used]

(8)          Remembrances for April 1835

    22  Whiteside John J. wants his deed he has
        paid fee.

    23d Canfield Buckman, says having purchased a
        part of the 16 mile point league and being
        entitled to land by certificate he applied
        for the balance of said league if for-
        feited by the first grantees - this appli-
        cation made to Mr. Williams in the Spring
        of 1833 he says.
[Written across]: I agree to let this matter rest
        until Williams --- home, it being in dis-
        pute.  Jack    24 Jany 1836

     "  Burleson James for
        Jonathan Burleson & selects Lea. No. 12
        Martin Ramsey       "       "      28
           New Survey
        South Antonio Road & West of the Colorado
        River. Jonathan Burleson is entitled to
        but 3/4 lea. His brother will take the
        balance of League No. 12.  See his letter.

        Wallace John Y. has selected League num-
        bered F on the head waters of the Yeagua
        New Survey.

30 Apl  Horton A.C. wants to locate League Nos. 4
        & 5 in the block of surveys near Mrs.
        Anderson.

Remembrances for May 1835

4  Nestor B. Hammat by his agent J.R. Lewis
applies for if forfeited League No. 9 on
East Fork Carancahua Bayou deeded to Geo.
W. Nixon.

4  Roberts Elisha wants his title for a
league of land conceded to him by the
government west of the Colorado - says he
has paid Surveying fees. Has paid 37 dol-
lars for fees on the same.

Kinney Louisa Ann now the wife of Danl
Perry wants the deed for the land which
was granted her by the government
Capt. Austin Agent.

Huff Martha wants land Tom Borden to select

20  Harrison Henry leaves with me a receipt
and memorandum relative to a copy of a deed
and settlement - "Is the copy written"

Remembrances for May 1835

David Ayres shows a receipt of money paid
on 3 league of land, to wit:
One league for Bird L. Hanks         $37.00
One    do        L.B. Franks          37.00
One    do    for himself              37.00
     Receipt dated 1st Apl 1833
He wants the copy of a deed for B.L. Hanks
& Franks.

Frederick Niebling applies for land on the
Cummins Creek.

20  David Fowler applies for land in the same
place.
Nancy J. Welch same as the above on
Navidad.
Hodge John wants a title written for a
tract of land on Oyster Bayou - Eli Micals
of Gonzales to execute it. Wm Hodge ways
he has paid for title.

22  Roberts Elisha paid Govt fees.

Head Benj by his agent E.G. Head applies
for League No. H  Chriesmans new surveys on
the Yeagua.

(11)

Remembrances for May & June 1835

May 30 Worthly Al. [This written above]
Whetherly, Alfred applies for a league of
land on the San Antonio Road being No. 5
of Chriesmans new surveys, his family now
in Alabama.
June 1st
Hodge William heirs of, want copy of deed.
Say they have paid for it.

"  Pevehouse James wants the copy of his deed
says he has a receipt for all the fees.

2 June Barker Jesse wants copy to deed - Little
Colony.

"  Standiferd James wants copy of deed -
Little Colony.

"  Avery Willis wants copy of deed - Little
Colony.

Demit Philip wants his deed out of the
office.

Thompson Wm for his sister applies for the
league above the heirs of Alley. He also
applies for the first vacant league below
him on the Navidad for 4 young men. And 3
quarters of league, below his father for
three other young men.

(12)

Remembrances for July 1835

6 July  Delgado Juan says he wants a title for No.
8 on the east side of the Sandy Bernard,
has been kpromised t him, he says for
several years.

14  Hall Edward from Missouri wants land. Aged
36 years. Applies for a quarter above &
adjoining the upper quarter on Chocolate.

"     Burgess M̲r̲ represented by Capt. Austin. Aged 35 years, has a family.

Brown Steel
M̲r̲ Drown applies by M̲r̲ Sims. Letter for League No, 3 west of the Colorado on San Ant. Road. See his letter. No. 8. Relinquishes in favor of Wolters.

16    M̲r̲ Shackleford says M̲r̲ Williams told him he could have league No. 4 on San Antonio Road E. side Colorado.

M̲r̲ Overton by M̲r̲ Sims applies for the same league.

(13)
July 25   Cartwright Jesse C. wants his title - copy of deed for 1/2 league on --- and his title for his league and labor Old Colony.

"     Rabb John G - Florida

"     Toy W̲m̲ H. Printer

Sept 14 McFarland M̲r̲ for M̲r̲s̲ White applies for her title. 4 or 6 Carankaway.

Murphy W̲m̲ wants his title for one fourth league on the LaBaca above Kerr. Says he gave his note for fees & has now paid me.

Overton Greenberry & others Col. Barret says applied for land through the letters of Sims.

Bridges W̲m̲ wants his copy of deed - land on LaBaca.

Webber J.F. wants his deed examied & corrected. Say his front is two hundred varas too short.

Sep 24 Winburn McHenry applies for a quarter of a league applied for by Hoth & Pendleton for the 29 Oct last. (Rem. old 14 p)

(14)

Parrot McNeas a S. Carolinian has applied
for land League D on the waters of Bidi
Bayou.

John McNeas - same do - same survey
Applies for League J

Ira McNeas - League M same place & survey

Blany McNeas - do - League N - do  do

Barnett Wm Applies by his agent Thos
Barnet for League No. 2 on San Antonio Road
E. Navasota.

Ward Wm Applies for League No. 2 south of
Highland Creek.

Robinson J.E.  Applied for the half moon
front on Matagorda Bay  and is deeded.

Dunn Patrick - Capt. Allen wishes to know
if he Dunn is entitled to land. Says he
died sme time since - find Mr. Williams
receipt for money paid for fees.

Whitehead & Foster. Foster applied for a
quarter of a league of land back of Isaacs
& Knight & White on the 4 May (Selections
p 29).  Whitehead applied for the same
(p 53) on the grounds that Foster has had
land granted him before - and says that Mr
Williams said he could have it & for evidence of this promises apply to C.C. Givins

(15)

Remembrances 1835

30 Sept

Richardson Geo F. wants his deed has got
the  money.

Dobie Wm wants title for 1/4 League 23 on
Middle Cr. They will send in two weeks.

Barnett William wants a league east of the
Brazos near Groces Retreat survey by Jesse
Barnett.

166

Lacy Wm D. for McCroskey, deceased, wants
the deed for one fourth league on Trespalacios.

Mann Marshall by his agent T.R. Jackson applies for League No. 20 on Middle Creek if
forfeited.

Mr. Jackson wants Mr. Chriesman to enter a
league for Mr. Mann the same league which
Mr. Jackson spoke to him respecting - say a
cedar hill on the left hand side of the
road leading to Bastrop.

Isaac Maiden & the widow San Pier want the
copies of their deeds - Show receipts for
the payment of fees.

Cartwright Matthew applies for a quarter of
a league (No.1) on Mound Creek. San Jacinto

(16)

Early James C. applies for a 1/4 of a
league entered by Roddy.  See Entries p 55.

Niebling Frederick applies for a tract of
land selected on the Brazos and San Antonio
Road upon which land he has made improve-
ments, said land lying above the road.

Mrs. Carnaghan applies also for a tract on
and above said road 4 miles more or less
west from Brazos River.

Dankworth William and Koyen Harmon apply
for land above San Antonio Road joining the
Tenoxtiteclan league on the Brazos River at
the south east corner of said league. This
for the first named. One quarter on the San
Antonio Road five miles more or less from
the river west side.

[An isolated entry without date]
Eleanor Living 50 years of age widow native of
Ireland. Family consists of 3 persons. Land on the
Navedad below Mr. Whiteheads.

PERSONAL NAMES INDEX

The original of the **Register** is in two bound volumes titled "A" and "B"
and each has numbered pages. These page numbers have been copied in
the text thus: (  ). In this book, the two volumes are called 1 and 2
in the order or writing, because "A" and "B" are actually in reverse
order. "R" refers to a short appendix of notes called "Remembrances".
They are at the end of this printed text.

| | | |
|---|---|---|
| Abbott Elizabeth 1-105 | Alley heirs  R-11,2-73 | Arnold William  1-39 |
| Abbott Josh 1-105,2-75 | Alley Abraham  2-47 | Arriola Edwardo  2-61 |
| Abbots Lancelot  2-9 | Alley Nancy  2-47 | Arrista Dolores  2-63 |
| Abrahams Alex  2-87 | Alley Ranson  2-47 | Atkins Phoebe  1-61 |
| Adair William J  1-11 | Alley Thos  1-57 | Atkins William  1-61 |
| Adams Francis  1-69 | Alley Wm M  1-23 | Atkinson Jesse B  1-39 |
| Adams Thos J  2-87 | Allison Patrick  1-17 | Atkinson Margaret 1-39 |
| Addison Isaac S  2-33 | Amelung Louis F  2-87 | Atkinson Robert  2-59 |
| Addison Jos J  2-33 | Anderson Mrs  R-8 | Atkinson Robt W  2-15 |
| Addison Lewis G  2-89 | Anderson Anna  1-79 | Atwell Wm  2-43,2-103 |
| Addsison Sarah  2-33 | Anderson Ephraim  1-81 | Austin Andrew Y  1-26 |
| Addison John  2-31 | Anderson John  1-79 | Austin Archibald  1-26 |
| Adkinson Mariah  2-31 | Anderson Milton J 1-81 | Austin David  2-73 |
| Adriance John  2-93 | Anderson Sarah Ann | Austin Henry 1-30,1-81 |
| Ainsworth A.C.  2-29 | 2-91 | Austin J.B.  1-93 |
| Aitken John  1-91 | Andrews Edmund  1-85 | Austin Joanna  1-105 |
| Aldrich Peter  1-63 | Andrews Isabelle  1-85 | Austin John |
| Aldridge Wm B  2-6 | Andrews Micah  2-57 | 1-15,1-16,2-13 |
| Alexander George  1-5 | Andrews Nancy  1-26 | Austin Thomas H  1-18 |
| Alford  2-61 | Andrews Reddin  2-47 | Austin Wm T 1-15,1-105 |
| Alford Eliza  2-5 | Andrews Richard  1-77 | Avery Elsina 1-37,R-11 |
| Alford Winfield  2-5 | Andrew Thomas  1-26 | Avery Willis 1-37,R-11 |
| Allcorn Elijah  2-79 | Andrews Wm  1-9 | Ayers Anne M  1-36 |
| Allcorn James D | Anthony D.W.  1-27 | Ayres  1-41 |
| 1-47,2-25 | Anthony Henry  1-35 | Ayres David |
| Allcorn John H | Anthony Jacob  1-27 | 1-36,2-41,R-3,R-10 |
| 1-53,2-25 | Applewhite Henry  1-25 | |
| Allcorn Lydia  2-25 | Archer Dr  1-47 | Babbett  R-1 |
| Allcorn Sarah  1-53 | Archer Branch T  1-107 | Babbit Benjn  2-83 |
| Allcorn T.J.  2-71 | Arcineaga M  1-36 | Babbitt Orange  2-99 |
| Allcorn Thos Jeff | Arenandis Joseph  2-73 | Bacchus John C  1-63 |
| 1-53,2-25 | Arlmut Amelia  2-4 | Bacchus Mary  1-83 |
| Allcorn Wm E  1-53 | Armistead Robt S  2-65 | Bailey Alexr  1-67 |
| Allen Capt  R-14 | Armour Nancy  2-69 | Bailey Gains  1-77 |
| Allen Artemisia  2-79 | Armour Robt  2-69 | Baine Cecelia  1-101 |
| Allen Clement  2-79 | Armstrong Delila  1-55 | Baine Moses  1-101 |
| Allen Jas  2-15 | Armstrong H.F.  2-79 | Baird  1-30 |
| Allen John M  1-103 | Armstrong Henry F | Baird Wm  2-61 |
| Allen Lydia  1-93 | 1-57,2-79 | Baire Henry L  1-49 |
| Allen R  2-45 | Arnold Daniel  1-53 | Baker Amaziah E  2-7 |
| Allen Richard 1-67,2-8 | Arnold Eunice  2-75 | Baker Anne  1-87,2-8 |
| Allen Samuel F  1-34 | Arnold Holly  2-75 | Baker Colbert  1-87 |
| Allen Wm  2-39 | Arnold Martha E  1-39 | Baker Danl D.D.  1-87 |
| Alley  1-15 | Arnold Rachael  1-53 | Baker Eliza W  2-8 |

167

| | | |
|---|---|---|
| Baker Hance | 2-8 | |
| Baker John | 2-101 | |
| Baker Joseph | 2-9 | |
| Baker Mosley | 2-8 | |
| Balkman Charles | 2-53 | |
| Bankson Fayett | 1-30 | |
| Bankston Blufad G | R-1 | |
| Bannister Chas B | 2-87 | |
| Bard Martha | 1-105 | |
| Bard William | 1-105 | |
| Barker Jesse | 1-37,R-11 | |
| Barker Lemon | 1-59 | |
| Barker Milinda | 1-37 | |
| Barksdale Lewis | 1-103 | |
| Barlow Rebecca J | 1-85 | |
| Barlow Samuel H | 1-85 | |
| Barnett Jesse | R-15 | |
| Barnett Tomas | | |
| | 1-15,R-14 | |
| Barnett Wm | | |
| | 2-63,R-14,R-15 | |
| Barney Anne Eliza | 1-83 | |
| Barney Jabez | 1-83 | |
| Barnhill Cinthia | 2-25 | |
| Barnhill Wm | 2-25 | |
| Barret Col | R-13 | |
| Barret D.C. | 2-29 | |
| Barret Elizabeth | 1-47 | |
| Barret Wm | 1-3,1-47 | |
| Barron Elizabeth | 1-91 | |
| Barron Thos | 1-91 | |
| Barrow Mrs. A | 2-71 | |
| Bartelson Caroline | 1-29 | |
| Bartelson P.K. | 1-29 | |
| Barten Elisha W | 1-57 | |
| Barten Susana | 1-57 | |
| Bartlett Francis | 1-18 | |
| Bartlett Jesse | 1-18 | |
| Bartlett John | 2-35 | |
| Barton | 1-55 | |
| Barton B | 1-63 | |
| Barton Joseph | 2-41 | |
| Barton Stacy | 1-55 | |
| Barton W | 2-97 | |
| Barton Wm | 1-55 | |
| Bates Henry | 1-12 | |
| Batterson Amelia | 2-81 | |
| Batterson Isaac | | |
| | 1-42,2-81 | |
| Batterson J [I] | 2-59 | |
| Baty Edwd | 1-51 | |
| Baudrano Amelia | 2-81 | |
| Baudrano Anthony | 2-81 | |
| Baugh Robt G | 2-65 | |

168

| | | |
|---|---|---|
| Baxter Henry | 2-23 | |
| Baxter William | 2-23 | |
| Baze Henry | 2-47 | |
| Beachamp John | 2-101 | |
| Beardslee Hester | 1-63 | |
| Beardslee James | 1-63 | |
| Beasley Rachel | 2-41 | |
| Beasley Wm | 2-41 | |
| Beaty Edward | 1-7 | |
| Beaumer Bern. H | 2-89 | |
| Beck Jno F | 2-101 | |
| Beckham Mary | 1-9 | |
| Beldin John | 2-87 | |
| Bell Mrs. | 2-9 | |
| Bell Abigail | 1-43 | |
| Bell George A | 1-73 | |
| Bell J | 1-59 | |
| Bell J.H. | 1-7,1-14,1-22 | |
| Bell James | | |
| | 1-51,1-61,1-79,R-1 | |
| Bell Jane | 1-105 | |
| Bell Joseph T | 1-105 | |
| Bell Thomas | 1-43,2-9 | |
| Bell Winsey | 1-79 | |
| Bellows Charlotte L | | |
| | 1-95 | |
| Bellows Geo L | 1-95 | |
| Bennet Chs H | 1-83 | |
| Bennet James | 1-55 | |
| Bennet Theodore | | |
| | 2-101,2-103 | |
| Berden Mrs | 2-3 | |
| Berry David | 1-19 | |
| Berry Elizabeth | 1-19 | |
| Berry John | 1-19 | |
| Berry John T | 1-59 | |
| Berry Lucinda | 2-31 | |
| Berry Nancy | 1-19 | |
| Berry Peter L | 1-24 | |
| Berry Radford | 1-33 | |
| Berry Thos O | 2-31 | |
| Bertrand | R-1 | |
| Bertrand Thos | 2-91 | |
| Bertrand Anne W | 1-59 | |
| Bertrand Peter | 1-59 | |
| Bess Ann | 2-101 | |
| Bess Elizabeth | 2-29 | |
| Best Humphrey | 2-29 | |
| Best Stephen | 2-7 | |
| Bettner C.A. | 1-27 | |
| Betts | 1-65 | |
| Biddy Abednigo | 1-21 | |
| Biddy Patsy | 1-21 | |
| Biegel Joseph | 2-1 | |

| | | |
|---|---|---|
| Biegel Margaret | 2-1 | |
| Billings | 2-71 | |
| Birch William | 1-79 | |
| Bird John | 1-89 | |
| Bird Nancy | 1-79 | |
| Bird Polly | 2-55 | |
| Bird Sally | 1-89 | |
| Bird Thomas | 1-79 | |
| Black John S | 1-85 | |
| Black Marcus L | 1-93 | |
| Black Mary | 1-85 | |
| Blair Alx | 2-17 | |
| Blair E.Alex.J. | 1-43 | |
| Blake Thos M | 2-53 | |
| Blakey Nancy | 1-27 | |
| Blanchet Pierre | 1-22 | |
| Bland Frances | 1-57 | |
| Blowne Wm | 2-87 | |
| Blythe | 2-79 | |
| Boatwright Anny | 2-77 | |
| Boatwright Barb. | 2-77 | |
| Boatwright Friend | 2-77 | |
| Boatwright Lydia | 2-77 | |
| Boatwright Richd | 2-77 | |
| Boatwright Thos | 2-77 | |
| Boatwright Wm | 2-77 | |
| Bohmer see Beaumer | | |
| Bond Henry | 2-99 | |
| Borden | 1-81 | |
| Borden Gail | 1-57 | |
| Borden Gail Jr | 1-59 | |
| Borden John P | 1-29 | |
| Borden Paschal | 2-23 | |
| Borden Paschal P | 1-57 | |
| Borden Penelope | 1-59 | |
| Borden T.H. | 2-21 | |
| Borden Tom | 2-77,R-9 | |
| Boren Matt | 1-93,2-29 | |
| Boren Nancy | 1-93 | |
| Bostic | 1-41 | |
| Bostic Mrs | 1-27 | |
| Bostic J.H. | 1-73 | |
| Bostic Levi | 1-49 | |
| Bostic Patsey | 1-49 | |
| Bostick | R-1 | |
| Bostick James H | 2-99 | |
| Bostick Sion R | 2-99 | |
| Boughan James G | 1-13 | |
| Bowen | 2-71 | |
| Bowen Almira | 1-53 | |
| Bowen Samuel A | 1-3 | |
| Bowen Sylvester | 1-53 | |
| Bowen Wm R | 2-19 | |
| Bowie James | 1-13 | |

Bowie Stephen 1-16
Bowles Benjamin 1-87
Bowles Betsey 1-87
Bowlin Jeremiah 1-7
Bowlin Solomon 1-7
Bowlin Wm 1-7
Bowman 1-91
Bowman Mrs 2-73
Bowman Abraham 1-65
Bowman John 1-81
Bowman Margaret 1-81
Bowman Samuel 2-61
Boyce Isaac D 2-85
Boyce John 1-3
Boyden Clarissa W 1-87
Boyden Wm 1-87
Boyle Wm 2-87
Braberry James 1-65
Bracy Macklin 1-36
Bradley James 1-32
Bray Cynthia A 1-91
Bray Thomas 1-91
Breeden Richard 1-32
Breedlove A.W. 1-95
Breedlove Susan J 1-95
Breen Charles 1-5
Bridge Wm 1-99
Bridges Hannah H 1-42
Bridges Thos 1-42,2-11
Bridges Wm 2-29,R-13
Brigham A 1-85
Brigham Elizab. S 1-85
Brister Nathl R 2-87
Brookfield Emma 1-20
Brookfield Wm 1-20
Brooks Blufad 2-7
Brooks Eliza Ann 1-103
Brooks Geo W
1-103,2-41
Brown 1-45,1-65
Brown A 2-45
Brown Alexr 1-89
Brown Jeremiah 1-79
Brown Joan
1-5,1-51,1-91,1-93
Brown Nancy 1-51
Brown Robert 1-5,1-53
Brown Sally 1-89
Brown Saml P 1-14,1-73
Brown Steel 2-51,R-12
Brown Susan 1-73
Brown Wm 2-49
Bruff Samuel 1-65
Bruning Adilaide 2-3

Bruning Henri 2-3
Brush John F 1-83
Bryan Wm H 2-69
Buckhannon James 2-65
Buckhannon Mary 2-65
Buckman Harriet 1-38
Buckner Eliz 2-23,2-31
Buckner John W
1-23,1-31,R-3
Buford Warren 1-1
Bullock Robert 1-59
Bundick S.C. 1-79
Bundick Thos W 2-53
Burdgess John
1-83,2-3,2-55
Burdgess Marg C 1-83
Burgess Mr R-12
Burgess John 2-3,2-15
Burleson Aaron 2-91
Burleson Ally 2-27
Burleson Edwd 1-75
Burleson Eliz 2-27
Burleson Gage 2-11
Burleson James 1-22
1-107,2-11,2-93,R-8
Burleson Jo 2-73
Burleson Jonathan R-8
Burleson Jos Sen 2-27
Burleson Jos Jr 2-27
Burleson Malinda 2-11
Burleson Sarah 1-75
Burnap Abijah L
2-23,1-105
Burnap L 2-23
Burnap Micajah L 2-95
Burnap Sarah 1-105
Burnett Anne 1-75
Burnett Crawford 1-75
Burnett D.G. 2-7
Burnett Mat 1-89,2-31
Burnett Nancy 1-69
Burnett Sally 1-89
Burnett Wm 1-69,1-83
Burney Robert 1-43
Burney Robert A 1-10
Burney Susan 1-55
Burney William 1-55
Burnham Stephen 1-103
Burton John M 1-69
Bury Charles 1-43
Busby Wm 1-79
Byrne John 1-91
Byrne Pamelia 1-91
Byrom J.J.D. 1-107
Byrom Mary J 1-107

Cady D.C. 2-49
Cahill J.B. 2-13
Calder James H 1-40
Calder Robert J 1-40
Caldwell Jas P 1-17
Caldwell Jane E 1-40
Caldwell John
1-12,1-95
Caldwell LucindaW 1-95
Calkins Simon 1-13
Callahan Joseph 2-81
Callender Syd S 2-87
Callihan John H 2-75
Callihan Malina 2-75
Calvit Fredk J 1-45
Campbell Anne 1-38
Campbell Cyrus 2-59
Campbell Eliz 1-57
Campbell H.O. 2-61
Campbell James 1-38
Campbell Jos. hrs 2-59
Campbell Lucinda 2-61
Campbell Rebecca 2-59
Canfield Buckman
1-38,R-8
Canter Josh 2-95,2-99
Capel Britton 2-5
Capel Jabez B 2-5
Carey Seth 2-87
Carleton Wm 2-91
Carlisl Robt 2-39
Carlton John 2-103
Carnaghan Mrs R-16
Carns Noah 2-31
Carr Harriet 1-101
Carr James C 1-101
Carrell Ed S 1-67
Carrol George 1-11
Carson Wm C 1-5
Carson Wm W 1-38
Carter Eliz 1-99
Carter Richd 1-27,1-99
Cartwright Eliz 1-32
Cartwright Geo W 2-85
Cartwright Jesse C
R-13
Cartwright Jesse H 1-1
Cartwright John 1-71
Cartwright Mary 1-71
Cartwright Matt R-15
Cartwright Nancy 1-1
Cartwright Peter 1-32
Cartwright Robt 1-1

169

| | | |
|---|---|---|
| Cartwright Willifred | Choate Thos 1-79 | Cocke Pleasant B 2-47 |
| 1-33 | Chriesman H 1-14,2-27 | Cockrill Wash J 1-12 |
| Cartwright Wm 1-33 | Christie Francis 1-99 | Coe Elizabeth 1-103 |
| Caruthers Eliz 1-101 | Church Eli 1-89 | Coe Philip 1-103 |
| Caruthers Mary 1-69 | Churchill Andrew 1-5 | Coibble Edward 1-20 |
| Caruthers Thomas 1-101 | Clampit Catherine 1-99 | Coker John 2-103 |
| Cash George M 1-65 | Clampit Ezekiel 1-59 | Coldwell John S 2-81 |
| Casner Isaac | Clampit Sarah 1-95 | Cole 1-51 |
| 1-34,1-114 | Clampit Susannah 1-59 | Cole J.P. 1-63 |
| Casner Jacob 1-37 | Clapp Wm 1-83 | Cole James 2-5 |
| Casner Mary 1-34 | Clare Abraham M 1-95 | Cole John 1-67 |
| Cass James M 2-87 | Clarisa Mary 1-89 | Cole Polly 1-67 |
| Castleman Andrew 1-7 | Clark Alvin B 1-57 | Coleman Ann 1-91 |
| Castlemen Andrew L | Clark Elizabeth 1-57 | Coleman Eliz 1-103 |
| 1-59 | Clark James 1-55 | Coleman Green H |
| Castleman Andrew Lewis | Clark John 1-9,1-63 | 1-107,1-114 |
| 1-9 | Clark Rebecca 1-79 | Coleman Lucy 1-63 |
| Castleman John 1-114 | Clark Rhoda 1-55 | Coleman R.M. 1-103 |
| Castleman Michael | Clark Silas 1-61 | Coleman Susan H 1-107 |
| 1-114 | Clark Wm C 1-79 | Coleman Young 1-63 |
| Castleman S 1-3 | Clark Anthy R 1-49 | Collingsworth Geo M |
| Cave Wm 2-8 | Clarke Bershela 1-99 | 1-93 |
| Cavero Mariano 2-95 | Clarke David 1-99 | Collins 1-77 |
| Cayce Hannah 1-65 | Clary Jesse 2-85 | Collins Wm 1-10 |
| Cayce Thomas 1-65 | Clary Susanna 2-85 | Colton Dan E 1-79,2-13 |
| Cazneau Wm L 2-11,2-49 | Clary Jno 2-13 | Colvin Aaron 1-47 |
| Chadoin see Shadoin | Clay Nancy 1-45 | Colvin Margaret 1-47 |
| Chamberlain Willard | Clay Nestor 1-45 | Cone Albert 1-67 |
| 2-87 | Clements A.L. 2-31 | Conklin Elijah 1-14 |
| Chambers Isabella 2-25 | Clements Letis 1-91 | Conkrite Lyman 1-89 |
| Chambers Talbot 1-75 | Clements Wm R 1-91 | Conkrite Sarah 1-89 |
| Chambers Thos 2-25 | Cleveland Horatio N | see also Cronkrite |
| Chambers Thos J 1-10 | 2-67 | Connell John H 1-81 |
| Chance Jos B 1-63 | Clifft Jesse 1-71 | Connell Matilda 1-81 |
| Chance Nancy 1-63 | Clifft Mary 1-71 | Conner Chas M 2-87 |
| Chance Samuel 1-15 | Clokey Anne 1-65 | Conner John G 2-77 |
| Chandler 1-85 | Clokey Robert 1-65 | Connelly E.M. 1-71 |
| Chandler Davis 1-57 | Clopper Andrew M 2-15 | Conrad Edward 2-101 |
| Chandler Hugh 2-77 | Clopper N 2-15 | Converse Thos F 1-43 |
| Chandler Prissa 1-57 | Clopper Nicholas 1-3 | Cook 1-45 |
| Chaney John 2-57 | Coates Samuel 1-17 | Cook Octavius A 2-25 |
| Chaney Lucy 2-57 | Coats Austin M 1-28 | Cook Wm C 2-85 |
| Chase Eliza 1-49 | Costs Lucinda 1-28 | Cooke Hamilton L |
| Chase Wm 1-49 | Coaty Francis 2-101 | 1-99,2-21 |
| Chatham Ditha 2-7 | Cochran Emaline 2-15 | Cooke Henry 1-35 |
| Chatham Thomas 2-7 | Cochran Jas 2-15 | Cooke Mary 1-35,2-21 |
| Cherney John 2-63 | Cochrane Benj 2-55 | Coonce Philip 1-81 |
| Chever Henry 1-43 | Cochrane Jas 1-77,2-13 | Cooper 1-34 |
| Chever John 2-17 | Cochrane Jeremiah 2-97 | Cooper Enos 2-97 |
| Chevers John 2-63 | Cochrane Robt 2-75 | Cooper Hannah 2-45 |
| Childers Hugh M | Cochrane Thos | Cooper James 1-18,2-45 |
| 1-36,1-114 | 2-13,2-97 | Cooper Miranda 1-18 |
| Childers Susannah 1-36 | Cocke Ann 1-57 | Cope Thomas 1-75 |
| Choate Jane 1-79 | Cocke John 1-7,1-57 | Copeland Dorcas 2-81 |

171

| | | |
|---|---|---|
| Dobie Wm | R-15 | |
| Dodd Aaron C | 2-103 | |
| Dodson Archolaus | 1-97 | |
| Dolan Anne | 1-69 | |
| Dolan Patrick | 1-69 | |
| Dominges Sixto | 2-5 | |
| Donaldson Danl F | 1-27 | |
| Donoho Charles | | |
| 1-14,1-99,2-37 | | |
| Donoho Isaac | 1-13,2-9 | |
| Donho Maria | 1-99 | |
| Donoho Mortimer | 2-35 | |
| Dooley Spirse | 2-51 | |
| Dorsey John | 2-61,2-85 | |
| Dottery | 1-22,1-85 | |
| Dottery Anne | 1-47 | |
| Dottery Bryant | 1-47 | |
| Douglas Anne Cath | 1-26 | |
| Douglass Saml C | 1-26 | |
| Dowdy Mary | 2-57 | |
| Dowdy Richd | 2-57 | |
| Downer Erasmus D | 1-105 | |
| Draughan Abijah W | 1-61 | |
| Drillard Vincent | 2-87 | |
| Drummond Thomas | 2-4 | |
| Duckworth Jacob | 2-79 | |
| Dudley Pulaskey | 1-12 | |
| Duff James | 2-79 | |
| Duff James C | 2-63,2-93 | |
| Duff Mary P | 2-79 | |
| Dunbar Isaac | 1-18 | |
| Duncan | 2-21 | |
| Duncan James | 2-17 | |
| Duncan Judah | 1-105 | |
| Duncan Peter J | 2-41 | |
| Duncan Sally | 2-41 | |
| Dundass Wm E | 1-67 | |
| Dunlap Dolly | 1-45 | |
| Dunlap Wm | 1-45 | |
| Dunlavy Mrs | 2-6 | |
| Dunlavy heirs | 2-75 | |
| Dunlevy D | 1-41 | |
| Dunn Eliza | 1-69 | |
| Dunn Patrick | | |
| 1-81,2-65,R-14 | | |
| Dunn R.L. | 1-69 | |
| Dunnahoe Chs | 2-85 | |
| Dupuy Wm | 1-85 | |
| Durbain Henry | 1-35 | |
| Durham Wm D | 2-87 | |
| Duty George | 1-71 | |
| Duty Joseph | 1-10 | |
| Duty M | 2-8 | |
| Duty Matthew | 1-10,1-47 | |

| | | |
|---|---|---|
| Duty Richard | 2-9 | |
| Duty Solomon | 1-10 | |
| Duty Wm | 2-59 | |
| Dwight Geo E | 2-91 | |
| Dwyer Edward | 1-97 | |
| Dwyer Eliza | 1-81 | |
| Dwyer Jeremiah | 1-81 | |
| Dwyer Mr | 1-29 | |
| Dykes Geo P | 1-23 | |
| Dykes Judy S | 1-23 | |
| Dykes Lovick P | 1-23 | |
| Dykes Roady V | 1-23 | |
| Dziaskoski J | 2-41 | |
| Dziekanski John | 1-5 | |
| Eagan Gabriel | 1-91 | |
| Early James C | R-16 | |
| Early M | 1-49 | |
| Earnest | 1-7,1-9 | |
| Earnest Felix P | 1-89 | |
| Eaton William | 1-25 | |
| Ebberle Catherine | 1-31 | |
| Ebberle Jacob | 1-31 | |
| Eblen Eliz | 1-103 | |
| Eblen John | 1-103 | |
| Echols Abner | 2-35 | |
| Echols Sarah | 2-35 | |
| Eckle Wm | 1-26 | |
| Eddings Abram | 1-73 | |
| Eddings Nancy | 1-71 | |
| Eddings Theophalus | 1-71 | |
| Edgar Alex | 2-75 | |
| Edwards Amos | 1-53 | |
| Edwards Chas | 1-69,2-41 | |
| Edwards Gustavus | 1-63 | |
| Edwards John | 1-10 | |
| Edwards John F | 1-49 | |
| Edwards John H | 1-53 | |
| Edwards John T | | |
| 1-5,2-37 | | |
| Edwards Martha | 2-37 | |
| Edwards Penelope | 1-53 | |
| Edwards Polly A | 1-69 | |
| Edwards Sarah A | 1-53 | |
| Ehlinger | 2-57 | |
| Ehlinger Joseph | 2-73 | |
| Ehlinger Mary A | 2-57 | |
| Eilers Rernhard | 2-95 | |
| Elam | 1-57 | |
| Elam John | 1-15,1-51 | |
| Elgin Albert | 1-32 | |
| Elkins Wade | 2-6 | |
| Elliot George | 2-49 | |
| Ellis Edmund | 2-19 | |

| | | |
|---|---|---|
| Ellis Richard | 1-14 | |
| Ellison James | 2-99 | |
| Ellison Moses | 2-99 | |
| Enderle John G | 2-2 | |
| Enderle Mariana | 2-2 | |
| Endt Lewis | 1-75 | |
| Endt Mary | 1-75 | |
| Ernst Frederick | 1-95 | |
| Ernst Louisa A | 1-95 | |
| Este Edwd E | 2-7 | |
| Estes John H | 2-4 | |
| Estis Anderson | 2-21 | |
| Estis Eliz | 2-21 | |
| Etherton Daniel | | |
| 1-45,2-21 | | |
| Evans Charlotte | 1-91 | |
| Evans Ephraim | 2-99 | |
| Evans Holdon | 1-91 | |
| Evans J.J. | 1-93 | |
| Evans Jesse M | 1-24 | |
| Evans John S | 1-45 | |
| Evans Martha | 1-101 | |
| Evans Polley | 1-93 | |
| Evans Sarah | 1-45 | |
| Evans Vincent L | 2-99 | |
| Evans Wm G | 1-101,2-41 | |
| Ewing Abbie | 1-59 | |
| Ewing Alex | 1-40,2-11 | |
| Ewing Charles W | 1-59 | |
| Ewing George | | |
| 1-10,1-14,1-47 | | |
| Fairchild Mahaley | 1-61 | |
| Fairchild Philo | | |
| 1-3,1-61 | | |
| Fann Eli | 2-63 | |
| Fanning J.W. | 2-13 | |
| Fanthorpe Henry | 2-1 | |
| Faris | 2-45 | |
| Farley Nancy | 2-31 | |
| Farmer Mrs | 2-71 | |
| Farmer Alexr | 1-65 | |
| Farmer James | 2-89 | |
| Farrel Emma | 1-20 | |
| Farrel James O | 1-20 | |
| Fay Thos F | 1-116 | |
| Fenn Eli | 2-41 | |
| Fenn Sarah | 2-41 | |
| Fennel G | 2-99 | |
| Fenton Chas H | 2-65 | |
| Field Joseph E | 2-6 | |
| Fields John | 1-7 | |
| Fike Nathan | 2-101 | |
| Finch John E | 1-105 | |

172

Finley Lydia V 1-45
Finley Wm D 1-45
Finney Nathan 2-49
Fisher 1-65,2-11
Fisher Anne 1-65
Fisher Eliz 1-73
Fisher Henry 2-89
Fisher John 2-99
Fisher Jorge 1-73
Fisher Reuben 2-97
Fisher S.R. 2-21,2-47
Fisher S.Rhoads 1-65
Fitch P.F. 2-81
Fite Ubetia 1-107
Fitzgerald 2-61
Fitzgibbons Nancy 1-71
Fitzgibbons Wm 1-71
Flack Elisha 1-75
Flanders John
1-15,1-85
Flanigan Joseph 1-30
Fletcher Joshua 1-43
Flewry Howard 2-11
Frewry Anthony B 2-11
Fogg John W 2-73
Foley B.M. 1-95
Foley M.B. 2-7
Foley S.T. 2-7
Fondervert 2-63
Ford D.S. 1-75
Ford James 1-89
Ford Wm W 1-89
Fordtran Charles 1-93
Foster R-14
Foster Franklin 2-97
Foster James 1-36,1-75
Foster James Jr 2-45
Foster James J 1-40
Foster James W 2-97
Foster John 1-39,2-103
Foster Mary 1-40
Foster Moses A
1-65,2-29
Foster Pamelia 1-36
Fowler Catharene 2-35
Fowler David 2-35,R-10
Frailey Nancy 1-67
Frampton Eliza S 2-37
Frampton W 2-37
Franks L.B. 2-21,R-10
Franks Littleberry 1-38
Fraser Danl M 2-19
Fraser Sally 2-19
Frazier Daniel M 1-3

Frazier Mary Ann 2-93
Frazier Moses B 1-3
Frazier Peggy 1-107
Freele 2-93
Fried Henry 2-81
Fulenwider 2-61
Fuller Hannah 1-105
Fuller Samuel 1-105
Fuller Eliz 1-63
Fulton M.L. 2-61
Fulton Saml 1-63
Fuqua Benj 1-93
Fuqua Ephraim 1-79
Fuqua Martha 1-79

Gage Burleson 2-11
Gage Calvin 2-73
Gage Elizabeth 2-73
Gage Malinda 2-11
Gage Moses 2-27,2-73
Gailbreth Geo 1-89
Gallatin Abraham 1-28
Gallatin Albert 1-28
Gandy Daniel R 1-93
Gandy Nancy 1-93
Garner Wm F 1-40
Garretson Thos 1-55
Gary Hary D 2-103
Gasley T.J. 1-9
Gates 1-14
Gates Amos 1-73
Gates Charles 1-65
Gates John 1-75
Gates Lydia 1-73
Gates Minerva 1-65
Gates Saml
1-49,1-65,1-73,2-55
Gay Thomas 1-75,2-71
Gazley Eliza 1-43
Gazley Thos J 1-43
Gee Alford 2-71
Geffray Irene 1-57
Geffray Louis 1-57
George Holman 2-51
George Jefferson
1-43,2-51,2-53
George Nancy 1-53
George Nicholas 1-53
Gerard Scott 1-101
Gervais Cath O 2-8
Gervais S.D. 2-8
Gibbons 1-61
Gieske Charles 2-3
Gill John P 1-103

Gill Mary 1-83
Gill Michael 1-83
Gill Presley 1-5
Gilland Geo M 2-87
Gillel Catherine 1-7
Gilleland Daniel 1-81
Gilleland Priscilla
1-81
Gillet heirs 1-83
Gilliland Dianah 1-53
Gilliland James
1-53,1-75
Gilmore Carolina 2-3
Gilmore Thomas 2-3
Gilmore Wm 2-77
Gilly Hays B 2-43
Gilpin Elias 2-79
Giraud Francis 1-7
Givens C.C. R-14
Glasgow Lydia 1-101
Gleason Cynthia 1-61
Gleason Cyrus 2-19
Gleason Phinneas 1-61
Gleason Wallis 2-99
Gleize Sarah 2-93
Goacher 2-73
Goacher Samuel 2-73
Goheen Michael R 2-91
Gonsales Maria G 2-2
Goodman John 1-17,2-35
Goodman James S 2-6
Goodman Rebecca
1-17,2-35
Goodman William 2-15
Gorden Horace 1-65
Gorden Elizabeth 1-69
Gordon John 2-103
Gordon Samuel 1-75
Gores Humphrey N 1-81
Gorham Isaac 2-57
Corham William 1-33
Graham Andrew 1-33
Graham Sibby 1-33
Graham Wm 2-87
Grammer David
1-14,1-83
Grant Hugh 2-51
Grantham Matt J 1-91
Grasmeyer F.W. 1-91
Grason P.W. 1-15
Gray Danl 2-95
Gray Francis H 2-87
Gray Joshua 2-95
Gray Mayberry B 2-73
173

Gray Thomas 2-95
Gray Wm Fairfax 2-99
Grayham Richd R-1
Grayson Benjn F 2-59
Greaves Richard 1-5
Green Benjamin 2-23
Green Geo 2-33,2-87
Green James 2-23
Green Mary Jane 1-81
Greene Elizabeth 1-51
Greene Patrick 1-51
Greenwood Anne 1-87
Greenwood Franklin J
1-81
Greenwood Joel 1-87
Gregg 1-75
Gregg Darius 1-53
Gregoire Ambrose
1-95,2-97
Grenville Benj 2-21
Grenville Mary 2-21
Grey James D 1-81
Grey Levina 1-81
Griffeth Ester 1-67
Griffeth Noah 1-67
Griffith Henry 1-83
Griffin Solomon 2-51
Grimes Disey 1-55
Grimes F 2-97
Grimes Fredk 1-7,1-55
Grimes Geo 1-7,1-55
Grimes J 2-77
Grimes Jesse
1-63,1-69,1-83
Grimes Rosanna 1-69
Groce Jared E Jr
2-37,2-45,2-97
Groce Leonard W 1-55
Grovesnor Geo H 1-7
Grymes George 1-9
Guild Alfred R 1-35
Guild John Jr 2-61
Guthrie Robt 1-3

Hablamaha Stephen 2-69
Hablamaha Thomas 2-69
Haddon Jackson 2-65
Haddon Wm 2-65
Haddy S.C. 2-3
Hadley Joshua 1-89
Hadley Obedience 1-89
Halderman David 1-34
Halderman Jesse 1-34
Hale Janie F 1-91
174

Hale John K 1-91
Hall E 2-51
Hall Edward 2-89,R-12
Hall Elisha 1-57
Hall Elizabeth 1-30
Hall G.B. 1-49
Hall George W 1-105
Hall J 2-9
Hall James 1-77
Hall Jemima 1-57
Hall John 1-93
Hall John L 2-49,2-87
Hall Joshua James 2-49
Hall Julietta 1-47
Hall Nancy 1-24,1-63
Hall Solomon 2-95
Hall Thos Jeff 1-63
Hall Warren D.C. 1-47
Hall Wm A 1-30
Hall Winneford 1-77
Hallett John 1-37
Hallett Margaret 1-37
Ham John 2-51
Hamer Rosila 2-101
Hamey Louisa 1-49
Hamilton David 1-1
Hamilton Dianah 1-1
Hamilton Fanny 1-87
Hamilton Josiah F 1-87
Hamilton Pascal B 2-59
Hammat Nestor B R-9
Hammer Rosalie 1-77
Hammond George 1-12
Hancock Patsy 2-55
Hancock Thos 2-55
Handy Robert Eden 2-7
Haney 1-47
Haney Berry 1-27
Haney Philadel 1-27
Hanks B.L. 1-37,2-21
Hanks Bird L 1-41,R-10
Hanks Sarah Anne 1-37
Hanks Wyatt 1-5
Hanson David 1-93,2-41
Hanson Thomas 1-93
Harby Julian J 2-89
Hardiman Thos J 2-91
Hardin 1-91
Hardin Caroline 1-87
Hardin Milton H 2-47
Hardin Sam 2-103
Hardin William 1-87
Hardy 1-23,1-69
Hardy Margaret 1-47

Hardy William 1-47
Harmon Daniel 2-7
Harmon E.D. 2-9
Harmon Mahala 2-7
Harper James 1-7
Harper Wm 2-89
Harrell Josiah F 2-83
Harril Dennis 1-105
Harril Nancy 1-105
Harrington Arabella
1-67
Harris David 1-16,1-59
Harris Dewitt C 2-59
Harris Gowin 1-25
Harris Isaac 1-22
Harris J.R. 2-91
Harris John 1-89
Harris Martha 1-22
Harris Wm P 1-79
Harrison 1-3
Harrison Henry
1-49,R-9
Harrison Jos D 1-67
Harrison Mary Ann 2-33
Harrison Rachel R 1-67
Harrison Wily 2-33
Harter Henry 1-79
Harvey David 2-85
Haskins Francis T 1-57
Haskins William 1-12
Hatch Harlem 1-71
Hatch Mary 1-71
Hatch Pamelia 1-47
Hath Sylvanus 1-37
Hatfield B.M. 2-43
Hatfield Caroline 2-43
Hawkins Ed St. J. 1-19
Hawkins Isaac R 1-18
Hawkins John 1-13
Hawkins Wm W 1-32
Hayden Eleanor 2-99
Hayn James 2-103
Hays Coleman 1-89
Hayslett Betsey 2-57
Hayslett Saml 2-57
Head Benj 2-39,R-10
Head E.G. R-10
Head Elbert G 2-39
Head Maria 2-39
Head Thos R-1
Head Wyly M 2-39
Heard America 1-101
Heard John M 1-97
Heard Maria 1-97

| | | | | | |
|---|---|---|---|---|---|
| Heard Nancy | 1-99 | Hinch Samuel | 1-67 | House Isaac | 1-49 |
| Heard Thos H.P. | 1-99 | Hines Mathew T | 1-107 | House James N | 2-67 |
| Heard Wm | 1-101,2-91 | Hinkson John | 1-63 | House John P | 2-79 |
| Heard Wm H | 1-12 | Hiroms Nancy W | 1-47 | House Joseph | 1-89 |
| Hearst Lewis | 1-57 | Hiroms Saml C | 1-47 | House Kizia | 1-49 |
| Heath Ebenr S | 2-67 | Hislop James | 1-93 | House Mary | 1-89 |
| Heath Joel F | 2-101 | Hodge Alexander | 1-49 | House Ransom | 2-81 |
| Heldenbrand Adam | 1-22 | Hodge Alexr E | 1-51 | Houjoa Anthony | 2-99 |
| Helm Thos P | 1-65 | Hodge Archie | 1-3,1-51 | Houston | 2-71 |
| Henderson | 1-43 | Hodge Charlotte | 1-51 | Houston David | 2-25 |
| Henderson Edwin | 2-8 | Hodge James | 1-89 | Houston Emily | 2-25 |
| Henderson Elvira | 2-8 | Hodge John | 1-53,R-10 | Houston Harriet | 2-25 |
| Henderson Francis | | Hodge Polley | 1-53 | Houston Saml | 1-32 |
| | 1-107,1-114 | Hodge Wm | R-10,R-11 | Houston Thos | 2-25 |
| Henry | 1-38 | Hodges Robert | 1-45 | Howard Chs | 2-11 |
| Henry M | 1-109 | Hodges Susan | 1-45 | Howell Elijah | 1-23 |
| Hensen Elisabeth | 1-89 | Hoffman David A | 1-35 | Hoya Anton | 2-91 |
| Hensley Betsey | 1-55 | Hoffman John | 1-40 | Hoya Franz vander | 2-4 |
| Hensley Harman | 1-55 | Hoffman Mary | 1-35 | Hubbard Matthew | 1-10 |
| Hensley Jackson | 2-97 | Hogan Edwd | 1-85 | Hubbell John | 1-22 |
| Hensley John M | 1-63 | Hogan Hannah | 1-85 | Hubbs Eliza | 1-67 |
| Hensley Johnson | 1-45 | Hoit Saml | 1-75 | Hubbs Levina | 1-67 |
| Hensley Mary | 1-63 | Holbrook Nathl | 2-87 | Hubert Frances | 1-73 |
| Hensley Sarah | 1-45 | Holcomb John D | 2-67 | Hubert M | 1-73 |
| Hensley William | 1-45 | Holden Mastin | 1-65 | Hudson George | 1-5 |
| Heron N | 2-93 | Holdridge Asa | 1-59 | Hudson H.G. | 2-101 |
| Heron Nicholas | 2-87 | Holland | 1-43 | Hudson Obadiah | 1-63 |
| Herrength Abella | 1-9 | Holland Franco | 1-49 | Huff Martha | R-9 |
| Herrington Daniel | 1-5 | Holland James | 1-55 | Huff Mary | 2-17 |
| Hickocke Horatio H | | Holland William | 1-49 | Huff Wm | 2-17 |
| | 1-43 | Hollgreon Francis | 2-37 | Huffman John | 2-67 |
| Higgins James | 1-24 | Hollingsworth Jas | 1-89 | Hughes Benj F | 1-14 |
| Higgins Maria | 1-24 | Holman George | 2-51 | Hughes Benj T | 1-107 |
| Highlands Saml | 2-63 | Holmes Asahel C | 2-15 | Hughes J.J. | 1-17 |
| Highsmith Abijah | | Holt Herman | 2-93 | Hughes J.W. | 1-14 |
| | 1-7,1-55 | Holtham John G | 1-75 | Hughes Jane | 1-107 |
| Highsmith Debora | 1-55 | Hope Adolphus | 1-53 | Hughes Peter M | 2-99 |
| Highsmith Samuel | 1-7 | Hope Prosper | 1-53 | Hughs Jas | 2-29 |
| Hill Elizabeth | 2-61 | Hopkins Joseph | 2-101 | Hughson James | 1-17 |
| Hill Ezra | 2-99 | Hornsby Malcolm | 2-13 | Hughson Temperance | 1-17 |
| Hill Js L | 2-13 | Hornsby Moses H | 2-13 | Hulbart R.O. | 2-31 |
| Hill Mary | 1-18 | Hornsby Reuben | | Hunt Herschel H | 1-29 |
| Hill Obedience | 2-3 | | 1-75,2-13 | Hunt J | 2-41 |
| Hill Stewart C | 2-87 | Hornsby Sarah | 1-75 | Hunt John C | 2-53 |
| Hill Thomas | 1-18 | Hornsby Wm | 2-13 | Hunt Mary | 1-40 |
| Hill Wm C.J. | 2-61 | Horton A.C. | R-8 | Hunt Rhody | 1-93 |
| Hillhouse Lucretia | | Horton Henderson W | 1-3 | Hunt William | 1-40 |
| | 1-34 | Horton Josiah | 1-3 | Hunt William R | 1-93 |
| Hillhouse Wm | 1-34 | Horton William D | 1-3 | Hunter Derrel H.M. | |
| Himer Geo W | 1-3 | Hoskins Isaac C | 1-30 | | 1-107 |
| Hinch | R-3 | Hoskins Nancy | 1-30 | Hunter Nancy | 1-49 |
| Hinch Leah Anne | 1-67 | Hotchkiss Anne | 1-75 | Hunter Wm | |
| Hinch Mary W | 2-8 | Hotchkiss Augt | 1-75 | | 1-16,1-49,1-51 |
| Hinch Michael | 2-8 | Hoth | R-13 | Hunter Wm L | 2-87 |

175

| | | | | | |
|---|---|---|---|---|---|
| Hunter Wm W | 1-12,1-91 | Johnson Francis | 2-87 | Kennard Anthony D | 1-29 |
| Hurry Edward | 2-51 | Johnson Francis W | 1-57 | Kennard Sarah | 1-29 |
| Hushan Thos | 1-23,1-107 | Johnson J.B. | 2-17 | Kennedy Absalom | 1-24 |
| Husted Henry | | Johnson Joseph | 1-85 | Kennedy Margaret | 1-71 |
| | 1-19,1-105 | Johnstone Chs.S.P. | 1-83 | Kennedy Rhody | 1-69 |
| Hutcheson Mary | 1-55 | Jones Benjamin A. | 1-11 | Kennedy Sarah | 1-57 |
| Hutcheson Nathl | 1-55 | Jones Betsey | 2-71 | Kennelly Jane | 1-95 |
| Hutchins A.C. | 2-95 | Jones Chs. S. | 2-27 | Kennelly Samuel | 1-95 |
| Hylan Joseph | 2-47 | Jones Gennet | 2-21 | Kenner Nancy | 2-27 |
| | | Jones Henry | 1-77 | Kenney John W. | 2-5 |
| Iiams John | 1-97 | Jones John | 1-5 | Kenney Louisiana | 1-59 |
| Ijams Basil C | 2-47 | 1-13,1-73,1-77,2-71 | | Kenney Maria E. | 2-5 |
| Iles Nancy | 1-85 | Jones John H. | | Kerley John | 1-21 |
| Iles Perry B | 1-85 | | 1-16,1-109 | Kerr | 1-59,R-13 |
| Ingram Ira | 1-3,1-77 | Jones Levi B. | 1-91 | Kerr Lacy | 1-19,1-31 |
| Ingram John | 1-59,1-87 | Jones Lewis B. | 2-77 | Kerr P.H. | 1-43 |
| Ingram Luke | 1-103 | Jones Mary | 1-73 | Keuass Chs. | 2-23 |
| Isaacs | 1-45,R-14 | Jones Milly | 1-107 | Kiggens Hamilton | 2-101 |
| Isaacs Harriet | 2-57 | Jones Myers F. | 1-13 | Kiggens Mary | 1-5 |
| Isaacs Thomas | 2-57 | Jones Phinneas | 1-71 | Kilgore Hugh | |
| Isaacs Wm | 1-65 | Jones Richard S. | 1-11 | | 1-55,2-101 |
| Ives Amasa | 1-59 | Jones Sarah | 1-91,2-77 | Killgore Joseph T | 2-99 |
| | | Jones Silas | 1-107 | Killen Levi | 1-73 |
| Jack Laura | 1-77 | Jones Simon | 2-29,2-79 | Kimball George | 1-77 |
| Jack Patrick C. | 1-95 | Jones Stephen | 1-65 | Kincade James | 2-45 |
| Jack S.H. | 2-13,2-17 | Jones Susannah | 1-65 | Kincade Jane | 2-45 |
| Jack Wm. H. | 1-77,1-85 | Jones Timothy | 2-21 | Kincaid | 1-51 |
| Jackson Elish | 1-49 | Jordan Margaret | 1-99 | Kincaid John | 1-77 |
| Jackson F.B. | 2-8 | Jurgens Conrad | 2-31 | King Grey B. | 1-38 |
| Jackson F.O. | 2-99 | Jurgens Heneike | 2-31 | King John G. | 1-67 |
| Jackson Francis W | 2-95 | | | King Pamelia | 1-67 |
| Jackson Isaac | | Kannon Agnes | 2-8 | King Susan S. | 1-38 |
| | 1-51,1-63 | Kannon William | 2-8 | Kinman Carey | 1-83 |
| Jackson Samantha | 1-51 | Karr Robert | 1-109 | King Samuel | 1-83 |
| Jackson T.R. | R-15 | Keass Steward | 2-23 | Kinnard Anthony D. Jr. | |
| Jackson Tilly | 1-63 | Kegans James | 1-7,1-55 | | 2-73 |
| James A.J. | 1-81 | Kegans Mary | 1-7 | Kinnard Michael | 2-45 |
| James Thomas | 2-71 | Kegans Nancy | 1-55 | Kinnard W.E. | 2-73 |
| Jamieson Isaac | 1-73 | Kelcey Elizabeth | 2-3 | Kinney Allen O. | 2-87 |
| Jamieson Margaret | 1-73 | Kelcey Leeman | 2-3 | Kinney Louisa Ann | R-9 |
| Jaques Adeline | 1-65 | Keller | 1-53 | Kinzy Peter | 2-49 |
| Jaques Benjn. F. | 1-65 | Keller Anne | 1-53 | Kinzy Sarah | 2-49 |
| Jaques Isaac | 2-85 | Keller Francis | 1-53 | Kirk Martha | 1-107 |
| Jaques Mary Ann | 2-85 | Keller Francis G. | 1-71 | Kleberg Louis | 2-103 |
| Jefferson J.R. | 1-79 | Keller John | 1-51 | Kleberg Robert | 2-69 |
| Jeffery Edward | 1-95 | Keller Levina | 1-71 | Klekamp John Birnham | |
| Jenkins | 1-14 | Kelly Nicholas | 2-95 | | 2-95 |
| Jenkins Barton | 2-9 | Kelso Alfred | 2-57 | Klonne Henry | 1-109 |
| Jennings GardingC | 2-15 | Kelso Martha | 2-57 | Kneass Chas. | 2-11 |
| Jennings Katherine | 2-15 | Kemp Caleb | 1-69 | Kneeland David | 1-75 |
| Jewell Benjamin | 1-107 | Kemp Charlotte | 2-53 | Kneeland Silence | 1-75 |
| Jinkins Edward | 1-55 | Kemp Jonathan | 2-53 | Knight & White | |
| Jinkins Sarah | 1-55 | Kendrick Burl | 2-61 | | 1-14,R-14 |
| Johnson | 1-85 | Kendrick Harvey | 2-61 | Knight Jane | 2-77 |

176

178

| | | |
|---|---|---|
| Martin John F. | 1-103 | Miller Simon |
| Martin Joshua W. | 1-89 | 1-7,1-27,1-49 |
| Martin Laurence | 1-67 | Miller Stephen | 2-77 |
| Martin Ramsey | R-8 | Miller William | 1-25 |
| Martin Robert | 1-83 | Millet Clementine 1-34 |
| Martin Toliver | 1-73 | Millet Samuel | 1-34 |
| Martin William S. | 1-103 | Millican Elliot M.1-69 |
| Martin Wyly | 1-16 | Millican Elizabeth |
| Martingly Philip | 2-99 | 1-69 |
| Mason J.W. | 1-107 | Millican Robert | 1-69 |
| Mason Malinda | 1-107 | Millican Wm. 2-81,2-85 |
| Mather Elisha | 1-101 | Mills Andrew G. | 1-23 |
| Mather Nancy | 1-101 | Mills R. | 2-17 |
| Matthews John | 1-95 | Mills Robert | 1-23 |
| Matthews Robert | 1-67 | Millsaps Isaac | 2-35 |
| Maverick Saml. A. | 2-43 | Millsaps Mary | 2-35 |
| Mayes Betty | 1-85 | Minser | 1-77 |
| Mayes Francis S. | 1-85 | Mitchell Jn. W. | 1-51 |
| Mayes Wm. D. | 1-75 | Moffitt N.C. | 2-67 |
| Mayo Jn. W. | 1-69 | Money John H. | 1-87 |
| Mays Thos. H. | 1-81 | Monroe Daniel | 1-87 |
| Medford Elizabeth 1-34 | | Monroe Sally | 1-87 |
| Medford Wm 1-34,2-55 | | Montgomery Andw. | 1-83 |
| Medley | 1-41 | Montgomery Wm. | 1-89 |
| Menefee George | 2-45 | Moore A.G. | 2-23 |
| Menefee John S. | 2-45 | Moore Armstead | 1-1 |
| Mercer Eli | 1-59 | Moore Cathrine | 1-91 |
| Mercer Elijah | 2-79 | Moore Davis | 2-25 |
| Mercer Levi | 2-79 | Moore Elisha |
| Mercer Nancy | 1-59 | 1-7,1-9,1-61 |
| Mercer Reason | 2-79 | Moore Francis | 1-59 |
| Merrill G. | 2-29 | Moore J.H. | 1-69 |
| Merry John | 1-42 | Moore James 1-45,2-71 |
| Merry Marrill | 1-42 | Moore James Walker1-85 |
| Messer Chs. | 2-53 | Moore Jane | 1-61 |
| Messoner Francis | 2-9 | Moore John 1-42,1-77 |
| Metcalf Alfred | 1-79 | Moore Jn. H. 1-14,1-31 |
| Micals Eli | R-10 | Moore John L. | 1-42 |
| Micoless Miguel | 1-61 | Moore Joh. S.1-91,2-81 |
| Milburn Allen T. | 1-87 | Moore John W. | 1-45 |
| Miles James | 1-89 | Moore Louis C. | 1-67 |
| Miles Sarah | 1-89 | Moore Luke 1-91,2-57 |
| Miliken George | 1-7 | Moore Martha | 2-25 |
| Miller 1-9,1-43 | | Moore Matilda | 1-85 |
| Miller Andrew | | Moore Nancy | 1-65 |
| 1-47,2-55 | | Moore Nathaniel | 1-103 |
| Miller Celia | 1-47 | Moore Olive | 1-45 |
| Miller Christopher2-95 | | Moore Rebecca | 1-103 |
| Miller Edmund | 1-49 | Moore Robert D. | 1-91 |
| Miller Hannah | 1-55 | Moore Sarah | 1-59 |
| Miller James B. | 1-43 | Moore Thomas | 1-65 |
| Miller Joseph | 1-55 | Moore William | 1-3 |
| Miller Lucinda | 1-49 | Morgan Celia | 1-85 |
| Miller Monte | 1-73 | Morgan James | 1-85 |

| | |
|---|---|
| Morris Catherine | 1-77 |
| Morris J.D. | 1-55,1-67 |
| Morris John | 1-81 |
| Morris Jonathan D. | 1-9 |
| Morris Nancy | 1-81 |
| Morris Richard | 1-77 |
| Morris Robert C. | 2-85 |
| Morris Wm. | 1-32 |
| Morse Eliza | 1-71 |
| Morse Henry | 1-71 |
| Morton | 1-49 |
| Morton Alexr. H. |
| 1-13,1-75 |
| Morton David S. | 2-91 |
| Morton Elanor | 1-75 |
| Morton Mary | 2-91 |
| Morton W.P. | 2-41 |
| Moseley | 1-103 |
| Mosely R.J. | 2-49 |
| Mosely Robert J. |
| 1-71,2-37 |
| Mosely S.J. | 1-71 |
| Mosely Susan Ann | 2-37 |
| Mosher Adam | 2-87 |
| Moss Matthew | 1-67 |
| Mouser | 1-93 |
| Mullins Braxton | 1-105 |
| Mullins Walter E. | 1-63 |
| Munson Anne B. | 1-43 |
| Munson Henry W. | 1-43 |
| Munson William |
| 1-7,1-9,1-43,1-63 |
| Murphee Wm. | 1-59 |
| Murphy James | 1-97 |
| Murphy Wm. | R-13 |
| Murray Rice F. | 1-45 |
| Muslim | 1-63 |
| Myrick E.P. | 1-51 |
| Myrick Niema | 1-51 |
| Nalls Robert | 1-1,1-9 |
| Nash C.M. | 2-6 |
| Nash David R. | 2-6 |
| Nash Francis M. | 2-39 |
| Nash Martha | 2-39 |
| Neal Lewis | 2-51 |
| Neill Harriet | 1-101 |
| Neill James C. | 1-101 |
| Nelson | 2-35 |
| Nelson Joshua | 1-73 |
| New William | 1-59 |
| Newall John D. | 1-105 |
| Newland John Alx. | 2-51 |
| Newman Jonathan | 1-49 |

| | | | | | | |
|---|---|---|---|---|---|---|
| Newman Polley | 1-49 | Palms John | 2-81,2-85 | Perry Ann | 2-79 |
| Newman Wm. | 2-81 | Panky | 1-57 | Perry Burrel | 1-83 |
| Nicholls Fanny | 1-109 | Panky Widow | 1-14 | Perry Daniel | |
| Nicholls John | 1-109 | Panky James | 2-31,2-49 | | 1-87,2-33,R-9 |
| Nicholson Mary Anne | | Panky Mary | 2-31 | Perry Eliza | 1-87 |
| | 1-73 | Panky Mary Ann | 1-49 | Perry Elizabeth | |
| Nicholson Peter | 1-7 | Park George S. | 2-101 | | 1-87,2-49 |
| Nicholson Roderick | | Parke | 1-79 | Perry Emily M. | 1-75 |
| | 1-13,1-73 | Parkenson Joseph | 2-77 | Perry James | 1-87 |
| Niebling Fred. | R-16 | Parker | 1-79 | Perry James F. | 1-75 |
| Nixon Fanny | 1-107 | Parker Aaron | 1-5 | Perry Jane | 1-83 |
| Nixon Geo. W. | R-9 | Parker Danl | 1-38,2-23 | Perry Lawrence W. | 2-33 |
| Nixon Jorge A. | 2-83 | Parker Henrietta | | Perry Wm. M. | 2-79 |
| Noble Fanny | 1-47 | | 1-41,2-27 | Peske John | 2-63 |
| Noble John W. | 1-47 | Parker Henry | 1-41,2-27 | Peters Lewis H. | 2-103 |
| Noland Eli | 2-43 | Parker John | 1-5 | Peterson James | 1-33 |
| Northington A. | 2-57 | Parker Joseph A. | 2-25 | Peterson John | 1-43 |
| Northington Andw. | 1-22 | Parker Patsey | 1-38 | Pettus Col. | 2-9 |
| Northington Andw. Jr. | | Parker Sarah | 1-51 | Pettus O. | 2-9 |
| | 2-57 | Parker Wiley | 1-99 | Pettus Patsey | 1-28 |
| Northington Eliza | 2-57 | Parks William | 1-109 | Pettus Samuel | 1-28 |
| Norton Allen | 1-40 | | | Petty George | 2-97 |
| Norton James | 1-73 | Parrott T.F.L. | 1-25 | Pevehouse Cinthia | 2-69 |
| Nowlan Daniel | 2-61 | Partin John | 1-45 | Pevehouse David | 2-69 |
| Nowlin James | 2-87 | Partin Nancy | 1-45 | Pevehouse Preston | 2-69 |
| | | Patching Tallcut | 2-43 | Pevehouse James | |
| OBrian Christopher | 2-89 | Pate John | 1-5 | | 1-51,R-11 |
| OConnor J.S. | 1-95 | Paterson Nancy | 2-2 | Pevehouse Mary | 1-51 |
| OConnor James | 2-47 | Paterson Neales | 2-2 | Pharr Samuel | 1-53 |
| OConnor Mary Frances | | Patino Anselms | 2-2 | Phelan John P. | 2-1 |
| | 1-95 | Patino Maria Catarina | | Phelps Dr. | 1-81 |
| OFarrel James | 1-20 | | 2-2 | Phelps Mrs. | 2-43 |
| OFlaherty James | 1-91 | Patrick George M. | | Phelps Abner | 1-93 |
| Odom Alexander | 1-14 | | 1-85,2-4 | Phelps T.A.L. | 1-77 |
| Oetkins Johann | 2-33 | Patton Robert | 1-1 | Philbrick Norris | 2-13 |
| Ogiest William | R-1 | Payton | 1-65 | Philips Abrham | 1-3 |
| Ormsbee Samuel B. | 1-67 | Peak Mrs. | 2-71 | Phillips James R. | |
| Osborn | 1-45 | Peak Eliza | 2-69 | | 1-15,1-69 |
| Osborn Benjamin | | Peaks | 2-55 | Phillips Sidney | 2-101 |
| | 1-3,1-51 | Peaks Eliza | 2-55 | Phillipson Jacob | 1-23 |
| Osborne Thos. | 2-47 | Pease Caroline | 2-81 | Phinney A.L. | 2-51 |
| Outlaw Z.B. | 2-101 | Pease E.M. | 2-29,2-91 | Phinney Andrew L. | 1-79 |
| Overton Mr. | R-12 | Pease L.T. | 2-29 | Pickens Elizab. | |
| Overton G. | 2-29 | Pease Lyman | 2-81 | | 1-36,1-103 |
| Overton Greenberry | R-13 | Pease S.M. | 2-29 | Pickens John H. | |
| Owen Christiana | 1-75 | Pebles Pamelia | 1-43 | | 1-36,1-103 |
| Owen John | 1-75 | Pebles Robert | 1-43 | Pieper Peter | 2-27 |
| Owens Mary | 1-63 | Peck Abraham | 1-81 | Pierce Demis Maria | 1-67 |
| | | Peebles Dr. | 2-21 | Pilgrim Thomas J. | 1-45 |
| Pace heirs | 1-77 | Peebles S.W. | 1-79 | Piper P. | 2-9 |
| Pace Wesley | 2-59 | Pendleton | R-13 | Pitts Obadiah | 1-91 |
| Page Benj. | 2-49 | Pepin V. | 1-77 | Pitts Polly | 1-91 |
| Page Lydia | 2-49 | Perkins Leonora | 1-63 | Ploger Ottilie | 2-4 |
| Paine Epps D. | 2-71 | Perkins Willi | 1-63 | Poe Geo. W. | 2-59 |

180

Polk Sally 1-97
Polk Thomas 1-97
Polke William P. 2-69
Pollard Amos 2-15
Ponton 1-38,2-71
Ponton Isabella 1-36
Ponton William 1-36
Pool B.B. 1-83
Pool Sarah 1-83
Porter B.A. 1-81
Porter Thomas K. 1-3
Powell Madam 2-3
Powell Anne 2-47
Powell Dorcas 2-41
Powell Elizabeth
1-47,2-95
Powell J.A. 2-95
Powell James 2-99
Powell John 2-41
Powell Joseph 1-97
Powell Thos. 1-57
Powell William 2-95
Powels Thos. 2-99
Prather Stephen 2-59
Prentiss Henry S. 1-40
Prest Jas. 2-11
Prest Jas. A. 2-11

Preusch Wm. G. 2-89
Price 1-63
Price James 1-99
Price Margaret 1-99
Price William 1-97
Pride William 1-12
Procter F. Junr 2-89
Pryor Thomas Jeff 1-49
Pugh Susan 1-107
Pugh Spencer A. 1-107

Queros Melena 2-65
Queros Pedro 2-65
Quinn John 2-1

Rabb John G. R-13
Ragsdale Jas. C. 2-49
Ragsdale John D. 2-99
Ragsdale Rebecca 2-49
Raleigh William 1-16
Randon David 1-16
Raney 1-42
Rankin 1-89
Rankin James 1-75
Rankin Sarah 1-73
Rankin William 1-75

Rankin Wm. M. 1-73
Ratcliff 1-18
Ray Andrew 1-97
Ray John R. 1-9
Ray Margaret 1-55
Ray Robert
1-55,1-69,2-93
Raysden De La F. 1-95
Raysden Nancy Adeline
1-95
Reams S.Y. 2-65
Reavell Nancy 2-69
Rector Amelia 1-101
Rector Claiborne 1-101
Rector Harriet 1-95
Rector Jos 1-12,1-95
Rector Morgan 1-101
Rector Pendleton 1-101
Redman John 2-49
Reed Jacob 1-97
Reed Martha 1-99
Reed Matilda 1-97
Reed Thomas J. 1-99
Reeder Mrs. 2-93
Reeder Benjn. C. 1-67
Reeder Mary 1-67,2-35
Rees John 2-87
Rees Joseph 1-65
Rees Margaret 1-65
Reese Charles K. 1-83
Reel 1-75
Reels Patrick 1-25
Reels R.J.W. 2-81
Reinerman J.G. 2-13
Reynolds A.C. 1-93
Reynolds Albert G.1-16
Reynolds Elizabeth
1-16
Reynolds Eliz. Ann
2-35
Reynolds Fabricius2-35
Reynolds George
1-7,2-103
Reynolds Harriet 1-93
Rice Alpheus 2-19
Richards Esteban 1-79
Richards Jesse
2-45,2-63
Richardson D.S.
2-37,2-41
Richardson G.F.
1-85,R-15
Richardson Sarah Ann
2-41

Rickhow Samuel J.2-103
Riddle Jos. P. 2-89
Rigby Benjamin 1-65
Rigby Catherine 1-65
Riggs Pleasant B. 1-85
Rion James 1-83
Rios Antonio 2-61
Rittrey Joseph 2-4
Robbins Cynthia 1-31
Robbins George 1-31
Roberts 2-17,2-37
Roberts Abraham 1-43
Roberts Andrew 1-53
Roberts Elisha
1-47,1-71,R-9,R-10
Roberts Elizabeth 2-43
Roberts Josiah 2-97
Roberts N. 2-99
Roberts N.F. 2-97
Roberts Patsey 1-47
Roberts William
2-43,2-97
Robertson J.E. 1-39
Robertson Jas. 2-5
Robinson 2-45
Robinson A. 1-47
Robinson Andw Jr. 1-63
Robinson Francis 1-28
Robinson J.E.
2-31,2-33,R-14
Robinson James 2-45
Robinson Jeremiah 1-69
Robinson John G.
1-28,2-93
Robinson John R.B.2-93
Robinson Martha 2-75
Robinson Mary 1-63
Robinson T.J. 2-73
Robinson Tuba 2-45
Robinson William
1-43,1-81
Robinson Zoraster 2-75
Roddy Ephraim 1-99
Roddy Hall
1-42,2-55,2-73
Roddy Harriet 1-99
Roeder Albrecht von
2-103
Roeder Anton L.S. von
2-103
Roeder Louis von 2-4
Roeder Otto von 2-103
Roeder Rosalie v. 2-69
Rodrigues Gertrudes1-1

| | | | | | | |
|---|---|---|---|---|---|---|
| Rogan Bernard | 1-19 | Sartuche Ignasia | 2-17 | Shannon Margart | 1-93 |
| Rogers | 1-89 | Saul Melissa M. | 1-51 | Shannon Owen | 1-93 |
| Rogers James | 1-95,2-93 | Saul Thos. S. | 1-51 | Sharp John | 2-101 |
| Rogers Joseph | 1-97 | Savage Emiline | 1-67 | Shaw John | 1-67 |
| Rogers Mary | 1-97 | Savage Mary | 1-67 | Shaw Polly | 1-67 |
| Rogers Nancy | 1-97 | Sawyer Mrs. | 2-67 | Shelby Jenkins | 1-1 |
| Rogers Rachael | 1-95 | Sawyer Elizabeth | 1-101 | Shelly | 1-81 |
| Rogers Raleigh | 1-95 | Sawyer John A. | 2-83 | Shepherd Elisa | 1-91 |
| Rogers Polly Anne | 1-95 | Sawyer Samuel | 1-101 | Shepherd Wm. | 1-91 |
| Rogers Samuel | 1-12 | Sayers John | 2-93 | Shinnault Walter | 1-24 |
| Rogers Samuel C.A. | 1-97 | Sayers Robert | 2-93 | Shipler Isaac B. | 2-97 |
| Rose Margart | 2-65 | Sayre Cathrine | 1-91 | Shipman D. | 2-91 |
| Rose Pleasant W. | 2-65 | Sayre Charles D. | 1-91 | Shipman Edw. | 1-75 |
| Ross James | 1-41 | Scanlon Michael | 1-81 | Shipman J. | 2-91 |
| Ross Richard | 2-89 | Schneider Bernhard H | | Shipman John M. | 2-13 |
| Rosseau | 1-21 | | 2-95 | Shreave John M. | 2-59 |
| Rosseau Moses | 1-53 | Schrier James | 1-61 | Shuff Washington T. | |
| Roulhac Wm. G. | 2-19 | Schrier Sarah | 1-61 | | 2-101 |
| Routh James | 1-107 | Schutte John A. | 1-91 | Shup Samuel | 1-5 |
| Rowland Frances W. | 1-26 | Scott | 1-10 | Silcriggs David | 2-81 |
| Rowland John G. | 1-26 | Scott Betsey | 1-97 | Silsbee Albert | 1-89 |
| Royall Anne | 1-51 | Scott James | 2-63 | Simmons Frances | 1-91 |
| Royall R.R. | 1-15 | Scott James W. | 1-97 | Simms Bartlett | 2-37 |
| Royall Richard R. | | Scott John | 2-99 | Simpson | R-2 |
| | 1-12,1-51 | Scott John H. | 1-81 | Simpson Pamela | 2-29 |
| Royster James M. | 1-95 | Scott Joseph | 1-97 | Simpson Wm. | 2-29 |
| Royster Sarah | 1-95 | Scott Joseph E. | 1-97 | Singleton | 1-59,1-63 |
| Ruble Fielding | 1-41 | Scott Lucy | 1-97 | Singleton Jefferson | |
| Ruble Francis | 1-41 | Scott Noah | 2-27 | | 1-61 |
| Rumpfeld Solomon | 2-17 | Scott Henry | 1-45 | Singleton Spyars | 2-71 |
| Russell Hiram | 2-89 | Scott Patrick | 1-43 | Singleton Wesley | 1-61 |
| Russell Luisiana | 1-61 | Scott Patsey | 1-45,1-97 | Skerrett William H. | 1-5 |
| Russell Reuben R. | 1-61 | Scott Phebe | 2-27 | Skinner James H. | 1-75 |
| Russell Wm. J. | 1-67 | Scott W.W. | 2-57 | Sleight Cornelius A. | |
| Ryan James | 1-35,2-103 | Scott William | | | 2-101 |
| | | | 1-107,2-71 | Sleight John L. | 2-55 |
| Sage Charles | 2-95 | Seale W. | 2-17 | Small James | 1-45 |
| Salinas Pedro | 2-2 | Seargent Jane Maria | | Smaley Abner | 1-5 |
| Sandefur Elisab | 1-61 | | 1-95 | Smaley Andrew | 1-5 |
| Sandefur M. | 1-61 | Seargent Jasper | 1-95 | Smaley Elizabeth | 1-5 |
| Sanders | 2-21 | Selkriggs David | 1-49 | Smaley John | 1-5 |
| Sanders Franklin | 2-35 | Sellers Robt. | 2-99 | Smaley Nancy | 1-5 |
| Sanders William | 1-39 | Sellers Robt. Jr. | 2-99 | Smaley Susana | 1-5 |
| Sandoval Jose | 1-1 | Sewall William H. | 1-5 | Smelser Abraham | 1-7 |
| San Pier Widow | R-15 | Sexton William | 1-73 | Smetser | 1-7 |
| San Pierre J. | 1-87 | Seymore James | 2-4,2-85 | Smith | 1-15,2-17 |
| San Pierre Joseph | 1-15 | Seymore Jane | 2-85 | Smith Adam | 1-28 |
| San Pierre Margaret | | Shackleford Mr. | R-12 | Smith Alona | 1-109 |
| | 1-87 | Shadoin Mahely | 2-47 | Smith Charles H. | 1-30 |
| Santi Augustin | 2-101 | Shadoin Thomas | 2-47 | Smith Charles S. | 2-75 |
| Santy Elizabeth | 2-79 | Shannon Cathrene | 1-101 | Smith Christian Jr | 1-9 |
| Sap John | 2-33 | Shannon Charlotte | 1-93 | Smith Daniel | 1-109 |
| Sargant Charles | 2-89 | Shannon Jacob | 1-101 | Smith Darkay | 1-47 |
| Sarton | 1-16 | Shannon John | 1-93 | Smith Elizabeth | |
| 182 | | | | | 1-77,1-79 |

| | | |
|---|---|---|
| Smith Henry | Springer A.E. 2-77 | Stiff Thos. R. 2-89 |
| 1-79 | Springer Elizab. | Stiffler Mairad 2-3 |
| Smith Henry S. 2-89 | 1-32,2-77 | Stockwell Elizab. 2-15 |
| Smith James 1-75 | Springer Erises 1-32 | Stockwell Jesse |
| Smith James N. | Springer Ezekiel 1-32 | 2-15,2-101 |
| 1-12,1-47 | Springer J.M. 2-7 | Stoddard 2-45 |
| Smith John | Springer John 1-32 | Stoddard David 1-77 |
| 1-77,1-83,2-27,2-101 | Springer John M. 2-77 | Stone Reuben P.F. 1-29 |
| Smith Joseph 1-99,2-35 | Squires Josiah 1-7 | Strickland Ira 1-81 |
| Smith Loretta 2-27 | Stack Florence 1-43 | Stringer Edward N.2-89 |
| Smith Margaret | Stafford Adam 1-57 | Stringer H.B. 1-83 |
| 1-93,2-59 | Stafford Elizab. 1-69 | Strodman A.A. 2-13 |
| Smith Mary 1-12,1-75 | Stafford Leroy 1-69 | Stubbins John O. 2-77 |
| Smith Missouri 2-79 | Standback Martha 2-91 | Stuart James 1-73 |
| Smith Narcissa 2-75 | Standeford Elizabeth | Stuart Zillah Anne1-73 |
| Smith Nelson 1-47,1-61 | 1-83 | Sullivan Dennis 1-69 |
| Smith Phinneas | Standeford James | Sullivan Eunice 1-71 |
| 1-29,1-87,2-65 | 1-83,R-11 | Sullivan John 1-71 |
| Smith Phinneas M. 1-29 | Standeford Sarah 1-83 | Sutherland 1-73 |
| Smith Richard | Stanford Alexander J. | Sutherland Frances1-47 |
| 1-93,2-59 | 1-101 | Sutherland George 1-12 |
| Smith S. 1-41 | Stanley Betsey 1-85 | 1-14,1-47,2-45,2-91 |
| Smith Sarah 1-77,2-59 | Stanley Willis 1-85 | Sutherland John |
| Smith Sarah Anne 1-47 | Stephen Jas. 2-43 | 1-12,2-91 |
| Smith Sophia 1-87 | Stephen Jas. R. 2-67 | Sutherland Susan 1-71 |
| Smith Susan Anne 1-30 | Stephen John M. Jr. | Sutherland Wm |
| Smith William 1-77 | 2-43 | 1-71,2-45 |
| Smith William J. 2-79 | Stephens 1-51 | Sutton Jesse 2-41,2-47 |
| Smith Wm. P. 2-59 | Stephens George 2-89 | Swearingen Elemeleck |
| Smith Wyly B.D. | Stephens Jacob 1-5 | 1-114 |
| 1-81,2-27 | Stephens James 1-51 | Swearingen Saml. 2-63 |
| Smither L. 1-77 | Stephens Mary 1-51 | Sweney S.W. 2-93 |
| Smithers Wm. 2-97 | Stephenson Amelia 1-43 | Swenny Wm. 2-99 |
| Smithwick Noah 1-77 | Stephenson Dimanes1-83 | |
| Snell Martin K. 2-89 | Stephenson James | Talbott John 1-21 |
| Snyder S. 2-93 | 1-5,1-43,1-83 | Talbott Susanna 1-21 |
| Solis Caliste de J. | Stephenson Thomas 2-79 | Tannehill 1-103 |
| 1-59 | Sterne Adolphus 2-2 | Tannehill J.C. 1-77 |
| Southmayd D.S. 2-9 | Sterne Maria Rosa 2-2 | Tannehill Jane 1-77 |
| Southmayd Joana 2-9 | Steritt 1-27 | Tanner Henry 2-49 |
| Sothers Thos. 2-17 | Sterrett A.B. 1-16 | Tarrant Edwd. H. 1-3 |
| Sparks Betsey 2-65 | Stevens 1-99 | Tate James 1-5 |
| Sparks Matthew | Stevens Ashley B. 1-89 | Taylor 1-49 |
| 2-29,2-65 | Stevens Jacob 1-7,1-51 | Taylor A.C. 1-105 |
| Sparks Sarah 1-37 | Stevens John R. 2-67 | Taylor Anna Maria 2-2 |
| Sparks William C. 1-37 | Stevens Mary 1-29 | Taylor Charles S. 2-2 |
| Spears 1-10,1-16 | Stevens Miles G. 1-29 | Taylor Christiana 2-71 |
| Spears Robt. 1-81 | Stevens Nancy 1-51 | Taylor James 1-107 |
| Speir Abner B. 2-15 | Stevens Sophia 1-89 | Taylor James W. 1-89 |
| Speir Betsey Ann 2-15 | Stevens Narcissa 1-33 | Taylor John 2-71 |
| Speir George W. 2-99 | Stevens Robert 1-33 | Taylor John B. |
| Spence William 1-69 | Stevenson Narcissa1-33 | 1-59,2-91 |
| Splane Peyton R. | Stevenson Robert 1-33 | Taylor John D. 1-15 |
| 1-9,1-49 | Stewart C.B. | Taylor John S. 2-71 |
| Splane Sallie 1-9 | 1-83,2-69,2-81 | Taylor Levi 1-89 |

183

| | | |
|---|---|---|
| Taylor Mary | 1-59 | |
| Taylor Rachael | 1-107 | |
| Taylor Robert Jr. | 1-85 | |
| Taylor Sarah H. | 1-99 | |
| Taylor Thomas | 1-99 | |
| Taylor Wm. H. | 1-71 | |
| Tenan Caleb | 2-55 | |
| Tennel Judge | 1-93 | |
| Tennell George | 1-79 | |
| Tennell Sally | 1-79 | |
| Tennille M.H. | 1-107 | |
| Thomas | 1-63 | |
| Thomas Jacob | 2-57 | |
| Thomas James | 2-71 | |
| Thomas John | 1-24,1-32 | |
| Thomas Nancy | 2-57 | |
| Thomas Phoebe | 1-32 | |
| Thompson | 1-14 | |
| Thompson Alexander | | |
| | 1-61,2-3,2-75 | |
| Thompson Asena | 1-61 | |
| Thompson Isham | 2-21 | |
| Thompson James | 1-7,1-49 | |
| Thompson John | 1-9 | |
| Thompson John A. | | |
| | 1-19,1-107 | |
| Thompson Joseph | | |
| | 1-30,2-33,2-85 | |
| Thompson Martha | 2-33 | |
| Thompson Nancy | 1-30 | |
| Thompson Sceney | 2-75 | |
| Thompson Thomas | 1-63 | |
| Thompson W.W.W. | 1-107 | |
| Thompson Wm. | R-11 | |
| Thonke Chs Ed | 1-101 | |
| Thorp Henry | 1-13 | |
| Tierwester | 1-91 | |
| Tierwester Henry | 1-67 | |
| Tinnin Caleb | 2-55 | |
| Tinsley J.J. | 1-91 | |
| Tobar Juan | 1-1 | |
| Tobar Teresa | 1-1 | |
| Tobin | 1-53 | |
| Tongate Meredith | 2-35 | |
| Toulson Thomas | 1-21 | |
| Townsend Gideon | 2-19 | |
| Townsend John | 1-91 | |
| Townsend Maria | 1-79 | |
| Townsend Nathl. | 1-79 | |
| Townsend Wm S. | 1-91 | |
| Toy Elizabeth | 2-57 | |
| Toy Wm. H. | 2-57,R-13 | |
| Trammell Burk | 1-103 | |
| Trammell James | 1-63 | |

| | | |
|---|---|---|
| Travis B. | 2-41 | |
| Travis William B. | 1-97 | |
| Treat Chauncey | 1-63 | |
| Treat Mary | 1-63 | |
| Trevino Antonio | 2-95 | |
| Truit Elizabeth | 1-99 | |
| Truit William | 1-99 | |
| Tumlinson John | 1-99 | |
| Tumlinson Laura | 1-99 | |
| Turner Amacy | 2-37 | |
| Turner Julia M. | 2-37 | |
| Turner Winslow | | |
| | 1-7,1-10 | |
| Tuttle James | 2-39 | |
| Tuttle James W. | 2-71 | |
| Tyler John | 2-69 | |
| Tyler Sally | 2-69 | |
| Tyley Jas. | 2-29 | |
| Tyley Matilda | 2-29 | |
| | | |
| Underwood Ammon | 2-17 | |
| Urban Joseph | 1-107 | |
| | | |
| Vaden | R-3 | |
| Vander Camp heirs | 2-31 | |
| Van d Hoya Anton | 2-91 | |
| Van der Hoya Franz | 2-4 | |
| Vanderwier Anne | 1-67 | |
| Vanderwier Cornelius | | |
| | 1-67 | |
| Vandorn Isaac | 1-5 | |
| Vanphebber J. | 2-101 | |
| Vanphebber S. | 2-101 | |
| Varrelman Catr. Henr. | | |
| | 2-2 | |
| Varrelman Joh.D.G. | | |
| | 2-2,2-81 | |
| Veeder Lewis L. | 1-67 | |
| Vernon Alexander | 2-43 | |
| Vernon Ann | 2-43 | |
| Vess Jonathan | 1-53 | |
| Vince A. | 2-3 | |
| Vince John T. | 1-87 | |
| Vince Susan | 1-83 | |
| Vince W. | 2-73 | |
| Von Dervert | 2-63 | |
| Von Roeder Albrecht | | |
| | 2-103 | |
| Von Roeder Anton L.S. | | |
| | 2-103 | |
| Von Roeder Louis | 2-4 | |
| Von Roeder Otto | 2-103 | |
| Von Roeder Rosalie | 2-69 | |
| Voss George | 2-89 | |

| | | |
|---|---|---|
| Votaw Elijah | 2-55 | |
| Votaw Francis | 2-55 | |
| Votaw Isaac | 2-23 | |
| Votaw John | 2-23 | |
| Votaw Liza | 2-23 | |
| | | |
| Wade David | 2-33,2-85 | |
| Wade John H. | 1-109 | |
| Wade Nancy | 2-33 | |
| Waldin Ann | 2-11 | |
| Waldrop Claiborne | 1-7 | |
| Waldrop Hezeka. | 1-7 | |
| Waldrop Wiley | 1-7 | |
| Walker | 1-63,1-75 | |
| Walker Gideon | | |
| | 2-19,2-101 | |
| Walker Hartwell | 2-89 | |
| Walker Henry T. | 1-79 | |
| Walker Jacob | 1-97 | |
| Walker James | 2-79 | |
| Walker John M. | 2-103 | |
| Walker Mary | 1-97,2-39 | |
| Walker Prudence | 1-79 | |
| Walker Sanders | 2-103 | |
| Walker Saran Anne | 1-97 | |
| Walker Tandy | 1-97 | |
| Walker William | 2-39 | |
| Wallace Eliza T. | 2-8 | |
| Wallace Gleason | 2-19 | |
| Wallace J.W.E. | 1-85 | |
| Wallace James | 1-49 | |
| Wallace John S. | 1-3 | |
| Wallace John P. | 1-3 | |
| Wallace John Y. | 2-8,R-8 | |
| Wallace Patsey | 1-49 | |
| Waller Edwin | 1-95 | |
| Waller Julieta M. | 1-95 | |
| Walters Gerdraut | 2-33 | |
| Walters Jacob | 2-33 | |
| Walters John B. | 1-59 | |
| Wamack Abram M. | 2-77 | |
| Wamack Elizabeth | 2-77 | |
| Ward Packson | 2-33 | |
| Ward Russel | 2-67 | |
| Ward Thos. Wm. | | |
| | 2-89,2-97 | |
| Ward Wm. | 2-31,R-14 | |
| Warner | 2-99 | |
| Warren David | 2-93 | |
| Warren John A. | 1-5 | |
| Waters William | 1-97 | |
| Watts Samuel B. | 1-107 | |
| Weatherby Alvan | 1-29 | |
| Webb Green | 2-25 | |

| | | |
|---|---|---|
| Webb Isam G. | 2-53 | Whiteside Elizabeth |
| Webb Sarah | 2-53 | 1-49 |
| Webber | 1-53,1-103 | Whiteside John 1-49 |
| Webber J.F. | R-13 | Whiteside John F. 1-34 |
| Webber John T. | 1-59 | Whiteside John J. R-8 |
| Weightman | 1-89 | Whittington Rosa 2-19 |
| Welch Henry J. | R-10 | Whittington Thos. M. |
| Wells | 2-21 | 2-19,2-93 |
| Wells Fleming T. | 2-103 | Wickson A. 2-103 |
| Wells Francis F. | 1-3 | Wickson Asa 1-61 |
| Wells James | 2-65 | Wickson B. 1-61,1-73 |
| Wells Martin | 1-59 | Wickson Barnabas 1-59 |
| Wells Sarah | 1-59 | Wickson Hutrah 1-59 |
| Welsh Gross | 1-71 | Wightman 1-77 |
| Wertzner Christian | 2-1 | Wightman Margaret |
| West James | 2-89 | 1-63,2-6 |
| Western T.G. | 1-29 | Wilbarger1-9,1-51,1-77 |
| Wharton John | 1-109 | Wilbarger Josiah 1-55 |
| Whatley Mahala | 2-15 | Wilbarger Margarette |
| Whatley S.T. | 2-15 | 1-55 |
| Wheaton Elizabeth | 1-87 | Wilhelm Richard 1-27 |
| Wheaton Joel | 1-87 | Wilhelm Sarah 1-27 |
| Wheeler Elisha | 1-38 | Wilkinson Amanda 1-35 |
| Whetherly Alfred | R-11 | Wilkinson James 1-35 |
| Whitaker Nancy | 1-71 | Wilkinson Leroy 2-47 |
| Whitaker Will | 1-71 | Willard Wm. C. 2-61 |
| White Mrs. | R-13 | Williams 1-57 |
| White Amy | 2-71 | Williams Absalom 2-97 |
| White Anne | 1-81 | Williams Augustus1-103 |
| White Archibald S. | 1-73 | Williams C. 1-65 |
| White Benjamin | 1-12 | Williams Geo. 2-51 |
| White Benjamin J. | 1-101 | Williams Job 1-45 |
| White Bethia | 1-91 | Williams John |
| White D. | 2-101 | 1-10,1-16,1-45 |
| White Dudley J. | 1-91 | Williams J.R. 1-79 |
| White E. | 2-9 | Williams John R. 1-28 |
| White Francis | 2-45 | Williams Joshua 2-43 |
| White James | 1-65 | Williams Levina 2-53 |
| White Jesse | 1-12,1-47 | Williams Love 1-103 |
| White Jno. | 1-71 | Williams N.B. 2-53 |
| White Margaret | 1-73 | Williams Nancy 1-45 |
| White Mary | 1-47 | Williams Rebecca 1-45 |
| White Nancy | 1-61 | Williams Samuel 1-116 |
| White Peter | 1-61 | Williams Sarah 2-93 |
| White Polly | 1-101 | Williams Thos. J. |
| White Rosa | 2-45 | 1-53,2-53 |
| White Saml. A. | R-1 | Williamson 1-79 |
| White W.B. | 1-57 | Williamson John W. |
| Whitehead | R-14 | 1-3,2-73 |
| Whitehead Edward P. | | Williamson Mary T.1-79 |
| | 2-53 | Williamson Robt. M. |
| Whitehead Nichs. | 1-61 | 1-45 |
| Whitehead Sidney | 1-87 | Williamson Wm 1-79 |
| Whitesides heirs | 2-97 | Williston Abraham 2-63 |

| | |
|---|---|
| Wilmans David | 2-27 |
| Wilson Charles | 1-97 |
| Wilson Elizabeth | 2-1 |
| Wilson George B. | 2-1 |
| Wilson Jane | 1-81 |
| Wilson Jesse | 1-81 |
| Wilson Robt. | 1-65,2-4 |
| Wilson Wm. K. | 1-61 |
| Winburn McHenry | |
| | 2-17,R-13 |
| Wingfield heirs | 2-67 |
| Wingfield Henry | |
| | 2-23,1-81 |
| Winn Elizabeth | 1-28 |
| Winn James | 1-28 |
| Winn Walter | 2-99 |
| Winston | 1-45 |
| Winston Anthony | |
| | 1-11,1-45 |
| Winston Edwd. | 1-18 |
| Winston Eliza C. | 1-95 |
| Winston Isaac | 1-11 |
| Winston Joel W. | 1-11 |
| Winston Milton | 1-11 |
| Winston Sally Anne1-45 | |
| Winston Thomas | 1-95 |
| Winston William | 1-11 |
| Winston William O.1-11 | |
| Winter Thacker | 1-12 |
| Witt Hughes | 1-73 |
| Wodwort Jonathan | 1-85 |
| Wolters | R-12 |
| Wood Alonzo | 2-9 |
| Wood John | 2-89 |
| Wood John L. | 2-79 |
| Wood M. | 2-97 |
| Wood Mandred | |
| | 1-105,2-89,2-103 |
| Wood Martha | 1-34 |
| Wood Reuben D. | 1-34 |
| Wood Samuel | 1-35 |
| Wood Sarah | 2-9 |
| Wood Tolbert | 2-101 |
| Woodruff | 1-27 |
| Woodruff John | 1-105 |
| Woodruff Rhody | 1-105 |
| Woods Gonsolvo D.S. | |
| | 2-31 |
| Woods Isabella | 1-55 |
| Woods John | 2-37 |
| Woods Leander | 1-53 |
| Woods Montreville | |
| | 1-5,1-9,1-55 |

185

| | | | | | |
|---|---|---|---|---|---|
| Woods Norman | | Wright J. | 2-91 | York John | 1-5,1-25 |
| 1-3,1-9,1-57,1-73 | | Wright James | 1-13 | York Thos. | 1-5 |
| Woods Zeddock | 1-3 | Wright James G. | 1-105 | Yorke Lutitia | 1-25 |
| Woodward Alvin | 2-21 | Wright Rufus | 2-19 | Young Mary | 1-32 |
| Woodward Nancy | 1-57 | Wright Sarah | 1-105 | Young Michael | 1-81 |
| Woodward Sandford | 1-57 | Wright Thos. | 2-91 | Young Rachael | 1-81 |
| Woody Samuel | 1-87 | Wright Wm. | 2-91 | Young Samuel | 1-105 |
| Wooldridge Ann | 2-75 | Wroe Nancy | 1-69 | | |
| Wooldridge Gibson | 1-11 | Wroe William | 1-69 | Zavalla Lorenzo de | 2-65 |
| Woolsey Abner | 2-9 | Wyatt C.C. | 1-83 | Ziekanski John D. | 1-61 |
| Wootten Paulina | 1-31 | | | Zimmerschmitt Frdk.A. | |
| Wootten Thomas J. | 1-31 | Yeagans | 2-63 | | 2-4 |
| Worthly Al. | 2-39,R-11 | Yeamans Asa | 1-71 | Zuber Abraham | 1-97 |
| Wrentmore Edwd. | 2-89 | Yeamans Daniel | 1-69 | Zuber Mary Anne | 1-97 |
| Wright Anne | 1-71 | Yeamans Jerusha | 1-71 | Zubic A. | 2-69 |
| Wright Claiborn | | Yeomans Joseph | | | |
| 2-4,2-27 | | 2-35,1-69 | | | |
| Wright Henry Q. | 1-71 | Yeomans Mary | 2-35 | | |

www.ingramcontent.com/pod-product-compliance
Lightning Source LLC
Chambersburg PA
CBHW070425270326
41926CB00014B/2939